The Ethics of Democracy

(1) A Made up Aristotle and Greeks — all early, and p83, 94

(2) serious about Hegel

(3) The democratization and non-rationalism goes too far.

(4) Basically accurate on much of Phil of Right

(5) p45 (6) A good discussion (pp 52 ff) of Hegel on Kant

(7) p55 criticism (8) pp 57-8 — a clear (if largely moral) discussion of why freedom requires the ethical life. (9) one good discussions of civil society (10) (11) he's never very clear on what freedom is. (12) pp 103-104 is a good summary and 124

(12) p111 for the criticism (13) see pp 122-123: A careful reading gives way to less passion, and less (no) attempt any more to defend Hegel and make him plausible (14) see my notes on pp 118-120 on other "completeness (and on what the state is.) (15) see 126-128 for criticism of his criticism of Hegel. (16) My p. 135 (17) see p138 criticism (18) nothing about religion at the end — only earlier matters of christianity. (19) see p 144 remarks and pp 145-146 (20) see 150, 151 (21) p192 (22) His p155 point — and mine (23) p 159 (24) p 162

The old attempt to "improve" Hegel by making him more democratic by reinstating his personal attitude and not saying why he agrees as he does.

SUNY series in Contemporary Italian Philosophy

Silvia Benso and Brian Schroeder, editors

The Ethics of Democracy

A Contemporary Reading of Hegel's
Philosophy of Right

Lucio Cortella

Translated by Giacomo Donis

Originally published as *L'etica della democrazia. Attualità della* Filosofia del diritto *di Hegel* (Marietti Editore, 2011)

Published by State University of New York Press, Albany

© 2015 State University of New York

All rights reserved

Printed in the United States of America

For information, contact State University of New York Press, Albany, NY
www.sunypress.edu

Production, Ryan Morris
Marketing, Anne M. Valentine

Library of Congress Cataloging-in-Publication Data

Cortella, Lucio, 1953–
    [L'etica della democrazia. English]
    The ethics of democracy : a contemporary reading of Hegel's philosophy of right / Lucio Cortella ; translated by Giacomo Donis.
        pages cm. — (SUNY series in contemporary Italian philosophy)
    "Originally published as L'etica della democrazia. Attualità della Filosofia del diritto di Hegel (Marietti Editore, 2011)"—Title page verso.
    Includes bibliographical references and index.
    ISBN 978-1-4384-5753-6 (hardcover : alk. paper)
    ISBN 978-1-4384-5755-0 (e-book)
    1. Hegel, Georg Wilhelm Friedrich, 1770–1831. 2. State, The. 3. Democracy. 4. Ethics. I. Title.

    JC233.H46C6813 2015
    320.01'1—dc23   2014038020

10 9 8 7 6 5 4 3 2 1

This book is dedicated to Donatella.
She knows how important she has been to me.

I wish to express my thanks to Giacomo Donis
for his passionate translation,
with its innovative and elegant solutions
to the many problems posed by my text and Hegel's.

Contents

Translator's Introduction

This translation is complicated by the fact that, in a sense, it is a complex—not simple—translation of a translation: my friend Lucio Cortella writes in Italian about Hegel's German texts, which he cites in Italian translation (always referring to the German original). I need to keep the Italian reading of Hegel's texts and terms in mind, along with the German—and, obviously, the English. Three sets of Hegelian terminology are always involved, and constantly ask to be reconciled with one another. Then, the English translations of Hegel date from the 1890s (Wallace, the *Encyclopaedia*—his *Logic* is from *1873!*) to the 1990s (Nisbet, the *Philosophy of Right*). Miller's two translations—of the *Logic* in 1969, followed by the *Phenomenology* in 1977, in which he changed his mind about the key Hegelian terminology—are quite readable but far—at times very far—from literal, *and* from the more literal Italian translations cited, and I have been obliged to modify them considerably (*but* not more than necessary). (*And* I owe a great deal to the Baillie translation of the *Phenomenology*: not only because I "met" Hegel through it, and read it three times, but also for its excellent and valuable insights into that extremely difficult text.)

Nisbet's (but I also constantly consulted Knox's) translation of the *Philosophy of Right* is, of course, the most important one for this book. I have discussed it, constantly and in depth, with *my author*, Lucio Cortella. I greatly respect Nisbet's translation, which makes Hegel's text readable but constantly attempts to be faithful, and have truly attempted to modify it as little as possible. But, in a sense, in this, my translation of this book, the "court of last instance" is what is in the mind of *my* author: which depends not only on the (*quite literal*) Italian translation of Hegel, but also on his expert (versus my by no means expert) knowledge of German. We have had interesting discussions! But the bottom line is this: I have at times (a few times) significantly modified Nisbet's translation, on the basis of the much debated and final judgment of Lucio Cortella. After all, it is *his* book that

ix

I translate, and my task is to translate *his* text and *his* reading of Hegel (and of Hegel's texts).

But then, apart from the Hegelian texts there are *many* other works by German authors discussed and quoted in this book, and here the situation is as complicated as it is with Hegel (if not more so). I have consulted all (I believe) the existing English translations of these works: on many occasions Lucio Cortella and I have not been in agreement with the published translations, and have modified them. As for the many German works not translated into English, I have translated them from the German myself—with Cortella looking over my shoulder every word of the way.

As for specific German terms, I have discussed a number of them in "translator's notes" (indicated by an asterisk) in the text. I have translated *Geist* as *spirit* and *Begriff* as *concept* on all occasions, and *aufheben/Aufhebung* as *supersede/supersession* on most occasions (see Nisbet, who interprets the word in various ways—a very complex matter). But the greatest difficulty resides in the fact that, while English has the term *actual* (*actuality, actualize, actualization*) corresponding to the German *wirklich* (etc.) as distinct from *real, reality, realize, realization* and the German equivalents, Italian has only *reale, realtà, realizzare,* and *realizzazione*. Lucio Cortella and I have discussed the translation of these terms every single time (the very many times!) they appear in the Italian text, because the distinction between *actual* and *real* is rarely clear cut, but is always important in the context of this book.

I need to say a few words about sexism in English. (It is uncritically rampant in Italian.) Given the absolutely legitimate demands to avoid the sexist use of the word *man* (*men*) (and *he* and *his*) and the complex linguistic and stylistic difficulties involved in getting around it, I attempted various solutions, but soon got myself into a bind. I used *she* and *her* instead of *he* and *his* a number of times, but perhaps not often enough? Perhaps I should have alternated: she, he, she, he? I may, perhaps, be guilty of a "token" use of *she*. I used plurals whenever I could, to avoid *his* and *her*. I shudder to think of how often I did end up using the word *man*. I used the expression *human being* (the somewhat unwieldy equivalent of the marvelous German word *Mensch*) as frequently as I deemed feasible. Nisbet uses it at times in his translation—almost invariably followed by a *he*! We translators (and all writers) must fight the good fight where sexism is concerned. But it is not easy, and success can be only partial, at best.

One last thing: I am firmly convinced that it is in the interest of the best possible English usage to distinguish, consistently and always, between a "defining" *that* and a "nondefining" *which*. This used to be a conflict between Brits and Americans, but I see it now as open warfare between reactionary and progressive linguistic thinking and practice. There will *never* be a "defining" *which* in any book of which I am the translator—not in my translation, but not in any quotation either.

Giacomo Donis
Venice, Italy

Preface to the English Translation

In recent years a new image of Hegel has been asserting itself in contemporary philosophical debate. Originating in the United States, this new reading has progressively challenged the prevailing European lines of interpretation. We have thus witnessed the advent of a "Hegelian paradigm" within contemporary ethico-political philosophy, after much of the second half of the twentieth century had been hegemonized by a pro-Kantian orientation (exemplified by such figures as Rawls and Habermas). This new paradigm is characterized, first, by a "concrete" notion of freedom, "situated" in practical and historical contexts and intimately connected with the natural character of our humanity; second, by a nonindividualistic conception of political and social life; and third, by a normativity that—unlike Kant's—is neither abstract nor formal but, rather, depends on a historical and individual process of formation. Here, the basic idea is that our freedom and our moral principles are not determined by pure reason (or by a purely procedural process of argumentation) but are historical products. Hence the importance of social institutions—the institutions Hegel had placed at the center of his *Philosophy of Right*: family, civil society, and state. It is on the basis of these spheres and within them that the original animal nature of human being goes through its process of formation and education, thereby gaining its specific freedom and its capacity for normative orientations. In this way it acquires what Hegel would call a "spiritual" nature.

This full-fledged "Hegel Renaissance" has been coupled (albeit not in all contemporary American Hegelians) with a "post-metaphysical" image of Hegel, flying in the face of the traditional interpretations that saw Hegelian philosophy as the restoration of those metaphysical demands that Kant had radically called into question. I refer here, in particular, to those philosophers (such as Pippin, Pinkard, Bernstein, Brandom, McDowell, to name just a few) who, based on the lesson of Sellars and Rorty, have proposed a reading of Hegel's thought in neopragmatistic terms. It is true that many aspects of Hegelian philosophy can be comfortably reconciled with the themes of American pragmatism: *antifoundationalism* first of all (Hegel's often repeated thesis that we cannot establish an ultimate foundation, be it empirical or logico-conceptual, and that there can be no immediacy that is not mediated in its turn); then, the *contextual* nature of our concepts, their constitutive referring to others, their perennial disputableness; and finally, the explicitly *historicist* seal Hegel impressed on his philosophy, as exemplified by his celebrated affirmation that philosophy is "its own time comprehended in thoughts."

My fundamental thesis in *The Ethics of Democracy* is based on an interpretation that keeps this Renaissance of a political Hegel separate from his postmetaphysical image. I believe it is possible and, indeed, extremely productive to repropose Hegel's theses on ethico-political questions and to show their contemporary relevance—*as long as* we neither forget nor minimize the "metaphysical" background that characterizes the whole of Hegelian philosophy. For this reason—as the reader will see—I have focused prevalently on studies by contemporary German philosophers, favoring them over the literature in English. Many of these studies, while acknowledging Hegel's critique of pre-Kantian traditional metaphysics (he often called it "old metaphysics"), hold fast to the idea that an ultimate ineliminable metaphysical residue does remain in his philosophy. In this context, my engagement with the checkered course of Hegel interpretations within the Frankfurt School will be an essential part of my analysis. In a certain sense, this book can be considered a child of that evolution and of its most recent developments. While in Adorno the contrast with Hegel is clear-cut and explicit, both with the *Logic* and with Hegel's philosophy of history and his theory of the state, ever since Habermas's works of the 1960s the judgment on Hegel has been more multifaceted: although the "closure" of the system characteristic of Hegel's mature works continues to be criticized, now the Jena Hegel, open to intersubjectivity and to communication, is valorized. Based on these premises the more recent members of the Frankfurt School have ended up by turning Adorno's judgment on Hegel on its head. In the works of Wellmer, Honneth, and Menke (the three authors I have discussed at greatest length) Hegel's practical philosophy—now completely rehabilitated—becomes the fundamental perspective for their ethico-political projects. And if it is true that Honneth in his early works still favors the Jena Hegel—with his focus on the theme of recognition—over the mature Hegel, in his more recent works it is, at last, the mature Hegel—the Hegel of the *Philosophy of Right*—who becomes the architrave on which he constructs his social philosophy.

In *The Ethics of Democracy* I follow this evolution closely. Its point of departure, constituted by the European interpretations (those of the Frankfurt School in particular), ultimately leads to conclusions that are particularly close to those of many contemporary Hegel scholars in the United States. However, my basic line of interpretation differs both from the conclusions of contemporary Hegelian neopragmatism and from the Hegel of the "new" Frankfurt School. The American Neo-Hegelians deserve great merit for having presented a comprehensive interpretation of Hegel that reclaims the entire corpus of his philosophical system, deeming it not only compatible with our postmetaphysical consciousness but advancing it as a theory that can respond adequately to some of the recurrent questions in contemporary philosophical debate. But, at the same time, understanding Hegel as our contemporary means minimizing the metaphysical content of his philosophy and reducing his logic to a sequence of *conceptual possibilities* that permit us to comprehend the natural and the sociohistorical worlds. But Hegel himself always opposed this Kantian manner of understanding logic, in which the categorial apparatus stands over against things and plays the role of a mere instrument capable of explaining them. Hegel, by contrast, explicitly presented logic as the in itself of things—as the ultimate nature and essence of totality. Of course, we are left with the open question of how *the essence of things* can be Hegelianly understood, in light of the fact that the *Science of Logic* itself calls the metaphysical notions of essence and of ground into question.

By contrast, the Frankfurt interpretation of Hegel appears to take precisely this Hegelian relationship with metaphysics univocally, deeming the fundamental core of the *Science of Logic* totally unacceptable for contemporary philosophical consciousness, precisely because it is intrinsically metaphysical. Hegel's topicality is therefore seen to reside exclusively in his philosophy of spirit and—in particular—in the doctrine of objective spirit. But this position, too, has its weak point: the philosophy of spirit and, in particular, Hegel's conception of freedom are rooted precisely in the *Science of Logic*. Hence it is not possible to render Hegel's practical philosophy topical without, first, seriously coming to grips with his logico-ontological assumptions.

The key to the interpretation I propose here is, precisely, the strict implication in Hegel's work between logic, ontology, and the ethico-political sphere. Hegel's conception of ethical life and his doctrine of the state are strongly conditioned by the logico-ontological assumptions of his thought. It is not possible to distance oneself from the authoritarian aspects of Hegel's conception of the political while failing to see his ontology as the root of his conception of freedom and, consequently, of his antidemocratic conception of the political.

Now, it is incumbent on me to explain what I mean by metaphysical conditioning of the Hegelian doctrine of ethical life. That Hegel radically distanced himself from traditional ontology is well known. His celebrated statement that it is a question of understanding *the true as subject* and not as substance is most certainly not to be taken as attesting to the existence of a supra-individual absolute subject of any kind. In Hegel we find no theorization of a macrosubject to which the totality of the real is to be traced back, just as for him no "cosmic spirit" or world soul can exist. Such a theory would take us back to the "old metaphysics," with its ontological substrate (albeit in a subjective guise). For Hegel "spirit" has a subjective dimension (our finite individual subjectivity), an objective dimension (the world of institutions and of history), and an absolute dimension (the sum total of the cultural forms represented by art, religion, and philosophy). Beyond these three realities there are no other "spirits"—neither divine nor supra-individual. Hegel's "metaphysics" resides elsewhere. We find it in the thesis, which recurs throughout the entire *Science of Logic*, that truth is of a conceptual nature—that is, logical and self-reflective. Absolute knowing is such not only because it represents the only knowledge capable of grasping this truth, but also because in it knowledge proves to be identical to its object—which is to say, the logico-cognitive "instrument" loses its instrumental character and becomes true because in the end it grasps its object as identical to itself. And precisely because there is no other true reality besides this one, and no entities or substrates that condition its existence, this self-reflective logical knowing is absolutely free and expresses the essence of freedom in the "purest" way possible. In Hegel freedom is synonymous with self-reflection and self-transparency. Where there is opacity there is no freedom, because "not-knowing" implies heteronomy.

This freedom, then, is not the property of a special subject, of a supremely perfect being, or of a supra-individual entity. Rather, it is the distinctive characteristic of finite human subjects who attain it through a long and complex process of formation, and without the decisive role played by relations of intersubjective recognition individual freedom could never be attained. But, precisely because freedom is not the original "property" of individual subjects, who in fact obtain it from the spheres of objective spirit in which their process of formation takes place, in Hegel freedom becomes an attribute proper to these spheres. This explains one of the fundamental theses that recurs in the *Philosophy of Right*, which I have called the "primacy of objectivity" and which means that the condition of perfect

self-transparency is attained not by individual subjects but by that objective *How.*
sphere which, more than any other, contains the conditions of freedom:
namely, the state. This explains Hegel's attributing the same characteristics
to the state that he does to the absolute: namely, to be "an absolute and
unmoved end in itself" in which "freedom enters into its highest right"
(§ 258). And this explains why the reciprocal relations of recognition that
characterize much of the process of formation of subjects almost entirely
disappear within the political sphere of the state, to be replaced by the
logic of the solitary self-recognition of spiritual ethical substance. In other
words, if it is true that the Hegelian doctrine of the state is characterized
by a deficit of subjectivity—that is, by a failure to attribute an active and *It would-*
critical role in determining the laws of the state and political decisions to *but is*
the citizens—this depends not on a specific defect of Hegel's political theory *this*
or on the historical conditioning of his time but, rather, on the ontological *true.*
background behind his practical philosophy.

This, however, is not to suggest that the project of "contemporizing"
Hegel be abandoned and that he be relegated to the philosophy of the
past. On the contrary, I am convinced that he can play an essential role in
contemporary philosophical debate. But on one condition: that we reopen
the question of his emphatic concept of freedom and the ontological background that sustains it. And this must be done without subjecting Hegel
to an external perspective—for example, our own conception of democracy—and forcing his philosophy to come into line with our own standards,
but rather on the basis of an *alternative concept of freedom* that we find in
Hegel's works themselves. I allude to his definition of freedom as "being-
with-self-in-being-other-than-self." This notion means that we can be free
not thanks to our own self-transparency but, rather, thanks to our relation
with otherness; that is, it entails the construction of a concept of *relational
freedom*, in which *individual autonomy* is guaranteed by maintaining the
other *in its otherness*. And, here, the "other" is to be understood in a broad
sense, comprising other subjects in their different roles, social practices in
which we participate, and the social and political institutions that permit
us to act and to think freely. Hence it is necessary to maintain and develop
intersubjective relations of reciprocal recognition in the various spheres of
ethical life over against their elimination in the sphere of the state, at least in
the way that Hegel delineates it. Accordingly, far from repressing individual
subjectivity on the strength of the primacy of institutional objectivity, the
constitution of the state ought to make provision for the *essential* contribution of the citizens to the making of political decisions. This involves the
reconstitution of a process of *reciprocal* recognition in which the citizens'

faithfulness to institutions (bottom-up recognition) entails an analogous recognition of the citizens by the state, in the form of an attribution of fundamental rights (top-down recognition).

What this book presents as a proposed "democratization of Hegel" is thus the result of my pressing to the extreme the logical and political consistency of an alternative concept of freedom to be found, albeit marginally, in Hegel's own works, and which finds its realization in the full development of the logic of recognition. The break with Hegel is thus nothing more than a distancing from the basic metaphysics that accompanies his dominant conception of freedom, in order to develop the democratic potentials implicit in his "heterodox" concept of relational freedom. Hence the intersubjective premises of this concept are fully compatible with the democratic political project, even if it is clear that the way in which Hegel conceives of his political constitution in fact moves in a different direction.

At this point it is fully legitimate to transform Hegel's doctrine of ethical life—his idea that social relationships, from the family to the political by way of the economic, have an ethico-normative foundation—into the project of a *democratic ethical life*. This project does not consist in proposing a decalogue of norms that ought to be followed by citizens and politicians who live within a democracy. For Hegel, such a proposal would continue to be afflicted with the limits of any Kantian type of morality; that is, it could do no more than propose an abstract list of duties that, in the end, the citizens would see as no more than a commandment from on high. What is more, it would run the risk of imposing a specific form of existence—a particular, and therefore controversial, way of expressing and experiencing democracy—on a culturally pluralistic social fabric. Democratic ethical life—the only *public* ethics possible in democracy—consists in this normative fabric, composed of practices, habits, and behaviors that all citizens have already internalized and made their own thanks to the relationship that has been established between the citizen and the public institutions. Here it is not a question of an external moral duty but of an ethics that we already practice and that philosophy has only to bring to light. We are all committed to the same observance of laws, just as we share the same sense of belonging to institutions, which is why we are held together by the norms implicit in them. These laws and institutions have taught us the *value* of freedom—the value of respect for ourselves and others, of a common belonging to the same destiny, of legality and rights, of justice and equity.

Here, no other authority is required to provide us with this orientation, be it religious authority, or the authority of past ethico-cultural traditions, or the authority of a philosophical conception designed to fill the void left by the disintegration of traditional ethics and by the impetuous advance of individual freedom. The only ethics possible is the one we all already share because it belongs to the juridico-constitutional system that shaped us, and on the basis of which we have developed our fundamental convictions. Only this ethics is *formal* enough that it not conflict with any individual substantial ethics, and it alone is *universal* enough to be shared by the entire society.

Hegel insisted that philosophy must not say how the state *must be*, nor what its ethics *must be*. Philosophy must limit itself to comprehending *what is already there*, and express conceptually that normativity which we already observe. An optimistic and conciliatory vision? A renunciation of the critical exercise supremely exemplified by Hegel's dialectic? An invitation to political conformism, with the plea to adapt oneself to an already existing ethical life? On the contrary, the modern ethical life of which Hegel speaks and the democratic ethical life that I propose are not tantamount to a specific ethical life, a particular historical tradition, or a set of cultural values to which we are invited to conform. Properly speaking, Hegel's *Sittlichkeit* and—all the more so—the one I am suggesting are no more than a process of formation, made possible by our inclusion within certain (social and political) institutions—that is, a *Bildung* by which we learn to *use* our freedom, our critical capabilities, our autonomy. This is exactly the opposite of a conformist ethics. It dictates neither moral behavior nor political orientation but only provides the *objective preconditions* (the normativity immanent in institutions) that permit individuals to decide on their life choices in true autonomy, while permitting institutions to implement deliberative politics.

One last question cries out for clarification. Despite Hegel's emphasis on the fundamental role played by the state within the entire sphere of objective spirit, it must be said that its tasks appear far more limited than those that most contemporary political theories attribute to state institutions. The state's superiority with respect to the family and civil society means no more than that the type of freedom the state transmits to its citizens is spiritually higher (and more complete) than the freedom that can be obtained within the other spheres. For Hegel, it is not the task of the state to govern the imbalances of civil society, or to deal with questions of the family and of education, or to implement economic policy, or even to administer the law. For him all these functions remain within the sphere of civil society, which has to find a way of self-regulation within itself (for example, through the institution of the corporation). As is well known, in the *Philosophy of Right* even the police are relegated to the sphere of civil society. For these very reasons Hegel has been reproached for his failure to deal with the problem of the vast social and economic inequalities (resulting in the creation of "a rabble") that he himself discussed in his analysis of civil society. When he affirms that there is to be no political "command" over the economy he appears to be implicitly accepting the theses of classical political economy and economic liberalism. It is paradoxical indeed that the great theoretician of the majesty of the state would seem to be endorsing neoliberal conceptions of the "minimum state." But Hegel has something else in mind. His response to the unsolved problems of civil society is not simply a self-regulation of economic mechanisms—no, it entails a *necessary* recourse to a higher sphere in which these citizens can *objectively* obtain (by their participation in political life) an education in ethically higher freedom. Thus, the (possible) solution to the problems of civil society will come from the heightened consciousness and autonomy of the citizens, not from direct intervention of the state. This is because, for Hegel, the state's ultimate end is, precisely, the full realization of a freedom that is ethically superior to mere economic freedom and to the exercise of human labor—in other words, a freedom that rises above the ethical designs of civil society. Political institutions, the action of the sovereign in maintaining the unity of the state, even war itself, are all designed for the full realization of this higher freedom. It is in this sense that Hegel's state has an ethical function—not in the sense that it imposes a certain system of values or a specific vision of life, but in the sense that its institutions contain the fundamental norms of freedom within themselves and thus prepare the citizens to behave according to these principles.

Hegel may be open to criticism on this point, since he appears to underestimate the impact of the economic sphere in guaranteeing the basic conditions that make a full exercise of freedom possible. If civil society in its inner self-regulation should fail to guarantee minimum conditions of subsistence, the moral constitution of the individual would be undermined. In this loss of self-respect and of confidence in the capacity to be autonomous the grand design of the state to shape free individuals would crumble. Let me say this: in delineating a political sphere released from economic conditionings and preoccupations, Hegel wished somehow to indicate a higher normative realm in which the sphere of merely natural needs is overcome, to give us an idea of a humanity capable of going beyond the merely technico-reproductive dimension. We may take this as a last, unexpected, utopian trait in a thinker known for his political realism.

Preface to the Original Italian Edition

Does Democracy Need Ethics?

The title of this book may seem paradoxical. Hegel, notoriously, does not belong to the tradition of democratic thought. Scholars debate whether his theory of the state can be considered liberal or antiliberal, but no one can seriously claim that the conception is democratic. To be sure, criticism since the mid-twentieth-century has taken decisive steps toward liberating Hegel's conception of the state from past interpretations that simplistically saw it as a legitimation of the Prussian state in the period of post-Napoleonic European restoration. If it is true that Hegel's work is unquestionably a child of its time, it is also true that the range of problems he deals with goes far beyond the specific context of the counterrevolutionary reaction in the first decades of the nineteenth century. What concerns Hegel is the question of *the foundations of the modern state*. In particular, his doctrine of ethical life is designed to solve a problem that has haunted modern political theory from its inception, only to become all the more acute in our contemporary democracies: Do abstract legal rules suffice to keep a society together and regulate its processes, or are a system of values, a shared tradition, and a common ethics also needed?

The theory of the liberal state, especially in its contemporary versions, resolutely denies the need for ethics as the basis of social life and the pillar of state institutions. For this theory, politics not only has no need of ethics, it must force itself to do without it. Precisely because contemporary states are drenched in an irreducible religious, ethical, and cultural pluralism they have no warrant to impose a particular system of cultural values on people who are foreign to it—people who have every right to live in the society. After all, the modern states were built on this basic option, after the wars of religion that had devastated Europe for decades—wars generated precisely by the assumption that a nation's identity resided in a specific religious faith.

The experience of that conflict between traditions and between opposing conceptions of life guided the formation of the modern liberal state, for which the basis of the pact of citizenship cannot be a specific conception of the good but exclusively of the abstract rules of justice. It is these rules alone that permit citizens with different value orientations to live together, to have the same rights, and to be treated impartially. The distinction drawn by contemporary liberal political philosophy between *the private character of the good* and the *public character of the right* is a theoretical synthesis of this goal of contemporary democracies. On the basis of this distinction, on the one hand individuals are allowed to conserve their own conceptions of the *good*—that is, their preferences, their life plans, their values, as long as such conceptions remain within the private sphere. On the other hand, the state has the task of establishing what is *right* for all—that is, of establishing by law the abstract rules on which individuals with conflicting conceptions of the good can nonetheless agree. Therefore, while justice is of political importance, the good remains a strictly private matter.

This solution—perfectly in line with the constitutions of contemporary democracies—appears reasonable enough. But, as the most acute minds of our time have noted, it does have a weak point: Can a state live and thrive without a shared fundamental ethics, without a reference to shared values, without an identification with precise historical roots? What is called into question is the effective capacity of contemporary politics to meet the challenge posed by liberal theories: the challenge of replacing traditions, identity references, and a shared common history with abstract rules, making the reference to justice and its laws the only shared identity. But, as the American communitarians have rightly observed, a society that has renounced a common idea of the good and cast off its historical identity fatally becomes a society without a soul, without a real bond between its citizens, without common ideas in which they can recognize themselves. At this point social ties will have grown so weak that care for the *res publica* and for the collective commitments of the nation fades away. Words such as *solidarity, common good,* and *general interest* become incomprehensible. In this context we can well understand the reaction that characterizes our societies, with their ever more frequent appeals to identity claims, collective symbols, and demands for the exclusion of all those who do not share the same historical past.

The best way of responding to appeals and demands of this kind cannot, however, consist in a return to preliberal forms of the state—the return to a single religion, value system, and cultural model of reference. Rather, the solution lies in the rediscovery of an *ethical ground that is common and shared*—an ethics that discriminates neither between nor against the diverse and plural conceptions of the good present in our societies. No intellectualistic effort is needed here to individuate the point of intersection between the different conceptions of the good and the different cultures that characterize us. There is no need of a new moral philosophy in search of a universalist conception of the good. It will be sufficient to individuate and make explicit *the ethics that is already incorporated and at work in the institutions of the democratic state* and that for this reason is already the basis of the social bond between citizens. Political institutions are not simply legal mechanisms or lifeless procedures. They are composed of laws, legal traditions, practices, habits, characteristics, and attitudes that make up an entire normative sphere. It is therefore in its political institutions that a nation's identity and its ideal references are to be sought. In short, there is an "ethical" side of state institutions that only a theory of democracy conceived as an instrument continues to ignore and to forget.

This is the fundamental meaning of the *Hegelian theory of ethical life*. When Hegel places the political within what he terms the sphere of *ethical life** he does not intend to call into question the neutrality of the modern state with respect to specific traditions or controversial conceptions of the good. Neither does he intend to propose an "ethical state," if this means the subjugation of the political to moral imperatives; that is, its dependence on given conceptions of life and of the good. What he has in mind is just the opposite: political institutions have an implicit ethical purpose—that is, they play an educative and formative role for the citizens. This purpose is "anchored" and "incorporated" in those institutions, which have imposed themselves in the historical process precisely because they have freed themselves from any controversial conception of the good and thus become transversal and shared.

Hegelian ethical life is not constituted by a particular system of values; it does not intend to impose a specific historical identity on the state; it does not seek to repropose traditional communal bonds. Hegel never called into question the *process of emancipation* that characterized the modern age, thanks to which humankind was liberated from the weight of past traditions, from communal ties, and from historical specificity. He knows that modern man [Mensch] recognizes himself in *one and only one identity*, namely *freedom*, by virtue of which he has taken leave of traditional bonds, assumed a critical attitude toward past history, and distanced himself from those values that were the basis of the old identities.

---

*Sittlichkeit in German, *eticità* in Italian.

But Hegel has more than this in mind. For him, once the old traditions and the ethos of the forefathers had been dissolved, *freedom* itself became ethos, taking root, objectifying itself in a legal system, a social practice, in political and civil institutions. For Hegel—and for us today— freedom in its turn has itself become tradition—the *tradition of freedom.* This has given rise to a practice, a mentality, a civil character, by virtue of which the modern individual puts independent judgment before conformism, accepts the coexistence of differents, takes responsibility as the point of reference for action. The capacity to be free and to accept the freedom and rights of others is not an innate human quality but presupposes a process of learning and education, activated precisely by the "ethical" character of political and civil institutions. *We have "learned" to be free,* and this learning process has now been consolidated and "institutionalized": the exercise of freedom, consciousness of our rights, respect for law, have become an essential part of ourselves—constitutive elements of our very nature.

The old traditions are now incapable of performing the role of formation and orientation they had always performed in premodern societies. But freedom did far more than simply destroy the old state of things: it created a new one, with freedom itself as its foundation. The institutions of the modern state have become our new world, our new homeland, the new source of our identity. Laws, rights and duties, political and civil institutions, procedures, the legal system: all this constitutes the *new community* of the modern human being—no longer historical community, ethnic belonging, cultural identity, but the practice of freedom, the legal and constitutional system, the institutions of the state of law. From this institutional world we have learned not only to be free but also to exercise our freedom together with others, to respect the rights, cultures, and values of others, and to unite tolerance with individual responsibility.

The term *constitutional patriotism* precisely expresses the new attitude of democratic citizens and the source of their new identity. The democratic citizen identifies with a community no longer based on specific traditions, religions, and controversial ethical options, but on institutions and practices generated by the constitution—that is, by the legal principles of freedom. Contemporary democracies will have ever greater need of a consolidation of this ethos. If they can no longer rely on the motivating force of the old conceptions of life then the traditional reference to a shared past history will prove increasingly problematic, as will any social bond based on cultural or religious conceptions, which have inevitably become plural and controversial. At the same time, however, the motivational force and the capacity for social coherence of mere universal rules of justice is clearly insufficient.

The solution lies in a common and shared ethos that is, simultaneously, *universal*—in principle participated in by everyone—and *concrete*, which is to say, already at work historically in the practice of political institutions.

The identity of the democratic citizen will therefore be a *posttraditional identity*, which will no longer make reference to the historical community, the homeland, the national history, but will recognize in the practice of freedom, beyond the borders of nation states, the new place of its rootedness and of its formation. The process of European unification will be consolidated only if it follows this path. Indeed, this process is not constitutively based on the sharing of a past history, made up more of nationalisms and conflicts than of peaceful coexistence, neither can it be reduced to mere economic and financial advantage. The search for distant religious and cultural roots risks producing more laceration than convergence. Only the valorization of a common legal and constitutional past and of a shared vision of individual rights—in short, only the practice of freedom—will make it possible to form a true common homeland and a European identity.

This is the substance of Hegel's lesson and the source of its great topical interest. Such a conclusion does not mean, however, that the entire Hegelian theory of the state is to be accepted without question. A contemporary reading of Hegel's *Philosophy of Right* must not lose sight of the inevitable limits his political conception presents today. There are two such limits in particular. First, the authoritarian features of a state in which, despite all the theoretical premises in defense of subjectivity, the individual plays virtually no active role in the determination of political institutions. The precedence Hegel attributes to objectivity over subjective dispositions means not only that the state takes priority over the citizens, but that the citizens' attitude to the state is one of recognition and acceptance of its superior rationality. The second limit regards the nationalistic closure of an ethos that is supposed to constitute the concrete realization of the universal idea of freedom. If ethical life is freedom's self-realization as tradition, why does Hegel nationalistically limit the realization of an idea that ought to know no boundaries (and thus should not lead to war between states)?

Hence the rediscovery of the fundamental themes of Hegel's political philosophy needs to be coupled with a second operation—namely, the necessary *democratization of his conception of ethical life*. Only in this way can his great philosophical lesson dialogue with the essential questions of the contemporary political constellation. This democratization, first, would give citizens an active role in constructing state institutions and deliberating on state policies and, second, would open up all the universalist potentials of ethical life, demolishing national limits and adapting them to the

multiethnic, multicultural and—ultimately—supranational reality of contemporary democracies. In this way, that which in Hegel is presented as a
theory of the ethical life of the *modern state* would become a theory of the
ethos that is necessary for the life of *contemporary democracy*.

Introduction

Morality and Ethical Life: Key Concepts in Hegel's Conception of the Political

With Hegel, a distinction not yet made by most philosophy before him became a systematic differentiation of great importance. But, at first blush, the etymology of the words *Moralität* and *Sittlichkeit* shed little light on Hegel's distinction. In fact the Latin *mores* correspond to the German *Sitten*, just as they correspond to the Greek *ethos*, from which our usual translation of the word *Sittlichkeit** derives. Just as *morals* derives from *mores*, *Sittlichkeit* derives from *Sitte*, and *ethics* from *ethos*—and all three signify "manners and customs." Hegel himself acknowledges this semantic equivalence in his Introduction to the *Philosophy of Right*—while, at the same time, stating his intention to make a distinction where none exists: "*Morality* and *ethics*, which are usually regarded as roughly synonymous, are taken here in essentially distinct senses" (PR § 33 R). He goes on to say: "But even if morality and ethics were etymologically synonymous, this would not prevent them, since they are now different words, from being used for different concepts" (§ 33 R).

As a matter of fact, there is one etymological element that distinguishes *Sittlichkeit* from *Moralität* and relates it to the *ethos* of the Greeks. Hegel refers to it in a handwritten notation in the copy of the *Philosophy of Right* he used for his lectures: "*Sitte* [custom]—*êthos*—the ancients knew nothing of conscience—Riemer: *êthos* Ionic *éthos*—habit, practice—(excellently, in Herodotus, 'dwelling') origin of humankind—*Sitte*—perhaps from *Sitz* [dwelling place]?" (RZ 302). While this connection postulated by Hegel— the notion that *Sitte* be linked to *Sitz* and to *sitzen*, that it indicate dwelling

---

*As "ethics" or, more precisely, "ethical life."

1

place, place of living—is only a hypothesis in German, it is unquestionably the case in ancient Greek. The original meaning of the word *ethos* is in fact precisely "dwelling place" and "place of living"; only later did it come to mean "custom."[1] Aristotle confirms this when he speaks of an *ethos of animals*, referring in this case to their dens and to the behavior connected with them.[2] *Ethos* in the sense of "custom"—the best-known and now the usual meaning of the word—is in fact an extension of that original meaning: the habitual place for our existence in fact consists in the practices, manners, and customs that provide us with the basic coordinates of our lives—that is, its "frame." This is why Aristotle himself[3] posits a connection between *êthos* [custom] and *éthos* [habit]: habit is in fact a habitual place, even if not a physical one. It is the environment in which we move.

This link between ethics and dwelling, prominent in Aristotle and later taken up by Hegel, indicates a conception of ethical life that is very different from the one we normally attribute to the moral sphere. It is the true key to an understanding of Hegel's distinction. Hegel writes, again in the Remarks to section 33 of the *Philosophy of Right*:

> Kantian usage prefers the expression *morality*, as indeed the practical principles of Kant's philosophy are confined throughout to this concept, even rendering the point of view of *ethics* impossible and in fact expressly infringing and destroying it. (PR § 33 R)

The opposition of morality and ethics thus takes the form of an opposition between Kant's and Hegel's moral philosophy. At the same time, however, this opposition is not absolute, since for Hegel himself the moral and the ethical are two equally essential dimensions of spirit. Indeed, both are part of that sphere of "objective spirit," which for Hegel includes all the spiritual (today we would say "cultural," in the broad sense) manifestations in which inner subjectivity has found a way to express itself objectively, outside itself.

In the *Encyclopaedia* Hegel writes that objective spirit is spirit "in the form of reality [*Realität*]" (ENC § 385), where the concept of *Realität* indicates the sensuous form of existence. Freedom of spirit has thus found a *sensuous world* (history, society, the concrete individual, the political, the economy) in which to externalize itself. This is a "*world* produced [*hervorgebrachten*] and to be produced [*hervorzubringenden*]" (ENC § 385) by spirit, in which freedom is found in the form of the *in-itself*; that is, in the form of external objectivity: "The objective spirit is the absolute Idea, but only existing *in itself*: and as it is thus on the territory of finitude, its actual rationality retains the aspect of external appearance [*äusserliches Erscheinen*]" (ENC § 483).

However, this external side, this form of appearing, must not be seen as a loss. Freedom's externalization is in fact its true purpose, its end: "The purposive activity of this will is to realize [*realisieren*] its concept, freedom, in these externally objective aspects, as a world determined by means of the concept" (ENC § 484). Without this objective world there would be no realized freedom; that is, there would be no freedom in history. Hegel calls this realized world of freedom *the world of right*.

> This reality in general [*Realität*], as the *existence* [*Dasein*] of free will, is *right*—the term being taken in a comprehensive sense not merely as limited juridical law, but as that which encompasses the existence of *all* the determinations of freedom. (ENC § 486)

This distinction between juridical law and the general sphere of right[4] (of which law is only a part) explains why in the *Philosophy of Right* Hegel does not simply deal with legal matters but is concerned with everything that is referable to the externalization of freedom.[5] "Right" taken as a whole is thus seen by Hegel as the objective manifestation of freedom, its realization as historical existence:

> "*Right* is any existence in general that is the *existence* of the *free will*. Right is therefore in general freedom, as Idea'" (PR § 29). And: "Right is something *utterly sacred*, for the simple reason that it is the existence of the absolute concept, of self-conscious freedom" (§ 30).[6]

Now, the reason why Hegel makes the world of right correspond to the entire sphere of objective spirit is because "rights" are rooted in the different forms of the objectification of freedom. As Axel Honneth observed, "all forms of social existence, insofar as they can be proved to be necessary conditions for the realization of 'free will,' may be called 'rights' because they are allocated a specific 'right' in each case."[7] The Hegelian notion of "right" can thus legitimately be understood as that comprehensive world of normativity which raises specific *validity claims* that can be tested on the basis of criteria of *justice*. For Hegel "right" is everything about which it can be asked whether or not it is just, and comprises the entire sphere of objective spirit (the legal in the strict sense, the moral, and, finally, the ethical, as we shall see). For this reason—Honneth goes on to say—according to Hegel "universal rights initially are not attributed to individuals but to those forms of social existence."[8]

When he articulates the various objective manifestations of freedom internally, differentiated in spheres, Hegel keeps the Kantian systematization clearly in mind. Kant, however, in the *Metaphysics of Morals* had distinguished between just two spheres: the domain of *right* and that of *virtue*. The former referred to the *external* (private and public) relations between individuals, the latter to the individual's *inner* sphere. Hegel introduced an important variation from this precedent, which Fichte too had substantially endorsed. For Hegel, the sphere of external relations between individuals is not to be seen as an *extra-moral* territory, completely delivered over to abstract right. His idea is that juridical rules regulate only a limited part of interpersonal relations (essentially, property relations). This makes a *third sphere* necessary, in addition to the spheres of right and of morality, which comprises all the other relations that come to be realized between individuals: *the sphere of ethical life*.

Hegel dedicates paragraph 33, which concludes the Introduction, to a detailed subdivision [*Einteilung*] of objective spirit into these three spheres, each seen as a different degree in the development of the "Idea of free will"; that is, of objectified freedom.

The *first stage* is that of "immediate will." Here, freedom is still in the form of the "in itself"; that is, it objectifies itself in an immediate external existence. Freedom becomes a *thing*, an "immediate external thing," and this immediacy in which the individual's freedom has been objectified is his *property*. Freedom is equivalent here to possessing something, to exercising one's lordship over objects. *This is the sphere of "abstract or formal right."* Such right does not regulate the inner life of individuals but only their external reciprocal contact, when they relate to one another as proprietors—that is, have a relation of possession with regard to a thing (property).[9] Thus, their reciprocal relation is itself merely thinglike and objectivistic, even if this objectivity is completely different from any natural objectivity since in these thinglike relations freedom has been objectified. Hegel goes on to say that "the will is *immediate*; its concept is therefore abstract, as that of *personality*; and its existence [*Dasein*] is an immediate external thing [*Sache*]' (PR § 33). Here, Hegel introduces the notion of "personality"—the legal person: in this sphere individuals lose all their specific traits, counting only as proprietors and therefore as abstract persons. Hence they exercise their freedom only in the figure of the legal person (which for Hegel is the "concept" of immediate will, while its "existence" is represented by the *Sache*, the thing).

The *second stage* is that of the "will reflected within itself"; that is, of the transition from the outward and thinglike side of freedom to the inward side. Here, we are in the *realm of morality*. In this regard, we have to wonder why Hegel chose to treat an inward dimension—morality—within objective spirit. The reason lies in the fact that, here, Hegel sees the sphere of morality as a practical disposition of the historical world; that is, as a form of life in which individuals discover this inner dimension of theirs and know themselves to be autonomous and responsible. In consequence, their objective historical life is itself influenced by this inner disposition. While freedom manifested itself in the previous stage in the form of the "in itself" here it takes the form of the *for itself*, that is, of reference to itself. In this way it inevitably tends to set itself against the external world, pitting subjective freedom against the universal (it is "determined as *subjective individuality* in opposition to the *universal*"). This leads to the "division" [*Entzweiung*] between the "right of the subjective will" and the "right of the world" (§ 33).

But the ultimate truth of objective spirit is represented neither by abstract right nor by morality. The Kantian division between a free inner world and a coercive external world does not do justice to the true nature of objective spirit. Only by understanding "the *unity* and *truth* of these two abstract moments," that is, the unity of the in-itself and the for-itself, will the Idea of free will manifest itself in its truth. *This third stage is that of ethical life*. In it freedom manifests itself in the form both of inner freedom and of objective reality: "freedom, as the *substance*, exists no less as *actuality* and *necessity* than as *subjective* will" (§ 33). Here, morality has penetrated into things—into the objects of the sociohistorical world. This is the *ethical* world: the world in which subjects recognize themselves as if in an inner world of their own.

Therefore ethical life is not simply the objectification of freedom, because freedom is already represented by abstract right. Ethical life is an objectified freedom that is not opposed to inner freedom: indeed, individuals do not experience it as alien. The distinctive feature of the ethical world resides in the fact that, in it, the moment of subjective freedom is not lost. While in the sphere of right the individual does not recognize the objectification of his freedom but only perceives its coercive moment (the legal sanction and the constraint of law), in ethical life this experience of alienation is overcome and subjective freedom comes to recognize itself in these objective forms. Hegel, accordingly, describes ethical life as "the *Idea* in its universal existence in and for itself" (§ 33).

Hence the Hegelian conception of ethical life presents itself from the very beginning with these three programmatic characteristics: (1) as a critique of the Kantian division of the practical sphere into just two domains, that of right and that of morality; (2) as a reunification of interiority and exteriority, of morality and legality; and (3) as an extension of the Kantian realm of freedom beyond the inner sphere of subjectivity.

But the particularity of this program consists in the fact that, in introducing his conception of *Sittlichkeit*, Hegel explicitly refers it to the Greek notion of *ethos*. We have good reason to wonder why he posits this idea of the historical world as a world of freedom in explicit continuity with the ancient conception of the practical sphere as *ethos*, that is, as the dwelling place of human beings. What possible relation can there be between the extension of Kantian freedom to the sociohistorical world and the ancient conception that rooted the practico-political sphere in the world of ethical *traditions*? Is there no incompatibility between the Hegelian idea of a sociohistorical world grounded in freedom and the ancient rooting of *ethos* in *physis*—that is, of ethical good in nature?

In fact *ancient ethical life* presents many points of contact with Hegel's conception, but there are also some significant differences. Both are *public* rather than private: that which the ancients called *ethos* regarded the network of behaviors, habits, and practical traditions within a community. Thus, it did not refer to private behavior (which, by contrast, has been the focal point of modern morality) but was essentially concerned with public practical traditions. For this reason the specific place of *ethos* is the *polis*. Hence the ancient unity of ethics and politics is not to be interpreted according to the modern canons of a "moralization" of politics; understood correctly, it is the rooting of political norms in an *ethos*—that is, in the *tradition* of a place.

In its turn, however, *ethos* is grounded in something that is beyond it: *nature*. "The roots of the *polis* are in *physis*" is the fundamental idea throughout Greek culture. But this is because the Greeks understood nature not as a neutral succession-connection of events but, rather, as a sphere that contains *prescriptions*. There is a *telos* immanent in nature—an end that makes it the essential source of normativity for the human world. In this framework the *good* is not simply an ideal of our subjectivity but, first of all, is an *ontological* reality, immanent in every natural manifestation.

The Platonic theory according to which the good is an Idea—indeed, is *the* Idea par excellence—means that nature in its highest manifestation and perfection is guided and oriented by the good. Aristotle, despite his criticisms of Plato's theory of Ideas, reconfirms this conception, explicitly affirming that the good is the culmination of the nature of things ("the good is that at which all things aim").[10] The actualization of the potentialities immanent in beings, that is, their passing from power to act, thus coincides with their good.

Aristotle's criticism of the Platonic concept of the good essentially calls into question its being understood as a universal Idea. For Aristotle the good is neither a universal substance nor a category but, rather, is transcategorial in nature, passing through all the genera and species. For this reason there can be no science of the good, neither can the norms for our acting be deduced from any supposed knowledge of this good. In his critique of so-called Socratic-Platonic intellectualism Aristotle insists that knowledge of the good is a mistaken response to the demand for a practical orientation. Not knowledge but will and the deliberation that follows it is what is decisive in a good action. For these deliberations to be "good," what is necessary is not wisdom but, rather, a practical context, a community, a city, that sustain the formation of a goodwill, educate it, and progressively allow it to meet the standard of the good that concretely exists in act. This practical context is, precisely, *ethos*.

"Man" [*anthropos, Mensch*] attains an "ethical" condition when he has realized the good that was immanent, bringing its *telos* to completion. This end is represented by the life in common with other men. Hence the *polis* represents the end of this journey, man's attainment of what he truly is. "Man is by nature a political animal [*zôon politikon*],"[11] which is to say, an animal that lives in the *polis*. In Aristotle, "nature" [*physis*] is not a simple de facto biological condition but, rather, indicates a being's *end* [*telos*]. Thus, the *polis* represents the conclusive and final condition of the human process of maturation and development. It is not to be understood as a mere succession of streets, squares, and houses, but as a network of traditions, habits, and practices that constitute man's *ethos*—his dwelling place par excellence. The end of man is therefore that of living according to these traditions, making them the guide for his communal existence.

An action is "ethical" insofar as it *conforms* not to abstract ideals and values but to these *traditions*. Only in this way does man live according to the dictates of his nature. Virtue is nothing other than the citizen's constant disposition to follow these traditions. This shifts the moral problematic from Socrates's and Plato's "theoretistic" approach (one must first *know and contemplate* the good, in order to apply it in practice) to the "practical" approach of Aristotle: what is essential is progressively adapting the will to the practices of all those who live according to the traditions of the *polis*. In this context the role of education, imitation, repetition, and habit is clearly decisive. Virtue is not acquired by theory but by practice—by progressively habituating one's character. This is the royal road for incorporating the good into the practice of one's life.

Since *ethos* is the sphere in which the good is embodied in communal practices, in ancient Greece no conflict between will and good or between human nature and ethics was possible. If human nature stayed its course and will was expressed within an active *ethos*, no external duty or command or constraint was possible. Here, indeed, the good is indistinguishable from our nature and our practical orientations.

As we shall see, Hegelian *Sittlichkeit* sets great store by these questions. At the same time, however, it aims to bring these elements into the context of the new historical conditions. In short: in Hegel, ancient ethical life will have to settle accounts with the acquisitions of modern morality, based on the subject and his freedom.

Kantian morality is the prime example of the "end"—the goal—of modernity, and of its radical opposition to the fundamental structure of ancient ethics. Kant calls into question two elements in particular. First, the *connection between morality and nature*. For Kant morality is such only insofar as it makes itself independent of nature; that is, autonomous with respect to sensuous inclinations, affections, and passions. Its ground is not in nature but in *freedom*. The result is a complete repositioning also of the good: it no longer resides in the nature of things but in the subject's capacity to be free.

The second element regards the *connection between morality and ethos*. Since it is grounded in freedom, morality is structurally independent of all historical, social, and family conditioning. It is pure *formality*—that is, "independence from all *material* of the law."[12] There is no morality if one follows the social conventions, traditions, and authority of the forefathers. It is possible, of course, that a tradition may realize what has been prescribed by moral law—but conscience will have to act only on the basis of the *autonomy* of moral law. Furthermore, since universality is the sole guarantee of morality (this is the very form of the categorical imperative), that which is prescribed by one tradition in opposition to another cannot be assimilated by moral conscience. Morality breaks the bond with the particularity of traditions and accepts only what has been raised above specific contexts. For a law to be *moral* it must be a law for *all* human beings.

The Kantian conception of right and of politics follow these same lines. They are grounded not in nature but in freedom. The foundations of right are pure practical reason and the "universal law of freedom."[13] This leads to an "artificial" conception of politics, its "constructive" character, its marking a break with nature. The process that began with Hobbes, who saw the state as a negation of the natural condition and an exiting from it, is here brought to its conclusion.

Also the universalist character of legal principles comes into collision with the ancient conception of politics. Such principles must prescind from the particularities of local manners and customs: justice is such only if it is able to remain neutral with respect to the ideals of "good life" held by different individuals. Kant's philosophy is based on that universalism which proved to be the solution to the *conflict between traditions*. The abstract universality of the moderns and the universal principles of freedom, justice, and equality arise as a response to the conflict that marks the origins of modernity: the wars of religion. Only the reference to abstract common values can bring conflicting visions of the good into agreement, in opposition to religious or ethnic inspirations and identity claims.[14] While ethos and belonging lead to division, universality unites: this conviction had to pass through the fire and the blood of the European wars of religion before it could assert itself and take root.

But even if artificiality and universalism do solve certain fundamental problems they also give rise to others, for which the mere viewpoint of modern morality has no answers. For Hegel these problems present themselves as irreconcilable oppositions: antinomies in reciprocal opposition.

1. Abstract universality cannot constitute the dwelling place of humankind that has been represented for centuries by living traditions and by the communities in which they were embodied. This gives rise to a feeling of alienation that is expressed precisely in the *opposition* that characterizes *the relation between the concrete individual and abstract moral universality.*

2. Morality is no longer rooted in the nature of the individual—indeed, it too is now characterized by a structural distance from this nature. This, in turn, gives rise to a further feeling of alienation in individuals who see something in moral laws that is opposed to their natural tendencies. This *second opposition* takes the form of *the conflict between morality and nature.*

3. Right asserts its universality by means of constraint, through sanctions. While the individuals' inwardness is free, their externality is subjected to constraint. This, in turn, gives rise to the simultaneous belonging of human beings to two

worlds: the free world of the inner dimension and the coercive world of the public dimension. Hence the *third opposition: the opposition between morality and right.*

Hegel's critical attitude toward Kantian morality stems from his awareness of these problems—an awareness that leads him to develop a new concept of ethical life, capable of reviving the ancient Greek harmony between individuals and public institutions within the new context represented by the free subjectivity of modernity. In this new context Hegel is faced with the necessity of rethinking the very notion of freedom. Only in this way will it be possible to connect the freedom of the moderns with the ancient conception of ethos.

Chapter 1

Freedom and the Absolute

Hegel inherits his concept of freedom from that philosophy of the modern age which, by conferring absolute centrality on the subject, ended up giving the individual dominance over nature, overturning the relation of dependence that had characterized ancient philosophy. Despite the distinction—also this typically modern—between an external natural sphere, marked by mechanistic relations of cause and effect, and an inner spiritual sphere, characterized by freedom, the individual, in relation to nature, had attained an essential supremacy, asserting his mastery over being and over things.

Hegel's enterprise can be seen as an effort to give radical consistency to this conception, in virtue of which freedom is no longer considered only a property of human inwardness and the sign of its superiority to nature but has become the ultimate logic of the real, the essence of totality. If freedom is the fundamental characteristic of the absolute and the absolute coincides with totality, it follows that freedom becomes the ground of all reality. Freedom is the profound truth of things, their hidden sense. Only insofar as the real is understood as essentially free is it apprehended in its truth. Nature itself is, in itself, *free*, since its truth is spirit, just as, inversely, conscious freedom is nothing other than nature that has come to be "with itself."* This results in an idea of the real that has been completely transformed with respect to the modern mechanistic conception. In this regard, Herbert Marcuse wrote: "But freedom is for Hegel an ontological category: it means being not a mere object, but the subject of one's existence;

---

*"Presso di sé"—in German "bei sich"—is translated throughout this book as "with itself."

not succumbing to external conditions, but transforming factuality into realization. This transformation is, according to Hegel, the energy of nature and history, the inner structure of all being!"[1] Objects are not in truth only objects, but subjects. If they are assumed in their factual condition of objects, things, pure substrates, they are not understood correctly—that is, they are not assumed in their true dimension. Nature is not true *as* nature. It is, in truth, freedom: it is the subject and not the object of existence.

But such an emphatic conception of freedom has need of a foundation. Hegel is well aware of this and by no means shrinks from the task. The terrain is that of the *Science of Logic*, and in particular the last pages of "The Doctrine of Essence," in which he prepares the transition to the "Subjective Logic."

1.1. Freedom and Ontology

The question posed throughout "Book Two" of the *Logic* is the question of *essence*, of ultimate nature, of the deep layer of reality, after the investigation in "Book One" of *being*, understood as immediacy, as presence, as what-is. From the very first pages of Book Two, Hegel referred to the investigation of essence as an *Erinnerung*—that is, as both a *remembering* and an *inwardizing*.[2] Such a movement implies a "backward-step" with respect to the investigation of being (but from the first pages of the *Logic* Hegel served notice that every true advance is a "*retreat into the ground*, to what is *primary* and *true*"[3]) and, at the same time, a step into a greater depth. It is a sort of journey in the *timeless past* of being—a past that is present in the etymon of the German word for essence [*Wesen*].

But this journey does not lead to any esoteric or hidden dimension of being. Indeed, the title of the last section of Book Two—presumably Hegel's last word on the subject—is *Die Wirklichkeit*. The Italian translation of the word as "reality" [*realtà*: the English translation is "actuality"] poorly expresses Hegel's meaning. *Wirklichkeit* is "reality" [actuality] insofar as it has developed all its potentialities—that is, has attained its completion, manifesting itself completely. In short: the deep and ultimate essence of the whole [*das Ganze*] is nothing other than its full and radiant manifestation. We are very close, then, to what Aristotle meant by the concept of *energeia*. This manifestation, however, must not be understood as something static (this would take us back to the very immediacy of being that essence supersedes) but, rather, as a continual self-manifestation, as the very process of showing. It is not fortuitous that the title of the last chapter of this section is "The Absolute Relation." Reality in act is nothing other than a relation—a movement.

It is here that Hegel broaches the question of freedom. In these last pages of the Doctrine of Essence he yields the floor to Spinoza—which means to the philosophical position that understood essence as substance and necessity. If Spinoza were right, then the truth of nature would be not spirit but substance, just as the essence of the whole would not be freedom—the free self-recognizing of thought—but blind necessity. The foundation of freedom—equivalent to a full and proper foundation of idealism itself—therefore presents itself as a *refutation of Spinozism*.

Hegel, then, takes Spinoza at his word[4] and assumes substance in its absoluteness, as *causa sui*. Substance is absolute precisely insofar as it does not depend on other than itself—that is, has no need of any other than itself to exist. It is, therefore, self-position. This conclusion entails the necessary speculative transition from substance to cause—the resolution of the relation of substantiality in that of causality.[5]

But this distinction between a (positing) cause-substance and a (posited) effect-substance, which corresponds to the celebrated Spinozian distinction between *natura naturans* and *natura naturata*, is in fact a purely nominal and abstract distinction, because the two realities are in truth only one. Consequently, substance can no longer be understood as substance alone or cause alone, but rather as relation between cause and effect, a relation in which the cause is immediately the effect and the effect is immediately the cause. Substance, then, is resolved in the reciprocal relation—namely, that *absolute relation*, which is the title of the entire chapter.

> Reciprocity displays itself as a reciprocal causality of *presupposed, self-conditioning substances*; each is alike active and passive *substance* in relation to the other. Since the two, then, are both passive and active, any distinction between them has already been superseded; the difference is only a completely transparent semblance; they are substances only inasmuch as they are the identity of the active and the passive. (WL11 407/SL 569)

In this case too, Hegel's "journey" consists in resolving ontological substantiality in a pure logical movement. But for this pure relatedness to show itself as the acquisition of the dimension of thought a last step is necessary: it is necessary that the absolute relation reveal itself as a relation of self-reflection, in which the relation is *transparent* and *self-aware*. This is a necessary step. If the reciprocity in which substance consists is to be truly absolute, the relation must be known by the substance itself—which is to say that the relation must be posited, not undergone, by the substance. Only if the process of self-causation is *thought* as a process of self-reflection—as a process that is transparent to the substance itself—will it be capable of positing its own absoluteness. But in this way substance reveals itself to be *concept* [*Begriff*]; that is, *subject*.

> The mutual opacity of the substances standing in the causal relationship has vanished and become a self-transparent *clarity*, for the originality of their self-subsistence has passed into a positedness; the *original* substance is original in that it is only *the cause of itself*, and this is *substance raised to the freedom of the concept*. (WL12 16/SL 582)

This is the true Hegelian foundation of idealism: the demonstration that the truth of ontological substantiality is nothing other than thinking—thinking reflected on itself. This act of self-reflection is the only true condition of absoluteness. The question of the ultimate essence of things has thus been answered: it is not ontological essence but logical concept.[6] Being *is* not in virtue of itself but in virtue of the reflectivity of thinking. The *Science of Logic* is, fundamentally, a journey from *being* to the *absolute Idea* as its condition: the last category is the ground of the first, its true raison d'être.

But this enterprise has also produced a *second important result*. In grounding substantiality in the concept, Hegel has at the same time grounded the blind and necessary self-causation of substance in the free and transparent self-reflection of the concept as its condition: "Accordingly the concept is the *truth* of substance; and since substance has *necessity* for its specific mode of relationship, freedom reveals itself as the *truth of necessity*" (WL12 12/SL 577–78). The transition from essence to the concept is therefore at the same time the transition from necessity to freedom. The movement immanent in Spinozian substantiality has refuted necessity and, at the same time, brought it to its consummation, to its truth.

> This infinite reflection-into-self, namely, that being is in and for itself only insofar as it is posited, is the *consummation of substance*. But this consummation is no longer *substance* itself but something higher, the *concept*, the *subject*. The transition of the relation of substantiality takes place through its own immanent necessity and is nothing more than the manifestation of itself,

that the concept is its truth, and that freedom is the truth of necessity. (WL12 14/SL 580)

Freedom, then, manifests itself as the truth of the whole: "In the *concept* the realm of *freedom* has thus been opened. The concept is free, since the *identity in and for itself*, which constitutes the necessity of substance, is at the same time superseded" (WL12 15/SL 582). The meaning of the *Logic* has been radically transformed: it is not simply the necessary journey made by the logical determinations but, since its ground is the freedom that reflects on itself, *the Logic manifests itself as the categorial system of freedom.* If it is "the exposition of God as he is in his eternal essence before the creation of nature and a finite spirit" (WL21 34/SL 50), God has revealed himself to be identical to freedom itself, and the processuality that characterizes him is nothing other than the cadenced journey of freedom. In fact, freedom does not consist in a single act, that is, in the self-position of thought (as it still did in Fichte), but in the totality of the categorial process. The absolute is freedom because it has superseded the totality of the finite categorial determinations that negate its self-positing. In conclusion: freedom (like thinking) is not an indistinct unity but is a process, a multiplicity, a journey, whose final destination maintains in itself the totality of the categories through which it has passed.

But let us understand Hegel's thesis correctly: in thinking the essence of the whole as freedom he does not intend to affirm the existence of an absolute that *in itself* is free, be it in the guise of a transcendent *supreme being* or in the guise of a spiritualistic *pantheism*. As he expressed it in the passage quoted above, "the identity in and for itself, which constitutes the necessity of substance, is at the same time superseded" (WL12 15/SL 582), which is to say: since the meaning of the whole is freedom, it *proves to be impossible to fix it in an essence.*

It is in this context that Hegel's claim, in the *Encyclopaedia*, that spirit is the ground of nature is to be understood: "*For us* spirit has for its *presupposition* nature, of which it is the truth, and for that reason its *absolute prius*" (ENC § 381). If "for us" (that is, for the reader of the *Encyclopaedia* or—more in general—for the self-consciousness that "knows itself" after having experienced the otherness of nature) nature comes before spirit, *in itself*—that is, in truth—spirit comes first: it is the ground, the raison d'être of nature. In other words, nature thought in its essence is nothing other than spirit: its truth is not in itself but in an other. Nature does not depend on itself but on an other—namely, on that spirit which is *the absolute prius*. This leads Hegel to conclude—perfectly in line with the fundamental thesis of idealism: "In this truth nature has vanished." Thought in its essence, nature has lost any trace of naturalness—of externality—and only spirit appears.

But what have we gained from all this? What is this essence of spirit that represents the truth of nature? Hegel's answer is crystal clear: "The *essence* of spirit is therefore, formally, *freedom*, the absolute negativity in the concept as identity with itself" (ENC § 382). Hegel's answer to the old ontological question, "What is the essence of spirit?" is that *spirit has no essence*. Precisely because it is freedom, spirit posits itself as the antithesis of everything that has a nature and a stable essence. Nature has now "vanished," and spirit shows itself to be "absolute negativity." It is so free that it can distance itself even from its own nature: "According to this formal determination, spirit *can* abstract from everything external, and even from its own externality, from its existence [*Dasein*]" (ENC § 382). Its freedom is the freedom to negate everything, all determinacy—even its own determinacy. Spirit cannot be an existing thing. But then, if spirit is the truth of nature and if the essence of spirit is freedom, then the truth of nature is that there is no substrate and that the only truth is the negation of every substrate. The essence of spirit is that of being the negation of all essence.

Nevertheless, this negativity stops short of negating this, its own negative activity: "it can endure infinite *pain*, the negation of its individual immediacy; that is, it can keep itself affirmative in this negativity and be identical for itself" (ENC § 382). Spirit can negate its external manifestations but not its free activity. In the same paragraph, a few lines earlier, Hegel wrote that spirit's "absolute negativity" was at the same time "identity with itself"; that is, the negativity was not directed against itself but maintained itself as negative, and this constituted its identity. This same concept is now expressed by the image of pain and its endurance. If the negative activity produces pain (precisely because it is also turned against its own manifestations, against its very positing itself as *existent*), this pain can be endured—it does not destroy the activity of negation. Spirit's self-negation can be endured.

Hegel focused on this relationship between freedom and pain in the famous "Conclusion" of his Jena essay *Faith and Knowledge*. His claim was that absolute subjectivity ("the pure concept") in its limitless freedom inevitably produced "infinite pain,"[7] and that "absolute freedom" led to "the absolute Passion, the speculative Good Friday in place of the historic Good Friday" (GuW 414/FK 191). Philosophy's task was that of comprehending this absolute freedom "in the whole truth and harshness of its Godforsakenness [*Gottlosigkeit*]" (GuW 414/FK 191).

But what is the relation between freedom and this "absence of God"? For Hegel this is all an inevitable consequence of the nihilistic nature of freedom and therefore of God himself. Indeed, God is freedom—which means that his relation with every determination is negative. His infinity is an "abyss of nothingness" (GuW 413/FK 190), and therefore entails the end of his own determinacy. The absolute that negates is, in its turn, negated by its own activity. Obviously this negating activity does not negate freedom itself, but is directed toward every *Dasein*, every existence, every immediate and empirical reality. It is at this point that Hegel writes the most famous lines of this early work: this infinite pain, before it was speculatively understood, "only existed historically in the formative process of culture. It existed as the feeling that 'God Himself is dead,' upon which the religion of more recent times rests" (GuW 413–414/FK 190).

The *death of God*—the passion and death of Jesus—is the religious representation of a speculative truth: the necessity that the absolute negate its own finite existence—that it pass through pain and death—precisely in order to assert its freedom. But the God that is put to death is the sensuous God—freedom as concrete and determinate existence: this reality cannot resist the process of negation. Jesus must be put to death. This story of "the death of God" represents historically the conceptual truth of the negative nature of freedom.

But this same story narrates the nondefinitive character of death. The negation is not absolute. Freedom, like Jesus on the cross, is able to endure the pain and maintain its identity at the moment of extreme forsakenness. The death of God is "a mere moment of the absolute Idea, but also nothing more than a moment" (GuW 413/FK 190), so that "the highest totality can and must achieve its resurrection solely from this harsh consciousness of loss, encompassing everything, and ascending in all its earnestness and out of its deepest ground to the most serene freedom of its shape" (GuW 414/FK 191). From death on the cross God rises again, no longer as sensuous existence but as spirit. For the spirit of freedom is capable of enduring negation, keeping itself "affirmative in this negativity" and thus showing itself to be "identical with itself" (ENC § 382).

1.2. Freedom and Self-transparency

Spirit's capacity to maintain its identity in spite of its eminently negative constitution is rooted precisely in Hegel's analysis of the nature of "*Begriff*" in the *Science of Logic*. As we have seen, in the "concept," the absolute independence of substance and the absolute self-transparency of the concept coincide. Indeed, the former—autonomy of the substance—is made possible precisely by the latter, that is, by the concept's transparency to, and full awareness of, itself. We are confronted here with one of the most distinctive features of Hegelian philosophy, in which freedom is always put into relation with self-reflectivity. Self-reflectivity is the special relationship that thought has with itself, thanks to which, referring to itself, it determines itself and makes itself independent of everything that does not coincide with it. This is the *first characteristic of freedom*, which Hegel expresses with the celebrated locution of *being-with-self* [*Bei-sich-selbst-sein*].

> [Spirit] does not find its content outside itself, but makes itself its own object and its own content. Knowledge is its form and function, but its content is the spiritual itself. Thus the spirit is by nature *with itself* [*bei sich*] or *free*. (PhWgI 54/PH1 47)

Spirit's relation to itself is the ground and the guarantee of its freedom. This is the principal difference between the freedom of spirit and the necessity of nature. While matter has its center outside itself (Hegel refers explicitly to the force of gravity that impels matter "to move towards a central point"), spirit has its center in itself.

> Spirit, on the other hand, is such that its center is within itself; it too strives towards its center, but it has its center within itself. Its unity is not something external; it always finds it within itself, and exists in itself and with itself [*bei sich*]. Matter has its substance outside itself; spirit, on the other hand, is being-with-self [*Beisichselbstsein*], which is the same thing as freedom. (PhWgI 55/PH1 48)

Joachim Ritter, in his comparative studies on Aristotle and Hegel, showed that this conception of freedom is rooted in the Aristotelian concept of "free human being": "Aristotle defined freedom by expressly differentiating it from the unfreedom of the slave: for him, 'that man [*anthropos*] is free whose end is in himself and not in another' (*Met.* 982b 25–28). Hegel draws first of all on this concept: freedom is the *Bei-sich-selbst-sein* of the individual."[8] Accordingly, Hegel's being-with-self is the idealist translation of Aristotle's having one's end in oneself. And this translation is possible because it is mediated by the Kantian theory of autonomy, according to which a human being is free when he is independent of every motive that is external to pure practical reason—that is, independent of any natural influence, be it internal or external, and of any coercion by another's will.

This first characteristic of freedom is fully consistent with the "modern" conception of freedom's essentially *self-referential* nature, grounded in the absence of relation with anything external (be it object or subject), since this would keep it from full autonomy, rendering it heteronymous. This is confirmed by a passage in the *Philosophy of Right*:

> Only in this freedom is the will completely *with itself, because it has reference to nothing but itself,* so that every relationship of *dependence* on something *other* than itself is thereby eliminated. (PR § 23)

Being-with-self is expressed here in terms of absence of relation with other (seen only as a relation of dependence and a source of unfreedom). Freedom, then, in this first formulation, appears to be monological, solipsistic, and self-referential—elements we shall find again in Hegel's second formulation of freedom.

1.3. Freedom and Negativity

The negative nature of freedom, emphasized in *Faith and Knowledge* and in the *Encyclopaedia*, is reaffirmed in the *Philosophy of Right*—in particular in the first of the three paragraphs that state programmatically the fundamental characteristics of freedom.

> The will contains the element of *pure indeterminacy* or of the 'I''s pure reflection into itself, in which every limitation, every content, whether present immediately through nature, through needs, desires and drives, or given and determined in some other way, is dissolved; this is the limitless infinity of *absolute abstraction* or *universality*, the pure *thinking* of oneself. (PR § 5)

The tendentially limitless nature of freedom is converted, for Hegel, into absolute abstraction—that is, into the impossibility of having determinate contents. Indeed, any determination would appear as a limitation of its universality and an external conditioning. Hegel refers to freedom in this sense as "*negative* freedom or freedom of the understanding" (§ 5 R): it manifests itself not only in the negation of all externality and of any object but also in the abstraction from all determinacy. Here, the dominion of the universal over the particular is radical, in the sense that it entails the negation of all particularity.

But the expression "freedom of the understanding" brings an element of caution to this presumed limitlessness. In Hegel the understanding [*Verstand*] is always a sign of finitude and limitation. And here limitedness is in some way the product of abstraction itself. Positing itself as limitless, freedom ends up by instituting, contrary to its own intentions, a new limitation and opposition—namely, between this indeterminate abstractness and the entire sphere of the determinate and the finite that it leaves outside itself. Hegel calls it "the freedom of the void," and he gives a couple of examples.

The first is the example of the "Hindu fanaticism of pure contemplation"; the second, of the French Revolution, "the fanaticism of destruction, demolishing the whole existing social order" (PR § 5). Hegel returns here to his celebrated analyses of the phenomenon of revolution, already prominent in the *Phenomenology of Spirit*; that is, to his claims that precisely the pursuit of universal freedom—universal equality—inevitably turns into the negation of any concretization whatsoever.

> It [freedom] may well believe that it wills some positive condition, for instance the condition of universal equality or of universal religious life, but it does not in fact will the positive actuality of this condition, for this at once gives rise to some kind of order, a particularization both of institutions and of individuals; but it is precisely through the annihilation of particularity and of objective determination that the self-consciousness of this negative freedom arises. Thus, whatever such freedom believes [*meint*] that it wills can in itself [*für sich*] be no more than an abstract representation [*Vorstellung*] and its actualization can only be the fury of destruction. (§ 5 R)

1.4. Freedom and Finitude

But freedom cannot be only this destructive limitedness of itself and of others. It feels free when it determines itself, when it creates and institutes something that depends on it alone. Freedom, as self-determination, thus has a *positive side*. It was Kant, in the *Groundwork of the Metaphysics of Morals*, who proposed a categorial distinction between *negative freedom* and *positive freedom*. The former characterizes the will when it can act "independently of *determination* by alien causes,"[9] thereby asserting its capacity to abstract from any sensuous and empirical influence. By contrast, positive freedom expresses its own law positively and by itself, and is thus "autonomy—the property that will has of being a law to itself."[10]

Hegel's comments in section 6, where he presents this second side of freedom, are to be read in this context. He remarks that freedom, if it posits itself as positive, necessarily determines itself in particular contents that it will end up seeing as its limitations, even if they come from itself. If, then, negative freedom asserted its absoluteness and its infinite nature at the price of its insubstantiality, positive freedom asserts its concreteness, but thereby ends up finding itself limited and finite.

> In the same way, '*I*' is the transition from undifferentiated inde-
> terminacy to *differentiation, determination,* and the *positing* of a
> determinacy as a content and object. [. . .] [This is] the absolute
> moment of the *finitude* or *particularization* of the 'I.' (PR § 6)

In the Addition to the paragraph Hegel explains that the "I" cannot express its freedom merely by willing, but only by willing something; that is, by determining itself in relation to concrete contents. But in so doing it finds its limitation and negation.

> I do not merely will—I will *something.* A will that, as described
> in the previous paragraph, wills only the abstract universal, wills
> *nothing* and is therefore not a will at all. The particular [thing]
> that the will wills is a limitation, since the will, in order to be
> a will, must in some way limit itself. The fact that the will wills
> *something* is the limit or negation. Thus particularization is what
> as a rule is called finitude. (RZ 54/PR § 6 A)

It seems that freedom, in the end, is unable to extricate itself from this aporia that makes it oscillate between two sides that are equally one-sided:[11] if it wants to be free in an absolute sense it cannot give itself concrete contents, and so its freedom becomes a freedom of nothing; but, on the other hand, if it wants to be freedom of something it loses its absoluteness and finds itself to be finite and unfree.

1.5. Freedom and Relation

Hegel gives his solution to this aporia in section 7, where freedom acquires a dimension that until that point had been hidden. His presentation of the solution is only formal at first, as "the unity of both these moments," in keeping with his distinctive manner of dialectical argument. It is "*particularity* [i.e., the second moment] reflected *into itself* and thereby restored to *universality* [the first moment]. It is *individuality* [*Enizelheit*]" (PR § 7). Hegel's idea (expressed here in a still only formal and indeterminate manner) is that freedom as "individuality" manages to be universal in its particularity, and therefore, finitizing itself, does not lose its universality, as hitherto had appeared to be inevitable. In short, the "I," even as it determines itself, manages to maintain its self-identity, without losing itself in the multiplicity of its contents. In other words, individuality—the "I"—"as *determinate* and *limited,* at the same time remains with itself, that is, in its *identity with itself* and universality" (§ 7).[12]

How can all this come about? How can two apparently irreconcilable dimensions of freedom be reconciled? Hegel answers this question in the Addition to section 7, leaving the formalism and vagueness of his initial formulation behind: "The third moment is that 'I' is *with itself* in its limitation, *in this other*; as it determines itself, it nevertheless still remains *with itself* and does not cease to hold fast to the *universal*" (RZ 57/PR § 7 A, my italics). That other in which freedom determines itself is no longer seen here as a limit for freedom but as identical to this freedom itself.

At this point Hegel broaches an illuminating example precisely of how an otherness can constitute not a limit to freedom but, rather, represent its fullest actualization: "But we already possess this freedom in the form of feeling [*Empfindung*], for example in *friendship* and *love*. Here, we are *not* one-sidedly within ourselves, *but* willingly limit ourselves with reference to an other, even while knowing ourselves in this limitation as ourselves." In affective relationships the other is *not* a limit to the individual's freedom, but is the condition of his or her development. In other words: while the individual is with the other he is at the same time with himself. As Hegel writes, "he regards the other as other" and, simultaneously, "attains a sense of himself [*Selbstgefühl*] for the first time": that is, *he is with himself precisely insofar as he determines himself in an other.* "*This, then, is the concrete concept of freedom*": in acquiring determinacy and contents freedom in no way loses its own universality and identity with itself, but gains concreteness without losing absoluteness. "Thus, freedom lies neither in determinacy nor in indeterminacy, but is both at once" (RZ 57/PR § 7 A).

In this passage Hegel is moving toward a concept of freedom that *corrects* the initial monological and self-referential paradigm he had introduced with the notion of "with itself," which was then essentially confirmed both by the negative and by the positive character of freedom. Freedom continues to be characterized as being-with-self, but this being is now understood as a *being-with-self-in-being-other-than-self.* In other words, freedom is now seen as *relational freedom.*

Hegel's reason for elaborating this more complex model of freedom lies in the limits a concept of freedom understood exclusively as being-with-self inevitably comes up against. As we have seen, a freedom that excludes otherness form itself and closes itself up within its relation with itself will always keep the other outside and see it as an insuperable limit. It will therefore be able to assert itself only in an infinite conflict with otherness from which it can never escape, and therefore will never attain its actualization. Only by including the other in its own project can freedom overcome this structural limitation.

It must, quite frankly, be said that this relational nature of freedom does not seem to be fully in line with Hegel's method in the *Science of Logic,* where the category of the Idea (and thus the essence of freedom) is fundamentally characterized by its self-reflective relation with itself (which is what accounts for its superiority to the category of substance). Nevertheless, despite the predominance of the monological model of freedom based on the exclusive and totalizing "for itself" [*für sich*], we do find some traces of this alternative (relational) model in the *Science of Logic.* In particular, in "The Doctrine of the Concept," after having at first described the "pure concept" as "the absolutely infinite, unconditioned and free" (WL12 33/ SL 601), Hegel goes on to say that, as *"free* power," this universal concept "encroaches on its other" (WL12 35/SL 603). But the impression that, here too, Hegel is endorsing a monological and exclusive concept of freedom is immediately corrected: the concept, in this encroachment, does not *"do violence"* to its other; on the contrary, in its other it is "calm and *with itself* [*ruhig und* bei sich selbst]." The concept's other is thus not seen as something alien to be defended against or to encroach on with violence, but rather as something in which the subject can find self-confirmation: in its other—outside itself—the concept is *bei sich.*

> We have called it free power, but it could also be called *free love* and *boundless blessedness,* for it relates itself to what is *different* just as it relates *to itself;* in what is different it has returned to itself. (WL12 35/SL 603)

The concept is presented here in the first place not as reference to itself but as *reference to another;* that is, as a "love" in which the concept does not lose its identity and freedom but, rather, finds them at a higher level. As we saw in the Addition to section 7 of the *Philosophy of Right,*

Hegel sees love not as dependence on another but, rather, as actualization of the self thanks precisely to its relation with the other.[13]

These conclusions, in "The Doctrine of the Concept," are fully consistent with Hegel's analysis in "The Doctrine of Essence," where he made it clear that absolute self-independence can be attained and posited only in the dependence on another.[14]

But Hegel had already discussed the relation of being-with-self with being-other in the last section of the *Phenomenology of Spirit*, titled "Absolute Knowing." Here, the superseding of the object's externality in relation to consciousness is not expressed simply with the usual formula of being-for-itself and of being-with-itself, but—rather—through the inclusion of being-other within being-with-itself as its moment: "self-consciousness has equally superseded this externalization and objectivity, and taken it back into itself so that it is with itself in its otherness [*Anderssein*] as such" (PhG 428/ PS 479). Analogously, the conceptual comprehension of its own content on the part of consciousness comes about when the "I" is with itself in its otherness: "it is only when the 'I' is with itself in its otherness that the content is *conceptually comprehended* [*begriffen*]" (PhG 428/PS 486). In the Preface, the notion of absolute knowing is presented as self-recognition in otherness: "*Pure* self-recognition in absolute otherness, this aether *as such*, is the ground and soil of science, or *knowing in its universality*" (PhG 22/PS 14). In other words: the immediacy of the unity with itself that characterizes the absolute (that which Hegel describes here as "pure self-recognition," and elsewhere as "reference to itself") is obtained not by *eliminating* otherness but only by *gaining* it—that is, by becoming-other and being-other-than-itself.

In conclusion, with this complex theoretical elaboration Hegel releases the concept of freedom from individual subjectivity and makes it a property of communicative relations. Freedom is something that is not originally within us, but that dwells first of all in the objectivity that surrounds us, from which we can then acquire it. This is the distinguishing feature of Hegelian doctrine.

1.6. Freedom and Objectivity

Hegel's elaboration of the Kantian concept of freedom can be understood as a progressive *desubjectivization of freedom*. As he writes in the *Philosophy of History*, freedom in the individual does not consist in following arbitrary will but in adapting to *true* freedom—that which he calls "freedom of the will" (PhWg IV 920/PH2 cf. 442 ff.). By this he does not mean "the particular will, as it is possessed by a determinate individual" but rather freedom "as it is in and for itself"—that is, "the freedom of God in himself, the freedom of spirit, not of this particular spirit, but of universal spirit according to its essence" (PhWg IV 920). Consequently, "if we would know what is truly right, we must abstract from inclinations, drives, desires, as particulars; we must know what the will is in itself" (PhWg IV 920/PH2 442).

If we do not allow ourselves be deceived by Hegel's theological tone (properly understood, "God" here is equivalent to truth in and for itself; that is, to the objective and universal essence of freedom), we may note that the notion of "the will in itself" does not seem to be very far from Kant. The release of freedom from the individual's arbitrary will—from sensuous inclinations and desires—had been a key element of Kant's philosophical enterprise. By the same token, in Kant, freedom—like duty—had become objective and independent of the empirical subject.

Hegel, then, does no more than draw the extreme conclusions of these Kantian theses: if true freedom is the objective freedom of duty then it cannot be understood as a property of the individual subject. In support of this conclusion he adduces the link between freedom and thought.

> *True* freedom, in the shape of ethical life, consists in the will's finding its purpose in a universal content, not in subjective or selfish interests. But such content is only in thought and through thought. (ENC § 469 R)

Just as thought in and for itself is the universal par excellence—is independent of particular subjects—the same is true of freedom. For Hegel, Rousseau had come to this conclusion even before Kant.

> It was the achievement of Rousseau to put forward the *will* as the principle of the state, a principle that has *thought* not only as its form (as with the social instinct, for example, or divine authority) but also as its content, and that is in fact *thinking* itself. (PR § 258 R)

As Hegel makes clear in the *Lectures on the History of Philosophy*, Rousseau's principle of the general will means that "the concept of freedom must not be taken in the sense of the arbitrary caprice of an individual, but in the sense of the rational will, of the will in and for itself" (GPh2 XV 477/ HP III 402). He goes on to say: "Freedom is just thought itself; he who casts thought aside and speaks of freedom knows not what he is talking of.

The unity of thought with itself is freedom, the free will." Thought is thus the condition for going beyond particular subjectivity: "It is only as having the power of thinking that the will is free" (GPh2 XV 478/HP III 402).

Hegel makes similar remarks in the *Philosophy of History*, where he endorses the principle "put forward by Kantian philosophy": namely, that "the will is free only when it does not will anything alien, extrinsic, foreign to itself (for as long as it does so, it is dependent), but wills itself alone— wills the will." (PhWg IV 921/ PH2 442). A concept emerges here that is central not only for Kant but also for Hegel, and which constitutes the true corrective with respect to the particular will: the concept of *the will that wills itself.*

As he writes in the *Philosophy of Right*, "the will that *has being in and for itself* has as its object the will itself as such, and hence itself as its pure universality" (PR § 21 R). And: "the absolute determination or, if one prefers, the absolute drive, of the free spirit is to make its freedom into its object" and, accordingly, "the abstract concept of the Idea of the will is in general *the free will that wills the free will*" (PR § 27).

Nonetheless, we know that Hegel does not think of this corrective to the particularistic will in the Kantian terms of pure universality. As we have seen, pure universality, precisely because it is capable of elevating itself above particularity and finitude, is incapable of determinations and dissolves into the void. Kant's proposal to overcome the particular wills can certainly be endorsed, "But the next question is: *How does the will determine itself?* For in willing itself, it is nothing but a relation of identity with itself" (PhWg IV 922/PH2 443).

Mere abstract universality is not the way to overcome the particularistic will. This is what emerges from Hegel's critique of arbitrariness, whose corrective resides in a concept of duty that is not merely universalist.

> A binding duty can appear as a *limitation* only in relation to indeterminate subjectivity or abstract freedom, and to the drives of the natural will or of the moral will that arbitrarily determines its own indeterminate good. The individual, however, finds his *liberation* in duty. On the one hand, he is liberated from his dependence on mere natural drives, and from the burden he labors under as a particular subject in his moral reflections on obligation [*Sollen*] and desire [*Mögen*]; and on the other hand, he is liberated from that indeterminate subjectivity which does not attain existence or the objective determinacy of action, but remains *within itself* and has no actuality. (PR § 149)

But in reasserting the Kantian critique of arbitrariness, pitting the true freedom of duty against that false freedom, Hegel characterizes this true freedom in a way that is very different from Kant's. The freedom of duty liberates the individual not only from "mere natural drives" but also from "indeterminate subjectivity that does not attain existence," and makes him fall into "depression" due to his "moral reflections on obligation." Duty is therefore something essentially different from a universalist imperative—a question that Hegel takes up in detail in his discussion of ethical life in the *Philosophy of Right*.

Analogously, arbitrariness is not simply dependence on natural drives but stems from the unfortunate combination of two elements: the indeterminate will on the one hand, and the will determined by natural drives on the other. Hegel writes: "The freedom of the will, according to this determination, is *arbitrariness*, in which the following two factors are contained: free reflection, which abstracts from everything, and dependence on an inwardly or externally given content and material" (PR § 15). Thus, when the universally free will comes up against empirical material it produces an arbitrary volition, as Hegel explains in the Addition to the same paragraph:

> The choice that I have lies in the universality of the will, whereby I can make this or that [thing] mine. This [thing] that is mine is a particular content and is therefore incompatible with me. [. . .] Because of this content, the will is consequently not free, although it has in itself the aspect of infinity in a formal sense. None of these contents is in keeping with it, and it does not truly have itself in any of them. (RZ 67/ PR § 15 A)

The content—that which is *other* than the will—makes the will unfree, and this gives rise to arbitrariness. Unlike the case of the "concrete will"—the will that stems from relation—here *the other*, instead of leading to greater freedom, makes the will dependent on it: "It is inherent in arbitrariness that the content is not determined as mine by the nature of my will, but by *contingency*; thus I am also dependent on this content, and this is the contradiction that underlies arbitrariness'" (RZ 67/ PR § 15 A). The relation to the other is here an unfree relation, governed by the logic not of freedom but of enslavement.

Arbitrariness, then, is "the will as *contradiction*" (PR § 15 R): it intends to be free, but in following its merely subjective inclinations it ends up by becoming unfree and dependent. It is therefore necessary to overcome both of the elements that determine it: the heteronymous nature of the content and the abstract character of the will. But to do so it is necessary to overcome the intellectualistic viewpoint that keeps them alive.

> The understanding stops at mere *being-in-itself* and therefore calls freedom in accordance with this being-in-itself a *faculty* [. . .] [In this way it] takes the relationship of freedom to what it wills, or in general to its reality, merely as its *application* to a given material, an application that does not belong to the essence of freedom itself. (PR § 10 R)

The error of the understanding lies in its instituting a relation between indeterminate freedom, on the one hand, and unfree contents on the other. The unfree relation instituted in this way in its turn generates an unfree—arbitrary—will. Hegel's enterprise consists in *thinking* freedom in a completely different way: not as the deliberation of a (free) subject with respect to an (unfree) object but as an *already existing network of free relations between subjects*. Here, what needs to be discovered is the *objective dimension of freedom* that makes it possible to realize a *relation between the free will and an other*—an other that becomes a moment of its freedom. Whether or not this other is part of freedom obviously does not depend on the will's subjective disposition, is not in its power, but depends on this network of objective relations.

Freedom of the will (or the freedom that wills itself) is to be understood not as mere abstract universality but as a *network of practices and objective relations* regulated by freedom and in which freedom is already embodied. This makes it possible to apprehend the nature of that *other* on which the freedom of subjects depends. This other is to be taken less—and not only—in the sense of another subject than in the sense of an *objective sphere* that becomes a guarantee of individual freedom. As we shall see, for Hegel this is the sphere of *ethical life*.

1.7. Freedom and Self-consciousness

While Hegel corrects the modern philosophers and Kant by denying that freedom is a property or a faculty of the subject, positing it as an objective and relational reality, at the same time he also reaffirms and radicalizes its subjective aspect. This aspect is implicit in the self-reflectivity and self-transparency that Hegel attributes to freedom. The condition for freedom to become real (and not a mere ideal outside of history) is that it be recognized, and that historical individuals become aware of it as their nature. "Freedom in itself carries with it the infinite necessity of attaining consciousness—since freedom, according to its concept, is self-knowledge—and hence of realizing itself" (PhWg I 63–64/PH1 55). The awareness of freedom is its realization. Freedom is activity, and hence is real only in the act of producing itself.

> [Spirit] is *its own product*, and is therefore its own beginning and its own end. The business of spirit is to produce itself, to make itself its own object, and to gain knowledge of itself; in this way, it exists for itself. Natural objects do not exist for themselves; for this reason, they are not free. The spirit produces and realizes itself in the light of the knowledge of itself; it acts in such a way that all its knowledge of itself is also realized. (PhWg I 55–56/PH1 48)

The consciousness freedom has of itself therefore coincides with its manifesting and realizing itself. Freedom cannot remain an ideal object of contemplation: if it remained an idea—that is, if it remained confined to the *Logic*—it would not be true freedom. It would lack the moment of its self-recognition, since the contemplating consciousness would remain outside it, thus infringing its *logical* nature. For it to be real it must be identical with the self-consciousness that recognizes it.

> If the spirit knows that it is free, it is altogether different from what it would be without this knowledge. For if it does not know that it is free, it is in the position of a slave who is content with his slavery and does not know that his condition is an improper one. It is the sensation of freedom alone that makes the spirit free, although it is in fact always free in and for itself. (PhWg I 56/PH1 48)

Freedom of the spirit is full only in its historical realization. Elevating itself above historical conditioning by no means guarantees its absoluteness; on the contrary, it can subsist only within history. Here, ontology forms a circle with history: its truth depends on the historical eventuality. God abandoned himself to the world and awaits his confirmation from the world. But the age of the complete self-recognition of the spirit is *the modern age*. Only here does freedom's being-in-itself come to coincide with its for-itself.

By contrast, the premodern ages are typically characterized by an absence of the consciousness of freedom. Spirit is always free, but its unawareness of its freedom entails its de facto unfreedom: "The *Orientals* do now know that the spirit or man as such are free in themselves. And because they do not know this, they are not themselves free. They only know that *one* is free" (PhWg I 62/PH1 54), namely, the despot. All the others are his subjects.

The consciousness of freedom first awoke among the *Greeks*, but with a decisive limitation. "Like the Romans, they only knew that *some*, and not all men as such, are free" (PhWg I 62/PH1 54). Their awareness went only to the point in which "it is only by birth (as, for example an Athenian or Spartan citizen), or by strength of character, education, or philosophy (—the sage is free even as a slave and in chains), that the human being is actually free." In short, "the Greeks and Romans, Plato and Aristotle, even the Stoics" never had the full and proper idea of freedom (ENC § 482 R).

True spirit manifests itself only with the advent of the *modern age*, in which it is realized "that man as man [*der Mensch als Mensch*] is free, and that freedom of the spirit is his very nature" (PhWg I 62/PH1 54). So, while for the Orientals *only one* is free and for the Greeks and Romans *some* are free, for the moderns *all* are free. This is the *greatness* of modernity: its having brought the journey of freedom to its final destination, thanks to the concept of self-conscious subjectivity.

Chapter 2

The Age of Universal Freedom

The modern idea that all human beings are free, independently of their specific race, language, religion, resources, or culture, is rooted—in Hegel's view—in a historical event that took place long before the birth of the modern world:

> It was through Christianity that this idea came into the world. According to Christianity, the individual *as such* has an *infinite* value, and as the object and end of God's love is destined to have his absolute relation with God as spirit and to make this spirit dwell within him. In other words: man *in himself* is destined to supreme freedom. (ENC § 482 R)

Thus, universal freedom has theological roots. It is based, however, not only on the special consideration broached by Christianity for the individual human being ("object and end of God's love") but on the far more radical idea that the incarnation of Jesus constitutes nothing less than the entering of God's freedom into the world. As Hegel tells us in his Remarks to section 482 of the *Encyclopaedia*, not only is the individual as such free but the freedom of the spirit "dwells within him" and has entered in "the sphere of *worldly existence*." Two consequences arise: the *consciousness* of freedom and, simultaneously, the *actuality* of freedom assert themselves. Modernity is characterized by both. It is the "*knowing* of the idea, i.e. the knowing by which human beings know that their essence, end and object is freedom." But modernity is also the actuality of this idea: "this idea itself as such is the *actuality* of human beings, not because they *have* but because they *are* this idea." Freedom is no longer an aspiration, an "ought" [*Sollen*], "a drive,

31

which demands its satisfaction, but is *character*—spiritual consciousness that has become *being* without drives." Freedom has become a world, a network of relations and of objective practices, from which subjective freedom draws its support and sustenance.

The greatness of the modern age lies in its having developed the idea of universal freedom in all the dimensions of objective spirit:

1. as *legal* freedom: the 'external' freedom of the *person* (2.1);

2. as *inner* freedom: the awareness of the inner autonomy of the *subject* (2.2); and

3. as *social* freedom: the freedom of *homo economicus*, the abstract *individual* of civil society (2.3).

2.1. "Person" and the Universality of Right

It is in the legal sphere that the idea of universal freedom—the attributing of freedom to all human beings independently of their specific character-istics—first manifests itself. The basis of right is *the idea of the person*; that is, consideration of the individual exclusively from the point of view of his rights and legal claims. Hegel refers to this initially as "the will's self-conscious (but otherwise contentless) and *simple* reference to itself in its individuality" (PR § 35). It is this self-reference that constitutes the identity of the "legal person," which therefore determines itself only in relation to itself, in the exclusion of all specificity and of any particular content. Hence the individual is considered a "legal person" when the characteristics that make him different from others are not recognized. From this viewpoint the use Hegel makes of the notion of person is strictly juridical—that is, without the moral sense that has become common usage in language today.

> It is inherent in *personality* that, as a *this*, I am completely determined in all respects (in my inner arbitrary will, drive, and desire, as well as in relation to my immediate external existence), and that I am finite, yet totally pure self-reference, and thus know myself in my finitude as *infinite*, *universal*, and *free*. (§ 35)

Even though the individual is particular and specific (because different from every other), only his universal and infinite side is considered, that is, his equality with all others. Considered exclusively from the viewpoint of freedom, human beings prove to be perfectly equal: *all* of them are free. Their formal relation with themselves makes each a "this" without any determination, equal to every other in simply being "this."

The person is therefore not a subject. In other words: the person is not the self-consciousness that—as Hegel had shown in the celebrated chapter dedicated to this figure in the *Phenomenology of Spirit*—attains self-awareness through a dialectical process of identification with the other but also of differentiation from it. The person has but one relation with other persons: that of equality.

> It is part of education [*Bildung*], of *thinking* as consciousness of the individual in the form of universality, that I am apprehended as a *universal* person, in which [respect] *all* are identical. A *human being counts as such because he is a human being*, not because he is a Jew, Catholic, Protestant, German, Italian, etc. (§ 209 R)

This idea is based on the convergence of two great cultures of antiquity: Christianity and Roman civilization.

> The principle of the *self-sufficient and inherently infinite personality* of the individual, the principle of subjective freedom, [. . .] arose in an inward form in the *Christian* religion and in an external form (which was therefore linked with abstract universality) in the *Roman* world. (§ 185 R)

In addition to Christianity, then, Hegel also considers the tradition of Roman law to be a source of modern subjectivity: it was Roman law that posited the legal notion of the *abstract person*. To this he adds a more recent contribution, namely Kant's idea that "what is of value is *thought*" (cf. § 209 R), where by *thought* he means abstract and universal thought— thought that prescinds from empirical particularities and is the foundation of the modern idea of the subject. This idea—Hegel remarks—"is of infinite importance" and is "inadequate only if it adopts a fixed position—for example as *cosmopolitanism*—in opposition to the concrete life of the state" (§ 209 R): in this case, freedom does not admit its own abstractness and does not recognize the need for its own completion in a context of concrete politico-institutional relations.

It is the consideration of human beings as persons that gives rise to the fundamental norm and specific imperative of right: "The [juridical-formal] commandment of right is therefore: *be a person and respect others as persons*"

(§ 36). Hence the concept of "person" includes a specific *relation of recognition*. We cannot consider ourselves persons if we do not consider others to be persons, since personhood entails universal equality: the condition for being a person is that *all* are persons.

This, however, is a circumscribed recognition, limited to the attribution of personality: "all" recognize all the others *only* as persons, approving and accepting one another's legal claims. Right prescribes no moral conduct, but limits itself to transmitting the norm of respect for the rights of others, without in any way prohibiting individuals from continuing to pursue their own interests. If this pursuit of one's own interests does not infringe on the rights of others, it must be considered perfectly legitimate and unlimitedly pursuable.

But even within these limits the other is, nonetheless, recognized, as we see in Hegel's treatment of *contract*, considered as a relation between owners who intend to exchange their properties. In a contract, then, the relation with the other becomes unquestionably more concrete than in the abstract exposition of the person. But, here too, the other is considered only in the guise of an owner of property. In this way the two contracting parties become equal to one another—they meet only insofar as they are equals, that is, insofar as they are only owners of property. All their other particularities are forgotten and set aside, because they do not determine the reason for their meeting. But this is paradoxical, since the owner of property presents himself as one who has *no* "property," *no* quality, *no* characterization. He loses his *Eigentümlichkeit*, his specificity and property, becoming identical to all others. By entering into the logic of contract-exchange he conforms to everyone else.[1]

> [Contract] is the process in which the following contradiction is represented and mediated: I *am* and *remain* an owner of property, having being for myself and excluding the will of another, only insofar as, in identifying my will with that of another, I *cease* to be an owner of property. (§ 72)

In acceding to a contract the property owner breaks his closure within himself and his particularity. He opens himself up to the other, recognizing himself as equal to another and, at this point, losing all his specificity: in "the unity of different wills" each of these wills "relinquishes its difference and distinctiveness [*Unterschiedenheit und Eigentümlichkeit*]" (§ 73). This explains Hegel's famous remark that "[contract] contains the implication that each party, in accordance with his own and the other party's will, *ceases* to be an owner of property, *remains* one, and *becomes* one" (§ 74). This means not only that, in an exchange, one property owner is lost and another is gained at the same time (ceasing to be and coming to be an owner at the same time), but also that the property owner ceases to be himself while, at the same time, remaining himself. Even though he relinquishes himself, he enters into this relationship only insofar as he *remains* an owner of property. At the same time he *re-produces* this state of his, becoming an indistinct member of the community of proprietors.

But the relation remains purely formal. To enter into relationship as property owners the two parties must negate their own identities: therefore, despite becoming equal to one another, they fundamentally remain strangers who know nothing of one another.[2]

This equality is so abstract that it proves to be substantially incapable of producing a relation with the characteristics of universality. The basis of a contract is the arbitrary will of individuals, not the universal will. The result is an agreement that is nothing more than the compromise between two arbitrary wills.

> The identical will that comes into existence through the contract
> is only *a will posited by the contracting parties*, hence only a *common* will, not a will that is universal in and for itself. (§ 75)

The world of right does not prescribe that *universality* which will be the criterion of the moral world, since its function is only that of allowing individuals to follow their particular arbitrary will—that is, to act strategically, without doing damage to others. The only legal universality is that of the person and therefore does not regard the ends of actions. What is attained, then, is only *communality*, not universality. Unlike universality, in communality particularities act on the basis of their interests and desires, which are never called into question in themselves. Indeed, the individual arbitrary will is substantially accepted and made compatible with the arbitrary will of all the others. Communality, in its essence, is therefore asocial; that is, devoid of effective intersubjective relations. This obviously does not mean that freedom of the person coincides with freedom of the arbitrary will. On the contrary: legal freedom prescinds from the arbitrary will and from the concrete individual, limiting itself to considering the individual only as an abstract person and guaranteeing him against the unlimited expansion of any arbitrary will.

Joachim Ritter, in his studies on Hegel, based his interpretation of the fundamental character of legal freedom on the Hegelian category of *diremption.** For Ritter, Hegel interprets modernity in the light of this category.[3]

> Modern society and civilization [. . .] all over the world are overturning the old historical orders of the past, separating individuals from these institutions and bringing them back to the equality of their constitutive human being.[4]

Modernity's realization of equality—that is, its assertion of the freedom of the legal person—entails a "break" with traditional man. It separates abstract man from the concrete man linked to status, culture, religion. In this way it produces a concept of the human being, the *person*, that completely prescinds from his sociohistorical concreteness.

> The future characterized by its equality has no continuity with the historical orders of the past. The historical being and the social being of man separate. That which in itself subsists in human existence conjointly is sundered.[5]

Historical being—the belonging to a class and to a tradition—is separated from social being, that is, from legal equality with all. The diremption of modernity from the past is therefore a *diremption within modern man* between his substantial inequality and his formal equality. Furthermore, it entails a diremption between the individual and the community, insofar as the legal person is the individual abstracted from communal ties, released from the historical context that gives him concreteness and specificity.

Ritter is convinced that Hegel was fully aware of the structural and therefore insuperable character of this diremption. For Hegel "there is no possibility of escaping from the diremption,"[6] but this represents neither a

---

*Entzweiung. In Hegel's *Differenzschrift* the term has been translated as: disunity, disunification, bifurcation, division, dualism, scission, split, dichotomy, diremption. (I think *cleavage* would be a better choice than any of these, apart from *diremption*.) R. D. Winfield, the translator of Ritter's *Hegel and the French Revolution*, follows the Cerf-Harris translation of the *Differenzschrift* and translates *Entzweiung* as *dichotomy*; I agree with J. P. Surber's choice of *diremption* in his translation of the same text. *Dichotomy* connotes a fixed opposition, a clear-cut and static partition into two mutually exclusive parts. Hegel has something completely different in mind: a forcible, even violent *separation*—and above all a *dialectical* one: interaction, not partition. *Entzweiung*, for Hegel, is the Spirit of the French Revolution. For Ritter (1957, p. 62 ff.), Hegel's *diremption* is of subjectivity and objectivity, but also of the romantic and the revolutionary, "of tradition and future"; it is "the form in which their original unity historically maintains itself under the conditions of the modern world."

definitive defeat of thought nor an insurmountable difficulty for the continuity of history. The task of thought is certainly not the unrealizable one of unifying what is dirempted but, as Hegel writes in the *Differenzschrift*, of "positing diremption in the absolute, as its appearance [*Erscheinung*]" (DFS 16/DIF 94). If diremption is already in the absolute, that which manifests itself in the modern world is nothing other than its historical expression: diremption must be thought, but not canceled.

On the historico-political plane the insuperability of this diremption from the past, far from making the break with history definitive, is precisely what makes historical continuity possible.[7] Modernity, by abstracting from the past, realizes that freedom which has been the unbroken thread of the West's historical experience. Abstract freedom is nothing other than the universalist extension of the freedom that in antiquity was reserved for a privileged few. Diremption marks an ineliminable transition on freedom's journey toward its final realization.

This analysis is substantially confirmed by Charles Taylor, for whom "the beautiful Greek synthesis had to die because man had to be inwardly divided in order to grow"[8]—that is, in order to discover his inner freedom. Without the break with concrete man it would never have been possible to attain the idea of self-reflecting and autonomous subjectivity—the idea of the abstract individual who is equal to himself and by virtue of which all are equal to each other. Hegel reaffirms this a number of times, in particular in his *Lectures on the Philosophy of History*, where he says that "the principle of free thought, of human inwardness, produced the rupture [*Bruch*]" that was absolutely necessary to go beyond Greek ethical life, which "so supremely beautiful, amiable and interesting in its appearance, is nonetheless not the highest standpoint of spiritual self-consciousness; it lacks the infinite form, the reflection of thinking in itself." In short, "the element of subjectivity, of morality, of reflection proper and of inwardness" was, indeed, a source of "corruption," but was also "the source of further progress" (PhWg III 638–639/PH2 cf. 267–270). In light of this, Taylor concludes, there was no way of healing the rift by reproposing a revival of that beautiful Greek *Sittlichkeit* which modern subjectivity, with its baggage of diremptions, had left behind: "The overpowering nostalgia for the lost beauty of Greece was kept from ever overflowing its bounds into a project of return."[9] The diremption had to be faced, and the solution to its problems had to be found within it, not outside it.

Earlier, in chapter VI of the *Phenomenology of Spirit*, Hegel gave us a wide-ranging analysis of the connection between diremption and the broaching of abstract right. Here, the world of Roman law was considered in its historical advent after the demise of the traditional community represented by the ancient *polis*. While the *polis* was characterized by the substantial unity of individual and community, its crisis gave rise to a model of the state in which the community dissolves into a merely formal universalism without substance and the individual acquires an autonomy that is only apparent, because devoid of all specificity.

> Now the substance emerges in everyone as a *formal universality*, no longer dwelling in them as a living spirit; on the contrary, the simple compactness of their individuality has been shattered into a multiplicity of points. (PhG 260/PS 289)

In the transition from the *polis* to the universal empire the community has dissolved and the individuals, who had been compact in the substantial unity of the ethical, have now become an indistinct multiplicity of points, a mere summation of persons equal to one another.

> The universal unity into which the living immediate unity of individuality and substance withdraws is the spiritless [*geistlose*] community that has ceased to be the substance—itself unconscious—of individuals, and in which they now have the value of self-essences [*Selbstwesen*] and substances, possessing a separate being-for-self. (PhG 260/PS 290)

The community has lost both its substantiality and its "spirituality," since the ethical structure that supported it has collapsed. This, however, gives rise to the independence of the individual, who previously had been dominated by and dependent on the community. Now the individual becomes "self-essence"—he finds his ground in himself and no longer outside himself—and "substance"—that is, he becomes independent *qua* individual, a characteristic that previously only the community could possess.

But this individuality conquered on the ashes of the traditional community is only apparent. The individual who is now opposed to the whole counts only as a "one" and not for what he is in himself, for his qualities and specificities. What arises from the dissolution of the ancient community is only the *abstract individual*.

> The universal, this lifeless spirit split up into the atoms of the absolute multiplicity of individuals, is an *equality* in which *all* have the value of *each*, i.e. count as *persons*. (PhG 260/PS 290)

The individual that emerges from the breakdown of concrete univer-sality is only an *atom*, whose only distinguishing mark is its equality with all the others—that is, its *legal equality*, in which, as we have seen, full-fledged individual characteristics are completely disregarded. What arises here is the *person* who is such precisely insofar as *all* are persons. In this sense what arises from the breakdown of the ethical community is not a new community but a new status of humanity, which Hegel calls "*legal status*" [*Rechtszustand*]. In it, abstract equality comes to replace the living relationships between the members of the old community. But this equality is not a relationship: it is, rather, the consequence and the reassertion of the absence of a relationship.

This condition gives rise to what the Hegel of the *Phenomenology* calls "the self" [*das Selbst*]—that is, the reflection of consciousness in itself and the discovery of the difference between self and social totality. To be sure, here we are still at the first, dawning form of the self, which will be followed by those of the modern world, but its fundamental characteristics are already present. Its characteristic trait is a sort of *immediate coincidence* between individuality and universality (while in the successive figures this relation will lose all immediacy).[10] Immediate coincidence means that the individual, although opposed to the abstract universality of which he is a part, is himself *a universal*—which is to say, a "point" that is equal to all the other "points" and is therefore devoid of particularity.

> Just as this person is the self that is empty of substance, so is its existence an abstract reality too. The person *counts*, imme-diately; the self is the point immediately at rest in the element of its being; it is without separation from its universality, and therefore the two are not in reciprocal motion or relation: the universal is without internal differentiation, and is not the content of the self, neither is it the self filled by itself. (PhG 341/PS 384)

Being universal on the part of the self means, here, being replaceable by any other. The universal that constitutes the self is "without internal differentiation": it is without contents apart from that of being a "whole"—which is to say, a multiplicity of individuals unrelated to one another. In fact, there is no relation (no "motion") between them, or between them and the universal. The totality to which they belong provides them with no content ("is not the content of the self") but is only the container con-stituted by these undifferentiated individuals. In this sense their relation is *immediate* ("is without separation")—that is, there is no middle term that gives the relation any concrete meaning apart from the mere coinciding of its members.

In this condition the individual, who at first—just after his liberation from the condition of communal compactness—had discovered his substantiality, immediately loses it again. This self is "empty of substance": while it sees its subsistence in its independence from the totality it also discovers its extreme emptiness and inessentiality.

> The consciousness of right experiences in its actually count-
> ing for something [*in seinem wirklichen Gelten*] the loss of its
> reality [*Verlust seiner Realität*] and its complete inessentiality
> [*Unwesentlichkeit*]; and to describe an individual as a *person* is
> an expression of contempt. (PhG 262/PS 292)

An individual who counts only for his abstract equality with everyone else counts for nothing. He has no quality or particularity, and thus discovers himself to be "inessential." Indeed, to describe him as a "person" is an "expression of contempt."

What is more: a society regulated by right alone and devoid of the substantial *ethos* that was the foundation of the *polis* is destined to give free rein to the arbitrariness of instincts and passions, and to unleash "the chaos of spiritual powers that, in their unfettered freedom, become elemental beings raging madly against one another in a frenzy of destruction" (PhG 263/PS 292). In such a context individuality is graphically confronted with its own contingency, and with its unmitigated exposure to the events that surround and threaten it. The diremption of totality put paid not only to the traditional community but exposed the individual to the danger of annihilation.

Hegel's analysis of legal status and of the abstract person dramatically reveals their *dual nature*. Yes, their advent gives rise to a new human condition that was completely unknown to the old world of substantial ethical life; but, at the same time, the price of this progress is an equally essential loss. The birth of modernity—which, for Hegel, took place within the ancient world itself—is marked by a process of *emancipation* and *alienation* at one and the same time.

With great conviction, Joachim Ritter emphasized the first of the two aspects. He brings to light the particular sense of liberation the "juridification" of intersubjective relationships takes on in Hegel. With its intervention relations between individuals come to be mediated by *things* [*Sachen*]*—that is, by the property relations individuals have with their objects. As we have seen, their reciprocal relations are, in the final analysis, nothing other than property relations.[11] But this means that right sanctions human lordship over things—sanctions, that is, the historical process "through which nature is transformed into a thing and taken into possession by man as a thing."[12] In this way freedom does not remain closed in a private inner world but *takes objective and historical form*. As Hegel puts it, "my will, as personal and hence as the will of an individual, becomes *objective* in property'" (PR § 46, my italics) and freedom expresses itself in the "external sphere" (§ 41). A thing, when it becomes property, is imprinted with the *sign* of human freedom, the seal of freedom's mastery over natural necessity (§ 58 and A). Hence, for Ritter, the sphere of property is "the condition of possibility for the realization of freedom in the entire range of its religious, political, and ethical substance."[13] Man "can first become free *in actu* when he frees himself from the unfreedom of the state of nature and makes nature a thing, breaking its power."[14]

The process of juridification leads, then, to two results: the objectification of freedom in the external world and the liberation of man from the dominion of nature. To be sure, for Hegel this process spells the destruction of every human and personal tie, but "beyond the negativity that characterizes it also for him, he maintains that the interpersonal relationship limited to things is not only the condition of liberation from nature, but simultaneously the positive condition of the freedom of individuals"[15]—that is, of this freedom's making itself objective. Here, juridical freedom essentially means the self-assertion of the spirit and its mastery over nature.

Ritter does not conceal the reification involved in this affirmation of freedom, insofar as the regulation of social relationships as mediated by things inevitably means reducing these relationships to things. Nevertheless, he insists that this reification is an advance over antiquity, since in the ancient world the condition of slavery meant the reduction of the entire human being to a thing. In the modern world, by contrast, the freedom of

---

*In his translation of Ritter's *Hegel and the French Revolution*, Winfield consistently renders *Sache* as "object of the will," distinguishing it from *Ding* (thing): he states his reasons for this in detail (p. x of his "Note on the Translation"). In the context of Hegel's *Logic* the distinction is important. However, here we are in the context of the *Philosophy of Right*, and I follow Nisbet (and Knox)—and, in particular, Cortella, whose discourse here centers on "*la cosa*" ("the thing") and *reification*—and render *Sache* as *thing*.

> a modern domestic servant or day-laborer [. . .] consists in that
> what they reduce to a "thing" and can "alienate" in the rightful
> form of contract is not themselves but only their labor power
> and the use of their skills for a limited time. [. . .] With this,
> freedom becomes, for the first time without restriction, the prin-
> ciple of a society. As a world of labor mediated through things,
> modern society frees man not only from the power of nature, but
> simultaneously raises freedom to the universal principle through
> the determination of labor and of all labor relations in such a
> form that skills can only be alienated as things, and property
> only for a limited time.[16]

It is legal freedom and the respect for the person it broaches that remains
irreducible to a thing, and therefore immune from the logic of reification.

Ritter clearly wants to distance himself from Marx. While the target of
Marx's critique is precisely the contradiction of modern man, torn between
formal freedom and the substantial unfreedom of the world of economy
and work, Ritter exalts this very diremption by showing the emancipating
side of formal freedom. But, in the modern world, these labor processes
take up most of human life, and the overwhelming power of their logic
invades nearly all the spaces of our lifeworld. The twentieth-century theories
of reification, in the variety of their conceptual and analytical forms, show
this clearly. Only an overestimation of the role of formal freedom in the
concrete life of individuals can make us believe that the moderns experience and perceive the reification of an essential part of their selves as an
emancipatory process.

What is more, Ritter's use of Hegelian philosophy to fuel his critique
of Marx only halfway achieves its objective. On this point Hegel proves to
be far more problematic than Ritter would like to admit. In Hegel's analyses the juridification of concrete life and its reduction to abstract relations
is presented more as a loss than as an emancipation. The development of
his thinking on the theme of diremption, from the *Differenzschrift* to the
Phenomenology, leads him to diagnose the diremption of modernity as a
full-fledged form of *estrangement*.

Hegel writes that the world of right and of the formal freedom of
the person appears to the concrete human being as a "reality from which
he is estranged [*entfremdete*]" (PhG 264/PS 293). The individual understood as a person equal to all other persons is not the individual in his
concrete reality—no, it is the individual as a juridical construction. Accordingly, individuals see this, their image, as something that most certainly is

attributed to them but that, at the same time, is deeply alien to what they really are.

> But this world is spiritual essence, it is in itself the interfusion of being and individuality; this its existence is the *work* of self-consciousness [Werk *des Selbstbewußtseins*], but it is also a reality immediately given and alien [*fremde*] to it, a reality that has a being of its own and in which self-consciousness does not recognize itself. This [reality] is the external essence and the free content of right. (PhG 264/PS 294)

Freedom has constructed a world, the juridical condition—but a world in which individuals do not recognize one another. Hegel refers to this work of construction as a *process of alienation* [*Entäußerung*]—that is, as self-consciousness's transferring its essence outside itself: "it [the reality of right] obtains its existence through self-consciousness's own *alienation* [*Entäußerung*] and *loss of essence* [*Entwesesung*]" (PhG 264/PS 294). Nevertheless, we must not take the concept of *Entäußerung* used here by Hegel in a negative sense. Subsequent uses of the term (Marx's in particular) are substantially different from Hegel's. In this context *Entäußerung* signifies—in a perfectly neutral sense—"externalization" (which is the translation that is technically closest to what Hegel has in mind);* that is, it indicates the process by which the individual transfers his essence outside himself.

Hegel makes it clear that this is not a negative process a few pages later, when he explains that this is the only way in which the individual manages

---

*In the passage considered here, Miller in fact translates *Entäußerung* as "externalization." Cortella, in his note at this point in the text commenting on the Italian translation of the *Phenomenology*, remarks that the translator "correctly" translates the term as (the Italian equivalent of) *externalization*, "thereby avoiding the negative meaning inevitably attached to the concept of *alienation*. Nevertheless *Entäußerung* has always been translated in Italian [and in English] as *alienation* and the use of the word *externalization* leads to a loss of all the connections with the subsequent history of a concept that has in these pages of the *Phenomenology* one of its principal places of origin." This is a point very well taken and, of course, is exactly the case in English as well. But, then, in Hegel *Entäußerung* is often not far from *Entfremdung*—it, too, generally translated as *alienation*. This is one reason why Miller translates *Entäußerung* at times as *alienation* and at other times as *externalization*—also to distinguish it from *Entfremdung*: which Baillie, in his "old" but always very interesting translation, renders as *estrangement*. I believe that *alienation* is the "necessary" translation of *Entäußerung*, for the good reason given by Cortella. It *may* also be the "best" translation of *Entfremdung*, but to distinguish between the two terms I shall follow Baillie and consistently translate the latter as *estrangement*.

to be real: "Self-consciousness is only a *something*, it has *reality* [*Realität*] only insofar as it alienates itself from itself" (PhG 267/PS 297). This is the condition of modern man—of man who has lost his traditional place within a community, who has become independent of the social totality, but who, finding himself alone and without his traditional supports, manages to be real only by "constructing" reality around himself and transferring his characteristics to it. Outside of these constructions, outside of this "work" he is mere naturalness—contingency that lets itself be overwhelmed by instincts and passions, a mere "plaything of raging elements."

> The self that is *immediately* valid in and for itself *without estrangement* [*Entfremdung*] is without substance, and is the plaything of those raging elements; *its* substance is therefore its alienation [*Entäußerung*] itself, and the alienation is the substance. (PhG 264–265/PS 295)

By means of alienation the self finally obtains the substantiality it had irremediably lost after the dissolution of the ethical community. Alienation is thus most certainly the loss of essence and its transferal to a world external to self-consciousness, but it is also the way in which natural self-consciousness, lost in its mere naturalness, recovers its substantiality and consistency.

"Legal status" is the first modality by which the natural self constructs an "artificial" world in which to be at home once more. But it cannot be satisfied with this status. This lack of satisfaction gives rise to the continuation of the process of alienation, and to the progressive creation of a world in which the self makes its home. For Hegel, *the fundamental characteristic of modernity* consists in its being a process of education [*Bildung*], thanks to which original natural individuality progressively becomes "civil." Modern man, who has now definitively left the traditional community behind, cannot accept being merely natural: he sees the radical insufficiency and contingency of an existence made up exclusively of instincts and passions. The fundamental principle of modernity is that *the state of nature must be left behind*, and the way to do so is by creating cultural, social, economic, and political products—in other words, by objectifying the self outside of itself. This objectification feeds back on the individual who produced it, acting on him as a process of cultural, institutional, ethical, economic, and political education.

> It is therefore through culture [*Bildung*] that the individual has value and actuality. His true *original nature* and substance is the

spirit of the *estrangement* of *natural* being [. . .] This individuality *molds* itself by culture [*bildet sich*] into what it is *in itself*, and only by doing so it *is in itself* and has actual existence [*wirkliches Dasein*]; the measure of its culture is the measure of its actuality and power. (PhG 267/PS 298)

In the modern world the individual counts not for his nature but for his culture, for the world he has managed to build for himself, for what he has made of himself through the process of "molding" and developing—in short, for the "products" of his spirit. His true original nature resides not in mere naturalness but in the products of his spiritual work, in the objectified results of his alienation. The true nature is the artificial nature of man's products. This is his true world.

But he achieves this result through *renunciation*. The individual must renounce his naturalness and his immediate instincts. This is the price he must pay to attain substantiality: "the renunciation [*Entsagung*] of [his] being-for-itself is itself the production of actuality" (PhG 267/PS 297). Transferal of the self outside itself is a process simultaneously of renunciation and of construction: the cultural world grows in proportion to renunciation of the natural world. Civilization is born and grows strong thanks to the repression of instincts—a question that will be at the heart of contemporary culture. But this is also the paradigm on which modern political theorists have envisioned the birth of the state: it is the renunciation of natural force by individuals struggling with one another that makes it possible for them to submit to the Leviathan and "creates" the "artificial" force of the state. In this way they regain their original strength—namely, by recognizing themselves in their product: in the political force of the modern state. Their "actuality consists solely in the supersession [*Aufhebung*] of their natural self" (PhG 267/PS 298), in the renunciation of their spontaneity and immediacy.

But Hegel gives us fair warning: at the moment in which self-consciousness produces its artificial world outside itself, it sees this world as *estranged*. This consequence may seem paradoxical, since this world is its product: there would appear to be all the conditions for accepting this objectification and recognizing the self in it. But this is not the case. The result of *Entäußerung* is not that the self finds itself once again in the other—no, it is the experience of *Entfremdung*, of *estrangement*.[17] Modern man has built an artificial world on his own scale, outside his self; but in this world he ends up *not recognizing himself*. Civilization, based on the repression of instincts and the renunciation of naturalness, produces "discontent" and a sense of estrangement. This is the fundamental characteristic of modern *Bildung*.

Paradoxically, the consequence of this situation is not an interruption of the process of *Bildung* but—on the contrary—its increase. In fact the individual continues to build his artificial world around himself because, in this activity, he sees the only way of overcoming his state of estrangement. Self-consciousness "divests itself of [*sich entäußert*] its personality, thereby producing its world, which it treats as something alien of which it must now take possession" (PhG 267/PS 297). Thus, the process of *Bildung* is simultaneously a process of alienation and reappropriation of what is estranged. It has a *dual* nature.

> This world is for self-consciousness something immediately estranged that has the form of a fixed and undisturbed reality. But at the same time, certain that this world is its own substance, it proceeds to take possession of it [*geht es sich derselben zu bemächtigen*]; [self-consciousness] gains this power over [substance] through culture [*Bildung*]. (PhG 268/PS 299)

The contradiction of the modern world lies in the fact that *Bildung* is the process by which the individual loses his essence and transfers it to another, but it is also the means by which he attempts to regain this lost essence. It is clear that the more he uses the "cultural" instrument the more he strengthens the process of alienation, and he will have all the more need of "culture" to take his essence back again. He seems to have no escape from this paradoxical circle.

With regard to the products that populate the world around us we moderns have developed an intimately antinomical *dual awareness*. On the one hand, we find *ourselves* in these products and we recognize our own essence in them. On the other, we experience estrangement from objects that are themselves *artificial*. Against an integrated and inwardly reconciled consciousness we pit a consciousness that is unreconciled and critical. Hegel theorizes this and calls the former "actual consciousness" [*wirkliches Bewußtsein*] and the latter "pure consciousness" [*reines Bewußtsein*]. The former experiences the unity of the self and the objectivity the self produces, "passing over" into the objective world it has created; the latter feels the full weight of the estrangement of this "fixed" and external reality.[18] The processes of modernity bear the signs of this unreconciled contradiction. The *Phenomenology of Spirit* passes through the many forms and modes this contradiction assumes, without ever arriving at a definitive solution to the antinomy. Here, the dialectic of *Bildung* presents the features of a structural insolubility.[19]

As we shall see, this problem that in the *Phenomenology* presents itself as an aporetic diagnosis of modernity (solved only "theoretically" in "absolute knowing") will find its full-fledged solution in the *Philosophy of Right*, and in particular in the doctrine of ethical life. But some Hegel scholars have taken this diagnosis as the truest image Hegel gave us of the modern world. Christoph Menke, for example, in his book *Tragödie im Sittlichen*,[20] claims that the condition of modern society, after the substitution of ethical life by legal status, has been characterized precisely by the distinctively tragic "no exit" situation theorized by the *Phenomenology*. For Menke, the introduction of right, beginning in the Roman era, entails an insuperable *diremption* between that which is universally valid (legal norms and the "person") and the concreteness of historical life. Individuals—he claims—cannot recognize themselves in the abstract image of the "legal person" that treats them all as equals, ignoring their particularities. Since an individual's identity stems from the context in which she grows up, from the values and the history she shares with others, when this context is characterized only by anonymous and juridically egalitarian intersubjective relations she has no more bases for determining who she really is. Her only identity is her equality with others. But this is the dissolution of all identity.

For Menke, this situation determined by the end of the "beautiful ethical life" of the ancients can find no "true" solution in the modern world. It is true that modernity compensates for the demise of the solidary relationships of the traditional community by conferring universal freedom upon individuals. As a result of the intersection between Roman law and the Christian valorization of individual freedom, we moderns no longer perceive right as an external imposition but as a product of our freedom. In short, in the modern world the conflict between individual freedom and legal compulsion is no longer meaningful, since it is in this very compulsion that the autonomy of the individual manifests itself. Nevertheless, if modern legal status manages to solve the problem of *equality* and of respect for individual *autonomy*, it gives no answer to the problem of *authenticity*—that is, to modern man's need for identity. Intersubjective relations founded on the criterion of equal respect for the other stand dumb before the demand to know what a good life is, and what values make it possible for the individual to realize herself authentically. Once the conflict between legal equality and individual autonomy has been resolved, in the modern world the conflict between the universalist dimension of autonomy and the particular sphere of authenticity flares up anew. Even though autonomous, the modern subject cannot find her realization in this equal freedom—she does not find what the ancients would have considered her "good." Here, the modern schema (less solidarity but more liberty, less common ethics but more individual autonomy, equal justice as a substitute for the good life) seems to find its structural limit.

Menke unquestionably deserves credit for having seen Hegel's works as an effort to deal with this fundamental aspect of the modern condition. But, as we shall see, he underestimates the solution that Hegel, with his theory of ethical life, intended to give. In any case, it remains to be seen how well the solution proposed in the *Philosophy of Right* can respond to the question raised by Menke and by contemporary theories of authenticity. I shall return to this in the concluding section of this book.

2.2. Freedom as Autonomy of the Subject

For Hegel the path that leads to the consolidation of the universal freedom of the legal person runs parallel to another process, that of modern man's *becoming aware* of his inner freedom. As we have seen, freedom must *know* of itself, otherwise it cannot *be* freedom. And modernity is the epoch of this self-disclosure of the freedom of consciousness: "The right of the subject's *particularity* to find satisfaction, or—to put it differently—the right of *subjective freedom*, is the pivotal and focal point in the difference between *antiquity* and the *modern* age" (PR § 124 R).

This new awareness produces a major change in the meaning of freedom. Freedom no longer resides exclusively in the *right* to be treated as a person (the "legal person")—in other words, it is no longer a *legal disposition* that recognizes the right of the person not to be subject to the will of others. Here, freedom becomes a *disposition of the subjective will*: "Only in the will as subjective will can freedom, or the will that has being *in itself*, be actual" (§ 106). In the Addition to this paragraph Hegel illustrates clearly the difference between *legal freedom* and *moral freedom*: while legal freedom is not concerned with the individual's intention but only with the effects of his action, for moral freedom what is decisive is precisely the subjective disposition.

> Human beings expect to be judged in accordance with their self-determination, and are in this respect free, whatever external determinants may be at work. It is impossible to break into this inner conviction of human beings; it is inviolable, and the moral will is therefore inaccessible. The worth of a human being is measured by his inward actions, and hence the point of view

of morality is that of freedom which has being for itself. (RZ
205/PR § 106 A)

The true difference between the legal sphere and the moral sphere
is therefore the difference between *freedom in itself*, that is, freedom as
objective right, and *freedom for itself*, that is, freedom as conviction and
subjective intention.

The moral point of view is the point of view of the will insofar
as the latter is *infinite* not only *in itself* but also *for itself*. (§ 105)

Here, freedom is no longer the *negative freedom* of abstract right—
protection of the arbitrary will and reciprocal limitation of opposed arbitrary wills—but the *positive freedom* of self-determination: *autonomy*. The
transition from right to morality is thus the *transition from person to subject*.

This reflection of the will into itself and its identity for itself,
as opposed to its being-in-itself and immediacy and the determinacies that develop within the latter, determine the *person* as
a *subject*. (§ 105)

Morality, delineated in these terms, is a specific characteristic of the
modern world—it is the conviction and practical disposition of modern
individuals: they know they are free, and make their conscience the ultimate
criterion of their actions. For this reason—as I remarked in the Introduction—Hegel deals with morality not within "subjective spirit" but as an
essential part of "objective spirit"—that is, of the external and historical
manifestations of freedom.

But this "objective" world of modern morality has been conceived
and prepared by *philosophy*. Indeed, philosophy is the acme of the self-
consciousness of freedom—the place in which this awareness assumes the
form of conceptual elaboration. After the advent of Christianity the second
phase of this development is represented, for Hegel, by the *Protestant Reformation* and by Luther's theological thought that Hegel sums up in these
few words: "Luther's simple doctrine is the doctrine of *freedom*" (PhWg
IV 878/cf. PH2 415). The Lutheran criticism of the redeeming value of
"external" works and its vindication of the fundamental meaning of faith
involves an opening of inwardness to the absolute: it is in inwardness that
the individual's salvation resides.

The simple difference between Lutheran and Catholic doctrine lies in this, that reconciliation cannot be accomplished through a mere external thing, the host, but only in faith, i.e. in the orientation of the spirit towards it. (PhWg IV 879/PH2 cf. 415–416)

And faith is not a certainty that is based on our sensibility or our opinions. It has to do not with the finite but with the absolute, it is "subjective certainty of the eternal, of truth existing in and for itself, the truth of God" (PhWg IV 880/PH2 415). In this way the subject discovers within himself the dimension of absoluteness.

He becomes a true subject only by renouncing his particular content and making this substantial truth his own. This spirit is the essence of the subject. Insofar as the subject relates himself to it as his essence, he becomes free, because he is absolutely with himself [*bei sich*]; in this way Christian freedom has become actual. (PhWg IV 881/cf. PH2 416)

The Lutheran doctrine of faith makes a new thinking of freedom possible. It consists in the recognition of freedom's nonsensuous and nonfinite nature. Man is free because the absolute dwells in his "heart": it is here that the modern journey of freedom starts. Indeed, if "the Middle Ages were the kingdom of the Son [. . .] with the Reformation the *kingdom of the Spirit* begins" (PhWg IV 881)—which is to say, the modern awareness of the essential freedom of human beings.

The modern philosophy of the subject, inaugurated by Descartes, is the legitimate heir of the Lutheran revolution. The principle of the *cogito* is in fact a principle of freedom. On the basis of the *cogito* one must accept no prejudice, no attestation that is made in an authoritarian and unfree manner; everything must pass through the sieve of doubt, of the calling into question of every presumed truth. The demand for a thinking with no presuppositions apart from thinking itself is the demand for a thought that is *with itself*, which is the fundamental category of freedom. "What is recognized as true must have the position that our freedom is contained in it, that we think" (GPh1 20 129; see also V9 93). *English empiricism* confirms this approach, reasserting the principle of freedom of thought and autonomy of judgment: "On the subjective side the important principle of *freedom* found in empiricism must also be recognized; namely that whatever a man admits in his knowledge he *himself* must see, he *himself* must know it to be *present*" (ENC-L § 38 R). Here, the vindication of freedom consists in reasserting the principle of evidence and of the priority of knowing over the object's presumed truth in itself.

This school of thought finds its maximum expression in *Kantian philosophy*. But, for Hegel, not in the doctrine of theoretical reason (which, in his view, reveals its unfreedom, since it cannot posit its own objects by itself), but rather in the doctrine of *practical reason*.

> Kant's idea of theoretical reason is that when reason relates itself to an object, this object must be given to it; but when the object is given by reason to itself, it has no truth; and in *this* knowledge reason does not arrive at independence. As practical, on the contrary, reason is independent in itself; as a moral being man is free, raised above all natural law and above all phenomena. (GPh2 XV 532/HP III 457)

Theoretical reason finds a limit to its freedom in the fact that it is dependent on the givens of sensuous experience. If it wished to give itself an object independently of these givens it would end up producing an apparent object—the idea. By contrast, practical reason posits its objects by itself, and in this it is fully independent: "here reason disdains all the given material that was necessary to it on the theoretical side" (GPh2 XV 532/HP III 457). Note well: the superiority of practical over theoretical reason does not lie, banally, in its practical character—that is, in the fact that the will *posits* its objects (i.e., is active) while consciousness *receives* them (i.e., is passive). No, it lies in the Kantian thesis that the pure will is capable of positing its determinations by itself without depending on the empirical will and sensuous inclinations. In this way Kantian practical reason attains—Hegel tells us—absoluteness, that is, a freedom freed of any kind of limitation: "Thus we have the standpoint of absoluteness revealed, since there is an infinite disclosed within the human breast" (GPh2 XV 533/HP III 458).

Subjective freedom—so important and essential in the journey of modernity—is nonetheless marked by *structural limits*. On many occasions Hegel criticized the reduction of freedom to the dimension of inwardness and, in particular, the conception of freedom in Kant. But it is above all in the *Phenomenology of Spirit* that he gave his critique systematic form, in two successive moments of the book: at the end of chapter V (in particular in the last two subsections of section C: "Reason as Lawgiver" and "Reason as Testing Laws") and then in section C of chapter VI, specifically dealing with morality. In these passages, Hegel's *objections to Kant* are particularly articulated and complex.[21] Nevertheless, it is possible to group Hegel's arguments around *three fundamental questions*.[22]

The *first objection* regards *the opposition between morality and nature*. For Kant the condition of what is moral is its independence from natural conditionings, both inside (sensuous drives, passions, desires) and outside the individual: without such independence the individual would in fact not be free, and therefore could not make moral claims. But this independence forces Kant to project morality into a dimension totally other than nature, in a supersensuous realm of ends. The result is a human condition inwardly split between a sensuous dimension, subject to natural necessity, and a supersensuous dimension, governed by freedom. In showing the intrinsic antinomicity and laceration of this condition Hegel remarks at the same time that for Kant himself this solution was less than satisfactory. In positing the separation between the two "realms," Kant simultaneously posits the "moral" necessity of their homogenization. His "postulates" of practical reason show the practical need for a unity between morality and inner nature (the immortality of the soul as the demand for a holy will—that is, a will no longer limited by sensuous drives) and for a unity between morality and external nature (the supreme good as the demand for a harmony between morality and an external nature that, no longer hostile, is a guarantee of happiness for every holy will). In short, such unity does not exist but *ought* to exist.[23] For a contemporary philosophical consciousness this objection of Hegel's is a critique that smacks of ancient metaphysics: not only is it not at all clear why nature and freedom ought to find a higher unity, but Kant's very doctrine of the two realms (the first sensuous and the second supersensuous) is very hard to accept. Nevertheless, properly decoded, Hegel's objection maintains all its validity. It intends to point out the substantial inefficacy of a moral law that has no place within our nature, which, indeed, is composed not only of our body but also of our habits, desires, practical interests, and values. The demand Hegel posits is, substantially, for a morality that is embodied within our lifeworld. In the end, Habermas himself is obliged to take Hegel's side in order to correct his own proposal of a morality inspired by Kant:

> This, then, is right: all universalist morality depends on *compliant* forms of life. It has need of a definite agreement with practices of socialization and education that embed strongly internalized controls of conscience in adolescents and promotes proportionately abstract ego identities. A universalist morality also has need of

a definite agreement with the political and social institutions in which juridical ideas and post-conventional morals are already incorporated. In fact, yes, moral universalism *arose* thanks to Rousseau and to Kant only in the context of a society that presents these *corresponding* characteristics.[24]

Hegel's *second objection* to Kant regards the *formalism* of morality and its incapacity to generate concrete practical contents exclusively on the basis of the form of law. In short, for Hegel "pure reason" cannot be "practical"—which is to say, it cannot generate maxims of action while totally prescinding from value assumptions of historico-empirical origin. This is the critique of what Hegel, in the *Phenomenology*, calls "reason as lawgiver." Pure reason can, at most, evaluate already-existing maxims but cannot generate new ones.[25] As Hegel makes clear in the following chapter, the difficulty consists in passing from pure universal formality to the historical multiplicity of maxims.[26] In other words, it appears to be impossible for the moral law to maintain its purity while it makes itself "plural"—that is, while "duty" becomes "many duties." But, here, although Hegel does raise the question of the decline of a morality that, differentiating itself, can no longer be "holy," the problem that really concerns him is the universal law's incapacity to make itself particular—that is, to differentiate and pluralize itself. This is a return, in a different form, of the young Hegel's critique of the dominion of the universal over the concrete life of individuals and of its violent and repressive nature—a critique that accuses Kantian universalist morality of an incapacity to recognize the pluralistic structure of modern societies and their increasingly differentiated interests. Put in these terms, however, such a critique could meet with serious objections. First of all, as Habermas rightly noted, it is precisely this differentiation of values and interests that makes the recourse to increasingly abstract and universal norms inevitable.[27] Mere formalism cannot make itself content: this is the real question Hegel raises. In the *Philosophy of Right* the objection is stated as follows: formalism cannot take as its criterion any standard other than inner consistency and absence of contradiction, "but it is impossible to make the transition to the determination of particular duties from the above determination of duty as *absence of contradiction*, as *formal correspondence with itself*, which is no different from the specification of *abstract indeterminacy*" (PR § 135 R). This leads, in the *first* place, to the inevitable recourse to already-existing norms and practices: without them, "reason as tester" would have nothing to test and therefore would produce no result. History and nature, kept outside the purity of moral law, once again become the condition for its functioning. In the *second* place, the pure testing of laws and the possible individuation of the right moral norm leaves the problem of its application unresolved. Here again, this leads to the necessary recourse to an additional faculty, alien to pure practical reason—namely, to the individual *capacity of judgment*, similar to the Aristotelian virtue of *phronesis*, capable of applying universal norms to the concrete case. This presents us with the problem of this faculty's *role*—that is, whether it can be considered merely applicative, or whether it brings back into play precisely those universal norms that, in Kant's formulation, ought to be tested only by pure practical reason.[28]

The *third objection* calls into question the productivity of Kant's *universalization test*—that is, the possibility of establishing the morality of the maxims on the basis of their extension to universal laws. In the *Phenomenology*, after showing the impossibility for practical reason to be a "lawgiver," Hegel also argues against the simple possibility of reason "as testing laws." With the help of a series of counterexamples, Hegel convincingly demonstrates the merely fictitious character of the generalization procedure, showing how it does no more than confirm what we *already* hold to be just or unjust.[29] This judgment is reaffirmed in the *Philosophy of Right*, where Hegel contests the effective capacity of the universalization test to add further elements of judgment to the merely formal criterion of consistency and absence of contradiction. This allows Hegel to extend the same objections raised against its "formal" character to the "universal" character of the moral law.[30] Quite rightly, objection has been raised against this criticism for its not fully doing justice to the Kantian criterion of universalization: the test Kant introduces is not purely *semantic* (the possibility of continuing to *think* certain maxims without contradiction once they have been universalized) but is *practical* (the possibility of everyone's *wanting* to universalize certain maxims).[31] Put in these terms the test would in fact demonstrate its heuristic validity—it could actually individuate the norms that can be universally shared. But in this case the universalization would do nothing other than confirm what all human beings *already* share *before* any universalizing procedure, and therefore "morality" would end up coinciding with "ethical life"—that is, with what is already at work and embodied in human practices and habits.

In conclusion, *Hegel's three objections can be condensed in a single fundamental argument*: pure subjectivity with its formal criteria (universalization, noncontradiction, consistency) is not capable of determining, from within itself, any moral content. As Honneth writes, "Hegel's objection to the idea of moral autonomy is that it does not help us in reconstructing how a subject will ever come to act rationally; for in trying to apply the categorical imperative, the subject will remain disoriented and 'empty' so long as he does not resort to certain normative guidelines drawn from the institutionalized practices of his environment."[32] In other words: *there can be no morality without ethical life*; there can be no moral autonomy without social conditions that by virtue of their ethical life have educated us to follow certain moral norms and to use our autonomy. But, by the same token, moral prescriptions cannot be founded on abstract subjectivity alone.

It is clear that, for Hegel, this conclusion does not call into question the moral process that has led to the idea of moral autonomy, neither does it entail the rehabilitation of a heteronymous morality. On the contrary, it means the opening up of a *broader concept of freedom* than was the case in Kant—a freedom that is not simply confined to the individual's inner sphere. Just as morality proves to be dependent on the institutional context that makes it possible, by the same token individual freedom constitutes itself on the basis of this context. It is thanks to the other, thanks to our ethical relations with other human beings, that we "learn" to be free—that is, learn to make concrete use of our freedom. Here the already important attainment of the "positive" freedom theorized by Kant—a freedom that determines itself positively on its own account—is further completed and enriched. This "positive" freedom can be obtained only thanks to a "relational freedom"—that is, a freedom embodied in the social practices and "ethical" institutions in which individuals ""grow up." In these relations an "objective freedom" is born and progressively takes shape: a freedom that is not reducible to individual autonomy but, at the same time, is its condition.

Hence *Kant's true limit* consists in *his failure to recognize this objective freedom* and his confinement of freedom to the inner and individual sphere alone. Against this sphere he pits the entire dimension of objectivity, in which he recognizes no "spiritual" value.

> This otherness [i.e., natural objectivity], because duty constitutes the sole essential end and object of consciousness, is, on the one hand, a reality completely *without significance* for consciousness. But because this consciousness is so completely locked up within itself, it behaves with perfect freedom and indifference towards this otherness; and therefore the existence of this otherness, on the other hand, is left completely free by self-consciousness, and it too relates itself only to itself. (PhG 325/PS 365)

Against the free world of self-consciousness stands the "self-subsistent whole" of the object: it is "in general, a *nature* whose laws like its actions belong to itself as a being that is indifferent to moral self-consciousness, just

as the latter is indifferent to it" (PhG 325/PS 365). But it is not only nature
that is seen to be abandoned by freedom: the entire historical world—the
world of objective spirit—is likewise abandoned.

> *The ethical world*, on the other hand, the state, or reason as it
> actualizes itself in the element of self-consciousness, is not sup-
> posed to be happy in the knowledge that it is reason itself that
> has in fact gained power and authority within this element, and
> that asserts itself there and remains inherent within it. The spiritual
> universe is supposed rather to be at the mercy of contingency
> and arbitrariness, to be *god-forsaken*, so that, according to this
> atheism of the ethical world, *truth* lies *outside* it. (PR Preface
> 8/12–14, my underlining)

Kant's true limit, then, consists not in his refusal to transfer inner
freedom to the historical world (wanting to subjugate historical reality to
subjective freedom would be "voluntaristic" presumption) but, rather, in his
inability to recognize the already-existing freedom at work in history. As
Joachim Ritter wrote, Kantian subjectivity "does not recognize reified reality
as its existence; it does not believe that God can be present in this reality"
and therefore its need to transmit itself to a world in its own likeness is
transformed into impotence: "morality, in the 'formalism' of the 'ought,'
must 'remain unrealized.' " [33]

In the light of these considerations it is clear that the intent of Hegel's
criticism of the Kantian "ought" is not to question the viewpoint of morality
but only the separation of the "ought" and reality. These two dimensions
are closely interwoven precisely in sociohistorical reality. Reality is rational,
for Hegel, precisely insofar as it "*is* as it ought to be," since "mere *being
without the concept*, without its own 'ought' to which it must conform, is
an empty illusion [*ein leeres Schein*]" (JW 17–18/JAC 18).

As Odo Marquard convincingly argued in a celebrated essay of the
1960s, Hegel on the one hand stands in perfect continuity with the transcendental philosophies of Kant and Fichte and with their "refusal to accept
the given as a court of last instance [*das Gegebene als Instanz*]." [34] On the
other hand his criticism of them was aimed at their "refusal to link universal ends, which therefore regard freedom, with the process of realization of
their mediation, and therefore to link the 'ought' with reality." [35] This refusal
was due to their fear of having to link the destiny of universal ends to an
uncertain historical reality: "It is to save universal ends from the uncertain-
ties of reality that Kant, Fichte, and the early Schelling trace these ends back

to postulates, to the mere 'ought,' and for this very reason can only find the universal in reality far from the real end, and the end far from the real universal,"[36] which is to say, the universal only in natural laws and the ends only in the world of inwardness. In the event, precisely this attempt to save the ends by distancing them from history turns out to be a subjugation to mere givenness—that is, a regression. It is against this outcome that Hegel posits the unity of being and the ought-to-be.

And it is here that the philosophies of Kant, Fichte, and the early Schelling show themselves to be *the fullest expression of the self-consciousness of modernity*, whose limit—the inability to recognize the objective dimension of freedom—consists precisely in an insufficient awareness of itself. This self-consciousness knows itself only as individual consciousness of freedom—as subjective freedom, as progressive discovery of the essential freedom of the individual—but fails to see in this the objective side of itself, the realization of freedom in history. In modernity "self-consciousness thinks of itself as being self-consciousness; in being self-consciousness it is for itself [*für sich*], but is still for itself in negative relative to its other" (GPh2 XV 620–621/HP III 549).[37] The new awareness of freedom remains confined within the subject and leaves the world of objective relations without self-recognition—that is, the world of nature and history, seen as domains ruled by mechanistic necessity and by causality. This subjective self-recognition, then, does not do justice to the *ontological nature* of freedom theorized by Hegel, which now appears in its true significance as not simply a metaphysical theory that conceives of the absolute and totality as free in and for themselves but—rather—as a historical diagnosis of the sociopolitical sphere and of the rootedness in it of the free spirit of modernity. But until this rootedness is recognized freedom cannot attain its completion. This is the foundation of Hegel's critique of modernity. Yes, he sees its greatness precisely in the discovery of universal freedom; but he also sees its limit in the restriction of this freedom to the subjective dimension. Hegel's theoretical project can thus be configured as an extension of the awareness modernity has of itself. The self-correction of modernity in which his project consists is therefore, essentially, a different awareness of what modernity has *already* become. Here, the moments of subjective and objective freedom ought to converge. The true realization of freedom is expressed adequately neither by its individual subjective side nor by its objective and suprasubjective side but, rather, by the self-recognition of objective freedom in individual self-consciousness. In other words, *the two movements must come together*: the self-determination of subjective freedom must coincide with the realization of the objective order. Individuals will recognizes their own essence in objectivity and objectivity becomes aware of its own freedom in individual self-consciousness. This is what takes place in the particular condition of objective spirit that Hegel call *ethical life*. In ethical life, freedom has "its actuality through self-conscious action, just as self-consciousness has its motivating end and a foundation that has being in and for itself in ethical being" (PR § 142). But this condition of complete interpenetration of the subjective and the objective is attained only in the last stage of ethical life, in the sphere of the state. The fundamental step on the way to this stage is the broaching of a new—typically modern—objective-historical dimension of freedom: the dimension of *civil society*.

2.3. Freedom of Civil Society

There is an essential link between civil society and the sphere of abstract right: civil society is the realization of this sphere on the social plane. In civil society, the abstraction represented by right becomes a concrete reality, takes sensuous form, and makes itself a social order—the *dwelling* of human beings. Here, once again, we have the connection between *ethos* and *dwelling*: civil society, by all rights, is part of the sphere Hegel calls *ethical life*. And while Hegel divides this sphere into the three distinct domains of the family, civil society, and the state, civil society is unquestionably the domain most characteristic of modernity and its condition of life. In civil society we find the phenomena of labor and the capitalist economy, industry and the liberal professions, the market and the distribution of goods, economic freedom and bourgeois individualism, social classes and the relation between poverty and wealth. Nevertheless, Hegel—despite his presenting civil society as the dwelling place par excellence of modern *homo economicus*—portrays it as a condition without any "ethical" content—as a savage realm of conflict without rules.

2.3.1. Civil Society as State of Nature

It is difficult to think of civil society as an ethical sphere—as a full realization of concrete freedom—when the type of individual that characterizes it is depicted by Hegel with the features of *natural man*, that is, of the human being seen from the standpoint of his *primary needs* alone. The fundamental attitude that characterizes the individuals who populate this sphere is that of the attempt to satisfy their needs. The first principle of civil society is "the concrete person who, as a *particular* person, is his own end" (PR § 182). We have moved on from the "abstract" person of right to the "concretely" living person of civil society, but his fundamental characteristic is still that of "particularity"—which is to say, of the individualistic personality exclusively concerned with its own interests (and, consequently, whose only end is itself). Described by Hegel in typically naturalistic terms, as a "totality of needs and a mixture of natural necessity and arbitrariness" (§ 182), such a personality proves to be the opposite of freely self-conscious and self-determining subjectivity.

Now, this "particularity in itself [*für sich*]," which is only an "indulging itself in all directions as it satisfies its needs, contingent arbitrariness, and subjective caprice," seems to have but one destiny: it "destroys itself and its substantial concept in the act of enjoyment" (§ 185). Capricious arbitrariness inevitably exposes itself to *contingency*: it produces a condition of life in which the individual is continually exposed to the arbitrariness of others, in addition to his own, and therefore to the inevitable limitation (if not the total obstruction) of that satisfaction which is the only aim of "natural man." In short: this society of the arbitrary gives rise to social conditions in which individuals have absolutely no control over their existence. Hence we can well understand why Hegel concludes that "in these opposites [i.e., necessary and contingent needs] and their complexity, civil society affords a spectacle of extravagance and misery as well as of the physical and ethical corruption common to both" (§ 185).

With these characteristics, the situation of civil society seems strikingly similar to that of the Hobbesian *state of nature*. We know, however, that the naturalness of civil society is "constructed," is the product of *Bildung*, of a process thanks to which the human being has "become" a single individual, on the ashes of the traditional solidary community. This immediate and particularistic naturalness is the typical "product" of modernity—a product whose characteristics were totally unknown to the ancient world, in which naturalness expressed itself in harmony with the social and the natural totality. The member of civil society is a result of the modern process of particularization, closely connected with the parallel advent of subjective freedom. His "naturalness" is thus the result of the process of *abstraction* by which the individual separated himself from the concreteness of the relations that bound him to the community and to his traditions. In the end, his distinctive characteristic was only his naturalness. The "natural man" is, in the end, the same as abstract man.

2.3.2. Abstract Freedom Becomes Reality

Civil society is the realm of abstraction; it is the becoming-concrete of what is abstract; it is abstraction that makes itself existence. Juridical universality is realized here as a form of material life. Here, again, the validity of Ritter's theses on the *centrality of diremption* is confirmed: it is by breaking with traditions that a human being can show himself to be pure nature—a needful being, seeking satisfaction. He has lost all "cultural" characteristics, connected with a social and historical status that has been totally erased by his break with the past. It is the historical process of modernity itself that has made it possible for the individual to lose all his historical traits, and to present himself as mere naturalness.

> The natural concepts of society, need and its satisfaction, and work and the division of labor, which Hegel adopts, remain "abstract" concepts for him; they entail the detaching of society and its practice from the history of tradition.[38]

Man as subject of civil society is "abstract" man, detached from his historical and spiritual relationships and left standing in the equality of his needful nature.[39]

"Abstract"—then—is man *separated* from the wealth of his characteristics and qualities, whose only identity is *limited to* "its restriction to the natural relationships of human existence and man's satisfaction of need through labor."[40]

Charles Taylor's position on this question seem more than reasonable. He affirms that civil society—thanks precisely to the principle of abstraction—achieves a singular *social equality*.

> There is a third trend in modern society that Hegel sees as being sustained by both these forces [individualistic liberalism and egalitarianism of the general will], and which is *that towards homogenization*. For it is not only the drive towards absolute freedom that sweeps aside all differentiations; the development of the capitalist economy has also meant the disruption of traditional community, the mass migration of populations, and the creation of a unified market and as much as possible a unified labor force. And all this has contributed to the homogenization of modern society, the creation of one large society in which

cultural subgroups are progressively eroded, or only survive at the periphery of life, in domestic customs or folklore.[41]

For Hegel, modernity is the *annulment of all difference*, not only from a juridico-formal but also from a sociohistorical standpoint. It is capitalist individualism itself that, attacking all forms of tradition, levels cultural differences and renders all individuality homogenous, precisely because it is characterized only by the needs and appetites that are the same in all individuals, since every other particularity has been dissolved. Taylor's position is that capitalist practice produces a *cultural egalitarianism*, different from the socioeconomic variety pursued by socialism but with equally weighty consequences for the concrete life of individuals.

Here, a *two-sided relationship* arises between legal equality and civil society—a reciprocal determination of the one by the other. *First*, the "freedom of all"—the universal consideration of every human being as a "person"—is a constitutive *condition* of civil society. Man presents himself in the world of work and the market essentially as a natural individual, independently of his institutional position (i.e., of his status): this is guaranteed by *right*. Ritter correctly states that in civil society "freedom has to count as the principle of labor"[42]—the condition for constituting a labor "market" is that individuals present themselves in it as mere naturalness, equal to one another and willing to pursue their interests freely. Freedom, here, is the same as naturalness.

Second, it is civil society that *makes possible* the practical and political constitution of the legal system. It is precisely because individuals have already "been made equal" (in Taylor's sense) that they are willing to accept the legal formalization of their equality.

> The *relativity* of the reciprocal relation between needs and work to satisfy these needs includes in the first place its *reflection into itself* as infinite personality in general, i.e. as (abstract) right. (PR § 209)

The relations of civil society, once they *reflect* on themselves and become *aware* of what these relations really are, are formalized in abstract right, which is thus the result of this self-reflection: civil society concretely realizes equality, and right manifests it reflectively with its normative system. Abstract right is therefore civil society's *knowing itself*, its self-consciousness. It is on the basis of civil society that right presents itself not as authoritarian imposition but as something *"universally recognized, known,* and *willed"* (§ 209). Civil society provides—so to speak—the basic condition, namely that equality of atomized individuals thanks to which right can be recognized and accepted as the regulation of what human beings already are: "naturally" equal persons who reciprocally enter into relation for the exchange of goods.

2.3.3. Primacy of Freedom Over Nature

There is another sense in which civil society is not a simple duplication of the *status naturae*: its members pursue *mastery over nature,* and the instrument of this mastery is *work.* In § 188 of the *Philosophy of Right* Hegel explains that civil society is, properly speaking, not characterized by immediate natural need but by "the mediation of need." In fact "the satisfaction of the individual" comes about "through his work and through the work and satisfaction of the needs of *all the others"* (§ 188). Hence there is an elevation from mere animal naturalness: unlike the immediate use that characterizes animal life, in civil society need passes through a mediation. Work imposes a deferral in the satisfaction of the need: instead of consuming the goods at his disposal immediately *homo laborans* defers the satisfaction of his need in anticipation of a greater one, and thus inserts an intermediate moment between his need and its satisfaction. But, here, the mediation is constituted not only by work but also by the social element: in civil society the needs of others come into play and thus, necessarily, also their work. I shall come back to this important relational element later on. For now it is sufficient to note how the introduction of this social element allows Hegel to speak of a "system of needs"—that is, of natural needs organized in a *system,* a *network of reciprocal relations.*

At this point, Hegel's approach to civil society begins to take shape. In civil society the individual presents himself in his abstract naturalness. And yet, through the mechanisms set in motion by the technico-instrumental approach to nature (work) and the network of relations with other individuals for the exchange of goods and for labor organization itself (interaction), he progressively emancipates himself from this immediate naturalness to gain awareness of his freedom and spirituality. Paragraph 187 represents a key moment in this strategy. Here, Hegel focuses on civil society's *education [Bildung]* of the natural man, in order to lead him gradually from his abstract individuality to that which Hegel terms "universality." In this context—especially in the long Remarks that follow the paragraph—Hegel explicitly vents his polemic with those philosophers (Rousseau first of all) who had pitted the "natural" against the "civil" side of man, magnifying "the ideas [*Vorstellungen*] of the *innocence* of the state of nature and of the ethical simplicity of uncultured [*ungebildeter*] peoples," implying that "*education will be regarded as something purely external and associated with corruption*" (§ 187 R). Hegel, by contrast, wants to show, on the one hand, the extreme intolerability of a merely natural condition but, on the other, he does not intend to pit against it a conception of civilization as radically antithetical to the constitutive naturalness of human beings. What he intends, rather, is to defend the thesis of a substantial continuity between nature and culture (*Bildung*), showing the processes at work in civil society that lead the individual from the immediacy of needs to the universality of his freedom.

> The end of reason is consequently neither the natural ethical simplicity referred to above, nor, as particularity develops, the pleasures as such that are attained through education. Its end is rather to work to eliminate *natural simplicity* [. . .] i.e. to eliminate the *immediacy* and *individuality* in which spirit is immersed [*versenkt*], so that this externality [*Äußerlichkeit*] may take on the rationality *of which it is capable*, namely the *form of universality or of the understanding*." (§ 187 R)

Also in the form of mere immediate naturalness spirit is not absent but only "immersed." It is through civil society that spirit can emerge from its unconsciousness. The instrument of which it avails itself is *work*. Hegel insists on the "external" character of civil society: its characteristic elements are nature and the appropriation of nature through "external" work and needs. And yet it is this very "externality" that educates the individual and raises him from immediacy.

> Only in this way is the spirit *at home* [*einheimisch*] and *with itself* [*bei sich*] in this *externality* as such. Its freedom thus has an existence [*Dasein*] within the latter; and, in this element that, *in itself*, is alien to its determination of freedom, the spirit becomes *for itself*, and has to do only with what it has impressed its seal [*Siegel*] upon and *produced* itself. (§ 187 R)

Civil society is an essential moment in the development of freedom, which even in external existence can make itself real—that is, can make itself *Dasein*. It is a spirit that succeeds in impressing its "seal" on the natural *thing*, which precisely by means of human freedom becomes an *object* of work. Hegel had insisted on this strict implication between work and freedom ever since his days in Jena. Work cannot be considered merely an instrument for the transformation of external nature, adapting it to human needs. Work also transforms inner nature, developing the identity of the subject and setting in motion a process of "formation" through which the individual gains awareness of his freedom and his spirituality. It is in this way that spirit emerges from its state of lethargy and unconsciousness, becoming "for itself" and recognizing civil society as its dwelling, its home, its "with itself." Work is thus a process through which freedom asserts its predominance over nature: "*Education* [*Bildung*] is *liberation* and *work* towards a higher liberation" (§ 187 R).

Freedom, for Hegel, does not reside in detachment from civilization, in returning to a mythical "natural freedom," but rather in the process of *Bildung* itself, in that interweaving of work and interaction thanks to which the individual frees himself from his naturalness. He reasserts this concept in section 194: "This social moment contains the aspect of *liberation*." Civil society is not only the locus of immediate and natural needs but is also where these needs become conscious, and are elaborated and socialized. By combining need with its "conscious" representation the individual emancipates himself from mere naturalness: "Within social needs, as a combination of immediate or natural needs and the spiritual needs of *representational thought* [*geistiges Bedürfnis der Vorstellung*], the spiritual needs, as the universal, predominate" (§ 194). The gaining of the universal consists in the transition from the rule *of* needs to the rule *over* needs: the human being now "relates not to external but to inner contingency, to *arbitrariness*" (§ 194). To be sure, we have not yet reached the stage of full freedom of the spirit—we are still in the domain of "contingency." But the process has been set in motion: need that is unconscious (and therefore governed by an external necessity) has been replaced by need that is aware of itself—by the inner will of individual arbitrariness. Once again, Hegel rebuts the idea of a freedom that would be possible only in nature—the notion that "in relation to his needs, man lived in *freedom* in a so-called state of nature in which he had only so-called natural needs of a simple kind" (§ 194 R)—insisting that in such a condition man would be dominated by nature and would live in "a condition of savagery and unfreedom" (§ 194 R). Nevertheless, it would be an error to oppose this false natural freedom with a spiritual freedom totally opposed to it, *other* than it (as Kant did). For Hegel, it is only through nature and thanks to the processes of civil society that true freedom can travel its road: "freedom consists solely in the reflection [*Reflexion*] of the spiritual into itself, its distinction [*Unterscheidung*] from the natural, and its reflection [*Reflexe*] upon the latter" (§ 194 R). The reflection of the spiritual does not pre-scind from nature but is the reflecting of the spirit on nature and on the basis of nature: it is the capacity of nature—thanks to the activity of the spirit—to project itself outside itself.

At this point we can return to section 187 and to its central thesis: we now have the elements to understand it adequately.

> The interest of the Idea, which is not present in the consciousness of these members of civil society as such, is the *process* whereby their individuality and naturalness are raised, both by natural necessity and by their arbitrary needs, *to formal freedom* and formal *universality of knowledge and volition*, and subjectivity is *educated* in its particularity. (§ 187)

In these few lines Hegel describes the entire process of the individual's emancipation within civil society. He also makes it perfectly clear that the subjects involved are in fact not *aware* of the process: they are *led* to "knowledge" but will only arrive at it at the end. While the process is going on they know only "natural necessity" and their "arbitrary needs"—and yet, these naturalistic elements produce a process of spiritual formation, a *Bildung*. As we have seen, the *transformation* of external nature is simultaneously a *formation* of inner nature. Now—this "education" conducted by civil society consists in leading the individual *first of all* to "formal freedom"—that is, to the rule of law: he learns to live in a society regulated by laws, and he learns to adapt to these laws. The *second step* is the acquisition of what Hegel calls "formal universality of knowledge and volition." Thanks to his work and his network of relations the individual acquires a *culture* (a universality of knowledge)—capacities, concepts, technical and theoretical knowledge, that permit him to orient himself in the socioeconomic world. But at the same time he also acquires a *practical knowledge* (a universality of volition)—he learns the moral notions and their relative universalist points of view.[43] Yes, it is true that these universalities are still "formal"—they are universalities of the understanding [*Verstand*]; but it is also true that they call into question for the first time the individualist standpoint with which man had made his appearance within civil society.

As Giuliano Marini wrote, in this elevation from naturalness to knowledge, the individual acquires "a theoretical and practical culture that makes him fit to be a member of this realm of work and of intellect [. . .] in civil society, man, emerging from the natural and immediate ethical life of the family, acquires the infinite refinement stemming from the intellect, from work, from the isolation in his individuality, which is also an advance in the development of his capacities."[44]

This, then, accounts for the *"ethical" nature of civil society*: it is the *habitual place* of modern man, capable of educating him *"to"* freedom and of freeing him *from* immediate needs. For this reason—as we have seen— here spirit is "at home." And for this reason this sphere (like every ethical sphere) is capable of setting in motion a process of emancipation of the individual that frees him from the slavery of his instincts and of capricious arbitrariness. And this comes about through the "hard work" that opposes the "immediacy of desire" and the "arbitrariness of caprice" (§ 187 R).

Modern man, to raise himself to full freedom, must therefore pass through the misery and physical corruption of civil society: here, he learns to discipline his needs and, in this way, to make the right use of his autonomy. It is perfectly true that, here, the individual is not taught to establish solidary relationships with others. *Civil society is the school of individualism* and its teachings lean toward a conscientious and disciplined use of the individual faculties. Nevertheless, the education to be *autonomous* is also an education to be *responsible*. As Albrecht Wellmer wrote, civil society "had a *positive* role with regard to the formation of individuals who would have the intellectual and moral qualifications that they would need as citizens of the modern state."[45] Hence only apparently does civil society lead to the loss of communal and solidary relations, because through its processes the foundations are laid for their reconstitution.[46] It is through the practice of individualism that the subject learns to overcome himself and open himself up to that broader sense of freedom which Hegel will present within the political sphere of the state.

2.3.4. Overcoming Individualism

Deeply marked by an individualist imprint, civil society—through this very individualism—prepares its members to become progressively aware of the universal dimension that goes beyond their immediate interests. And it does so by forcing individuals to enter into relation with one another, and so to engage with a point of view different from their own. If, in fact, the first principle of civil society was the "particular person," now Hegel presents us with the *second principle*:

> But this particular person stands essentially in *relation* to other similar particulars, and their relation is such that each asserts itself and gains satisfaction through the others, and thus at the same

time through the exclusive *mediation* of the form of *universality,* which is *the second principle.* (PR § 182)

The individual pursues his own ends and is able to attain them only insofar as he utilizes his relations with others. While this does not mean that individualism as such is called into question, what Hegel is saying is that its necessary condition is precisely the relation with other individuals: it is thanks to others that every human being attains his own ends. This is why Hegel writes that the particular person is "mediated by the form of universality," since every member is in a certain sense "delivered" to the others.

Returning to section 187, we find that Hegel himself makes similar remarks: if "individuals are *private persons* who have their own interest as their end," nevertheless "this end is mediated through the universal," in the literal sense that the universal "*appears* to the individuals as a *means*" by which to attain their end. In other words: the end can be attained only if each individual *relates* to the other in a system of forced universal collaboration. For this reason, individuals must "determine their knowledge, volition, and action in a universal way and make themselves *links* in the chain of this *continuum* [*Zusammenhang*]" (§ 187). In these paragraphs Hegel broaches his celebrated thesis of modern society as a *system of all-round interdependence.*

> The selfish end in its actualization, conditioned in this way by universality, establishes a system of all-round interdependence [*System allseitiger Abhängigkeit*], so that the subsistence and welfare of the individual and his rightful existence [*rechtliches Dasein*] are interwoven with, and grounded on, the subsistence, welfare, and rights of all, and have actuality and security only in this context. (§ 183)

But in this condition in which each one of us comes to depend on all the others our independence is not lost: on the contrary, it is strengthened precisely by its reference to an other. It is thanks to the other that we strengthen the feeling of our autonomy, precisely because it is the action of the other that permits us to realize ourselves. Here—also within the system of needs—Hegel's conception of *relational freedom* is confirmed: the subject can be with itself only in its other.

Therefore only in appearance does modern civil society represent the realm of the autonomous and independent individual, because in reality it ends up creating new dependencies, thanks to which the feeling of autonomy can develop and grow stronger. If civil society "tears the individual away from family ties" and "alienates the members of the family from one another, and recognizes them as autonomous persons," it nonetheless institutes a new dependence: dependence on society itself, on the "social" universal:

> It substitutes its own soil for the external inorganic nature and paternal soil from which the individual gained his livelihood, and subjects the existence of the whole family itself to dependence on civil society and to contingency. Thus, the individual becomes a *son of civil society*, which has as many claims upon him as he has rights in relation to it. (§ 238).

The old natural family has been replaced by a new one, far more extended and anonymous, certainly less solidary and not as ready to take care of us, but able to raise us as autonomous individuals, capable of living on our own precisely because always forced to live in relation with all the others. This reciprocal estrangement accompanied by reciprocal dependence produces the independence of modern man, the "son of civil society," this mixture of selfishness with an altruism not willed and not pursued, but no less necessary.

> But in this dependence and reciprocity of work and the satisfaction of needs, *subjective selfishness* turns into a *contribution towards the satisfaction of the needs of everyone else.* By a dialectical movement, the particular is mediated by the universal so that each individual, in earning, producing, and enjoying for himself, thereby earns and produces for the enjoyment of others. (§ 199)

The individual does not pursue the universal voluntarily, does not act for everyone's welfare, he wills only his own exclusive welfare and nevertheless obtains, without willing it, the universal—that is, the welfare of everyone. This is the mechanism by which modern society functions: it is not necessary to be altruistic to produce social wealth, it suffices to pursue one's own interest, and this will produce welfare for everyone else.[47]

Roberto Finelli has quite rightly pointed out that in this conception, in which individuality and universality harmonically combine without this reconciliation's being consciously intended, Hegel returns to a conception of modern civil society that is close to the natural world, in which the order of the whole is not produced consciously by the single natural moments and thus appears alien to them, even though it is their product.[48] In this context we can well understand Hegel's famous expression in the *Encyclopaedia*, where he refers to civil society as the "system of *atomistic*" (ENC § 523): "atomistic" because in this society each individual is seen as separate from the others and lives concentrated only on himself, but also "system" because, in fact, he is unconsciously connected with all the others.

2.3.5. Civil Society as "the External State"

The action of the universal within civil society broaches some characteristics typical of the sphere of the state, even if, here, the state is of a particular type. Hegel calls it "*the external state*" (PR § 183): it remains external to individuals, and is not the condition of their individuality and subsistence but, rather, is produced and constituted by them. It is the individuals who construct this system of all-round relations, just as it is they who determine its regulation through laws, courts, legal proceedings, and punishments.[49] Consequently, this state is not the full realization of freedom but remains within the dimension of naturalness and need. It originates in the necessity for regulation of the needs and appetites of individuals. Hence Hegel refers to it as "*Notstaat*" (§ 183), the *state of need*: its end is to provide the juridical instruments necessary to regulate the satisfaction of natural needs.

This external state and state of need is, however, also the "state of the understanding" (§ 183): it serves to guarantee that "formal freedom" (§ 187) which is the endpoint and goal of the process of civil society. And formal freedom is merely an *external freedom*: it is the freedom to not be invaded and coerced by others; it is the negative freedom against the intrusion of the other; it is, precisely, the *freedom of the understanding*. The fundamental characteristic of civil society is always that of individualism, even if this selfishness is—willy-nilly—*relational*, but not *explicitly*, not *consciously*, not *voluntarily* relational. The universality of civil society thus remains subordinate to the individual: it "ensures at the same time that particularity *becomes* the genuine *being-for-itself* of individuality" (§ 187). Its end stands outside it, in the individuals it is designed to serve.

In civil society, universality is never recognized by those who contributed to producing it. None of its protagonists see it for what it is. Hegel expresses this concept, saying that "it is not as *freedom* but as *necessity* that the *particular* rises to the *form of universality*" (§ 186). Which means: the transition from particularity to universality is a *necessary and uncontrolled consequence, not a freely willed and pursued end*. Rather than sought after, the universal is *suffered* by the protagonists of civil society. In conclusion:

the conjunction here is *of the understanding*, and the two terms—even in conjunction—remain, in the end, separate and unrelated.

2.3.6. The Realm of Appearance

We find Hegel's thinking on the relation between universality and particularity condensed in just two paragraphs of the *Philosophy of Right*. However, to properly understand these paragraphs we need to read them in the light of the speculative categories of *essence, appearance, semblance,* and *reflection,* as Hegel presents them in the *Science of Logic*.

We begin with section 184. Returning once again to the relation between universality and particularity, Hegel reaffirms the difficulty of reconciling them on the basis of civil society. The "Idea" (i.e., the reality of the ethical and of freedom) seems to have split (Hegel speaks of *Entzweiung,* diremption) into these two moments. If, on the one hand, universality shows itself to be the "ground" (*Grund*) and "ultimate end" of particularity—its "necessary form," the "power over it" (*Macht über sie*) that, it seems, particularity must conform to and obey, on the other hand, this particularity has taken possession of "the right to develop and move in all directions" (§ 184). No universality seems able to control this incessant motion of particularities referred only to themselves, and the harmony that this combination of egotisms seems to realize is as contingent and fortuitous as anything to be found in history. Ethical life, which represented the fundamental characteristic of the previous moment—that is, of the *family,* which produced the autonomous personalities who went on to constitute society—breaks into two, with individuals on one side and the universalist result of their actions on the other. "It is the system of *ethical life lost* [*verlorene Sittlichkeit*] in its extremes" (§ 184—my italics). The totality that results from the action of the particularities is certainly not a *false* totality, but it is not the genuine reconciliation of the egotisms either. Hegel refers to it as a "*relative totality*" in whose external manifestations (which he calls *Erscheinungen,* "appearances" or "phenomena") an ""inner necessity" appears.[50] What in fact appears are the conflicting egotisms, but behind this appearance a "whole" reveals itself while remaining partially concealed—a ""whole" with the character of "necessity." The universal that would seem to be something merely contingent and totally dependent on the caprices of individuals here appears less precarious: it is in fact the *absolutely necessary,* even if the individualities do not recognize it and do not know it for what it is.

Three paragraphs earlier Hegel had connected this external appearing with an inner truth that was still concealed. In section 181 he said that in civil society universality was the "fundamental basis" [*Grundlage*] of the particular, albeit in a "still only inner and formal" sense, concluding that this universal was present in the particular "only seemingly [*nur scheinende Weise*]."[51] Like the necessity of section 184, also the universality appears here as something *beyond* the empirically visible social phenomena: there is only the *semblance* [*Schein*] of this universality in them, not its reality. In the end, what Hegel calls the "ethical Idea"—the full and proper reality of ethical life—manifests itself in civil society only in the form of semblance. Hegel introduces here—as any reader of the *Science of Logic* has already remarked—some fundamental categories of the *logic of essence*. The conclusion of the paragraph refers explicitly to that text and can be understood only in its context.

> This relation of reflection accordingly represents in the first instance the loss of ethical life; or, since the latter, as the essence, is necessarily *seeming* [*als das Wesen notwendig scheinend ist*], this relation constitutes the *world of appearance* [*Erscheinungswelt*] of the ethical, i.e. *civil society*. (§ 181)

The logical category with which Hegel introduces civil society is thus that of *reflection*. Unlike the family, which constitutes its immediate precedent, civil society becomes possible only insofar as that immediate unity is broken by reflection—that is, by a becoming aware that is also a distancing, which broaches duality where there had been compact unity before. But reflection inevitably spells the end of that ethical life: it is "lost" and—as Hegel will say three paragraphs later—lost "in its extremes," which are now dirempted and opposed.

From the "being" of the family the "essence" of civil society has emerged but, as is the case with logical essence, also this essence fails to keep its promise to show itself as a fuller and a more compact truth: indeed, it shows itself to be exactly the opposite. Reflection has made the transition to essence possible but, instead of making being more visible, has dissolved it in a play of references in which every trace of it is lost. At the moment in which the essence of being—its deepest and most hidden truth—was to manifest itself, this essence seems fatally to keep out of sight, loses every feature of being, and shows itself as being's negation. The same thing occurs with the transition to civil society. The unity of the family has faded and diremption has come into the world, with the result that the essence in which civil society consists now shows itself only as a *semblance of reality*. Ethical life has vanished, is lost, is dirempted: in the form of essence it

has become "necessarily seeming." Obviously "semblance" does not mean "nothingness"[52]—in fact, Hegel immediately adds that this is a "world," constituted by phenomenal appearances [*Erscheinungswelt*] that allow a truth, a necessity, a hidden universality to shine through them.

We have every reason to believe that if Hegel broached the two logical categories of *semblance* and *appearance* one right after the other he intended to give them different meanings. Indeed, if we follow the scansion of his argumentation in section 181 ("since ethical life as the essence is necessarily *seeming*, this relation [of reflection] constitutes the *world of appearance*"), we see that he develops the following thesis: *since ethical life is "seeming," the world the relation of reflection constitutes will be a world of "appearances."* In other words: the "seeming" nature of the ethical does not entail the nothingness of the world but its *real* constitution as an appearance that—at the same time—reveals and conceals the truth of the ethical.[53] In Hegel's *logic*, while *Schein* [semblance] is the negation of being, i.e. its nothingness and mere reference, in *Erscheinung* [appearance] this "referring" character is rooted in a real subsistence.[54]

On this basis, it seems legitimate to conclude that there is a precise correspondence between the three moments of ethical life (family, civil society, state) and the great tripartition of the *Logic* (being, essence, concept). Which is to say: the *family* represents the immediacy of *being* and the unity of particularity and universality; *civil society* represents the reflection and thus the split between reality and appearance typical of *essence*; while the *state* constitutes the moment of the fullness of the reality represented by the *concept*—the unity of being and essence, immediacy and reflection, objectivity and subjectivity.[55]

However precise or imprecise these correspondences may be, what is indisputable is the transitory and intermediate character of civil society: it has features that in some respects anticipate the state but, at the same time, it is unable to solve the problems that face it by itself. Indeed, its characterization as *appearance* confirms the *intellectualistic* structure we noted earlier. As we have seen, in civil society a form of reconciliation between particular and universal is realized, but this unity, as a product of the *understanding*, proves to be partial and inadequate. Only *reason* would be able to realize it, but in civil society—Hegel warns—reason, too, is subject to semblance.

> Consequently, the semblance of rationality [*Scheinen der Vernünftigkeit*] in the sphere of finitude is *the understanding*. This is the chief aspect that must be considered here, and that itself constitutes the conciliatory element within this sphere. (§ 189)

The same understanding that Hegel refers to here is the basis of the viewpoint that governs *political economy* (explicitly cited by Hegel in the Remarks to the paragraph), whose "thought" manages to trace "the simple principle of the thing [*Sache*]" and to make explicit "the activity of the understanding that works within it and controls it." So, for Hegel, as long as one remains within the sphere of civil society it is useless to expect to reach a viewpoint higher than that of the understanding: it is senseless to oppose this partial reconciliation with a subjective viewpoint that "gives vent to its discontent and moral irritation." The only conciliatory element one may expect consists in "recognizing this semblance of rationality" (§ 189 R), while acknowledging the fact that in this sphere the reconciliations will be intellectualistic—that is, partial and contingent—and the only modality in which reason will be able to manifest itself is that of semblance. This is the structural limit of civil society. It will always have two sides. It will always be an essential moment of ethical life and, at the same time, its dissolution—the homeland of modern man, but also a homeland in which he feels estranged.[56]

Hegel's attitude to civil society is thus neither of uncritical endorsement nor of moralistic rejection but, rather, of a *unity of exposition and criticism*. As Michael Theunissen wrote, the critical perspective runs through much of the *Philosophy of Right*, characterizing in particular the sections on abstract right and morality,[57] but then entering into the very sphere of ethical life: "The theory of civil society is not divorced from Hegel's critique in the doctrines of abstract right and of morality"; indeed, in this theory "the critique is consummated."[58] The particularity of the doctrine of civil society consists, for Theunissen, in the fact that in it truth manifests itself in untruth itself. That is: negativity and positivity show themselves to be tightly intertwined. While Hegel does criticize the type of freedom and universality that are realized in civil society, at the same time he shows in that negativity the appearing of a freedom and a universality that are true in and for themselves.[59]

This interweaving of exposition and critique becomes particularly evident in the question of the relation between historical individualities and social universality—a question that, as we have seen, plays an essential role throughout this section of the *Philosophy of Right*. On the one hand, we have Hegel's *exposition* of the progressive development of individual freedom within civil society, its strengthening and its full realization, made possible by the very conditions of civil society itself. On the other hand, we have his *critique* of the limitedness of the subjectivist horizon, in which we see the individual overcoming himself in the universal, in social totality. Now, this self-overcoming consists in the continual *reference to other*, which is the relation that characterizes the sphere of abstract right, the sphere of morality and, then, the sphere of civil society as well.[60] On this subject Michael Theunissen broached the notion of "*Veranderung*," in which the assonance with the word *Veränderung* [change, transformation] fuses with the meaning of the word *Andere* [other], which it contains. "*Veranderung*" is the transformation undergone by the individual while he becomes other and is referred to the other that stands before him. For Theunissen, this movement is one of the key concepts of the entire *Philosophy of Right*. In civil society in particular it consists in the necessity for the single individual to integrate himself in the system of omnidependence, within which he can earn his self-subsistence and independence thanks to the work and the needs of all the others. Here, individualist freedom shows itself in all its limitedness—or, more precisely, its content of truth and profound essence is made visible in the universal. Here, the universal will reveals itself as the ultimate truth of the particular will.

This consideration, for Hegel, already contains the necessity of the *transition to the state*—the necessity of the transition to a condition in which the universal will is the object of the particular wills *explicitly*, not only implicitly. Let us not forget that the protagonists of civil society remain completely unaware of their "*Veranderung*"—of their being referred to other and of their shared construction of a universal will. In the transition to the state this lack of awareness is superseded. But for this last step to be taken the work of civil society is absolutely indispensable. Civil society is the irreplaceable condition for the constitution of the state—the indispensable transition for the individuals to become aware of the truth of the universal.[61]

For this reason Hegel maintains that civil society, together with the family, is "the *scientific proof* of the concept of the state" (§ 256). *Proof* is to be understood here, first of all, as the "development of immediate ethical life through the division of civil society and on to the state, which is shown to be their true ground" (§ 256). In other words, it must be understood as the *process* that leads to the state and to its true universality as the *result* of civil society. Second, however, this proof is to be understood as a *confutation* of the two moments that precede the state—that is, as the supersession of their claims to truth and to priority. From the "critique" of family and civil society emerges *ex negativo* the positive truth of the state. The state, then, does not "depend" on the moments that precede it, in the sense in which a consequence depends on premises and first principles, but—on the contrary—makes the moments that preceded the state dependent on it. The *state* is the true "premise" and the true "first principle": only in light of the state can the limited truths of family and civil society be understood. Therefore not even the process of mediation that gave rise to the state can act as a premise: that mediation is "superseded" at the moment in which it constitutes the state.

> Since the state appears as the *result* of the development of the scientific concept in that it turns out to be the *true* ground [of this development], the *mediation* and semblance [already referred to] are likewise *superseded* [*hebt auf*] by *immediacy*. (§ 256)

The mediation is a semblance of mediation, just as the state is only apparently mediated (i.e., produced) by what precedes it. In reality the state is an immediacy (i.e., the true premise) on which the process of mediation depends: it is the ground, the reason, of the subsisting of all the moments that preceded it. "In actuality, therefore, the *state* in general is in fact the *primary* factor" (§ 256). Thus, the "necessity" glimpsed in the phenomena of civil society, like "relative" universality, were foretastes of the implicit presence of the state, even before the state showed itself as such.

2.3.7. From Subjective Freedom to Relational Freedom: Family, Civil Society, Corporation

Despite the "*Veranderung*" undergone by the subjects within civil society, as long as one remains within this sphere individualism is never completely overcome. Hegel reasserts the uselessness and the empty abstractness of any attempt to repress this individualism and to pit the "ought" of equality against the inequalities produced by selfish interests. Indeed, civil society is *founded* on the *right of particularity*, on its inviolability,[62] and the development of this right—which "manifests itself in every direction and at every level" (§ 200)—necessarily produces inequalities. And these inequalities are not combated but, on the contrary, are increased all the more, through a reproduction of the basic natural inequalities and their strengthening and multiplication as "spiritual" inequalities.

> The spirit's objective *right of particularity*, which is contained within the Idea, does not cancel out [*nicht aufhebt*] the inequality of human beings in civil society—an inequality posited by nature, which is the element of inequality—but in fact produces it out of the spirit itself and raises it to an inequality of skills, resources, and even of intellectual and moral education. (§ 200 R)

In this sense the structure of *status naturae* is never really overcome. The particularity of civil society "retains [. . .] the remnants of the state of nature" (§ 200 R): suffice it to think of all the elements of contingency that can produce a state of inequality between human beings—contingencies that are not combated in the least.

In civil society, then, we find a specific model of freedom—individualist and *negative*, which recognizes only its own particular interest and ignores the needs of all the others. This society seems to have forgotten and canceled out its sphere of origin, the family, in which a different model of freedom had been realized—a *relational* model. But the condition for the concretization of that model was the profoundly different nature of the ethics governing that sphere.

The *family* realizes ethical life in the form of *immediacy*—that is, in an unconscious form; and this absence of reflection keeps its members from isolating themselves and repelling one another. In the family, then, even within the modern constellation, we find some features of *ancient ethical life*, in which an indistinct unity of individual and community was in force and in which the totality held absolute sway over the individual. Also in the "modern" family (as long as it remains the individual's sole reference—i.e., prior to his contact with society) individuality does not know itself as "person" but only as "member" (see § 158). And the reason for this lies in the fact that "the family is a *single person*" whose members "are its accidents" (§ 163 R). Only in the case of its "ethical dissolution" (which comes about when the children come of age and leave their family of origin) do its members become "legal [*rechtliche*] persons" (§ 177).

But in spite of these characteristics, in which the family is similar to the ethical model of antiquity—in spite of the basic immediacy—Hegel places his conception of the family within the coordinates of modernity. His is in fact the family of the bourgeois world, in which all the "economic" features that characterized it in its traditional version have been lost, and have now been replaced by the "modern" characteristics of feeling and of private relations.[63] But the fundamental point regards the type of "ethical" function Hegel attributes to the family: its purpose is that of *educating* its members in *individual freedom* and of establishing relations that, rather than annulling the individualities in the compactness of the family unit, prepare them to use their freedom in an autonomous and responsible manner. This is a typical feature of the modern age. "Their union [in marriage] is a self-limitation, but since they attain their substantial self-consciousness within it, it is in fact their liberation" (§ 162). The limitation determined by this demanding relationship with the other that is realized in the bond of the family is, here, not a restriction of freedom but its expansion. In this union both partners are *freed* from their limits: the two persons come to be themselves more than they would have been if they had remained outside the union.

On this subject, the Addition to section 158 is even more significant. Here, Hegel makes it clear that the specificity of love consists in gaining "my self-consciousness only through the renunciation of my independent existence [*meines Fürsichseins*] and through knowing myself as the unity of myself with another and of the other with me" (§ 158 A). In other words: it is the renunciation of myself that allows me to gain "my self-consciousness." While the "first moment in love" is the decision not to be autonomous and the will to give my self to the other, losing my autonomy, its "second moment"—the actual result obtained thanks my giving up my autonomy— is that "I find myself in another person" (§ 158 A).

This is why Hegel adds that the understanding cannot apprehend what actually happens in love. The understanding cannot endure this contradiction in which autonomy is *negated* and at the same time *reaffirmed*. But, here, what is at work is precisely that concept of *relational freedom* in which "I" am free not "against" but "thanks to" the other.

Hegel shows us an analogous interweaving of freedom and relatedness in the relationship between parents and children. The discipline imposed on the children is by no means designed to reduce them to elements inseparable from the family. On the contrary, it is designed to educate them in freedom—that is, to prepare them to abandon the very family that generated and raised them. While the immediate task of the education of children ("the *positive* determination") is to "give ethical life the form of immediate *feeling*" in them, the second function ("the *negative* determination") is that of "raising the children out of the natural immediacy in which they originally exist to self-sufficiency [autonomy]* and freedom of personality, thereby enabling them to leave the natural unit of the family" (§ 175).

Ethical life in the sphere of the family is thus characterized as the realization of *intersubjective relations* that are the condition of freedom and autonomy. In establishing themselves between the spouses (§ 163) these relations are characterized by a reciprocity regulated by *love, trust,* and *sharing* [*Gemeinsamkeit*], while in the case of the children the relationship is characterized by *love, trust,* as well as by *obedience* (§ 175).

---

*Nisbet translates *Selbstständigkeit* as *self-sufficiency* or, at times, *independence,* but Cortella uses the word *autonomy* [*autonomia*] (and *autonomous* [*autonomo*]) throughout the book.

With the transition to *civil society*, while the result of the ethical development realized by the family—that is, the autonomy of the individual—is
maintained, the reciprocity of the relations this result made possible are
completely lost. In the intersubjectivity that characterizes this sphere there
is no sign whatsoever of relations or intentional references to the other. The
individual is led toward the others almost against his own intentions, since
these intentions are turned exclusively to the pursuit of his particular interests. This results in the absence of an effective relation with the other that is
capable of forming the identity of each in communality with and difference
from the other individualities. Here, the reference to one's other is resolved
in a universal interchangeability, in a making oneself indistinguishable, and
in a complete renunciation of one's specific individual characteristics. The
individual is brought to universality, but the price he pays for this elevation
is that he himself becomes "abstract." This loss manifests itself in particular
in the domain of *work*, in which the individual becomes the link of a chain
in which each is for the other in a wholly indeterminate manner.

> Through the division of labor, the work of the individual becomes
> *simpler*, so that his skill at his abstract work becomes greater, as
> does the volume of his output. At the same time, this abstrac-
> tion of skill and means makes the *dependence* and *reciprocity* of
> human beings in the satisfaction of their other needs complete
> and entirely necessary. Furthermore, the abstraction of produc-
> tion makes work increasingly *mechanical*, so that the human
> being is eventually able to step aside and let a *machine* take his
> place. (§ 198)

The mechanization and simplification of work, the universal replace-
ability of workers ever more similar to machines, the all-round dependence
in the satisfaction of needs—all this produces a general leveling of society.
In this regard, Rüdiger Bubner wrote:

> The system of the satisfaction of needs seems to suggest that in
> this context the particularities are respected as such. But in fact,
> through the perfecting of the system they find themselves con-
> sumed and leveled. Each believes that he is the important one,
> but then when he looks at the whole he sees that he functions
> as an element of exchange with all the others.[64]

In short: the particularities, apparently valorized and flattered, are in
fact *consumed* to such a degree that they return to the condition of natural

Is this word the author? from Hegel?

equality from which they started. Civil society, on one hand the locus par excellence of inequalities and of the multiplication of natural differences, on the other realizes a new type of equality—an anonymous leveling that further increases the pressure of dominion over every member of society. Universality, which the individuals refused to recognize and tenaciously kept outside their aims and their interests, not only imposes itself on these intentions but effectively makes itself identical to these very individuals, taking possession of their identities and stripping them of all specificity. The human being loses all concreteness, becomes identical to the social universal, and thus alienates himself from *himself*—from the identity most fully his own. In the end, abstraction and estrangement become the specific qualities of intersubjective relations.[65]

The loss of the relational dimension of freedom and the relapse into a solipsistic model provokes, first, the diremption of particularity and universality, and then their forced uniformation. In the end it is individual freedom itself, laboriously pursued by the protagonists of civil society, that is called into question: the individual loses his autonomy and becomes, himself, indistinct and abstract universality.

Despite all of this, Hegel is convinced that civil society has within it the resources to correct this tendency to individualism, to naturalism, and to abstraction. These resources can be utilized to bring the protagonists of civil society back to *caring for this universal* that they have ignored, and to making it the object and end of their action.

This comes about in a first—still limited—manner with the assignment of this task to the *authority of the "police,"* a "social" institution whose functions—in the meaning Hegel attaches to *Polizei**—go far beyond our current meaning of the word. Hegel refers to the *Polizei* as the "authority [*Macht*] of the universal that guarantees security" (§ 231): it is responsible for guaranteeing not only protection from crimes but, above all, a political economy—a regulation of the markets, a social policy. In essence, in the "police" Hegel sees something similar to today's welfare state. In fact, it is entrusted with the task of solving the problem of the *diremption* between "disproportionate wealth" and the "great mass of individuals" who "sink below the level of a certain standard of living" (§ 244). Since the irreducible individualism of civil society renders the universal it produces wholly contingent, and since "despite an *excess of wealth*, civil society is *not wealthy enough* [. . .] to prevent an excess of poverty" (§ 245), this intervention is not only right and proper—it is necessary. Nevertheless—as Hegel tells us—the action of the "police" remains "an *external order*" (§ 231), insofar

---

*On the meaning of Hegel's *Polizei*, see the Nisbet translation, pp. xlii–xliii.

as it is not civil society itself in its organicity that sets itself the goal of the universal.

> What the police provides for in the first instance is the actualization and preservation of the universal that is contained within the particularity of civil society, [and it does so] as *an external order and arrangement* for the protection and security of the masses of particular ends and interests that have their subsistence in this universal. (§ 249)

Only when the preservation of universality is no longer carried out externally but becomes the *inner end* of civil society itself—only then is the foundation laid for the *reconstruction of ethical life*. This is the element that characterizes the activity of the *corporation*.

> In accordance with the Idea, particularity itself makes this universal, which is present in its immanent interests, the end and object of its will and activity, with the result that *the ethical returns* to civil society as an immanent principle; this constitutes the determination of the *corporation*. (§ 249)

Hegel, here, presents us with the rehabilitation of a *medieval* institution, on the wane in his own time. What is more, he entrusts it with a specific task closely linked to the dynamic of *modern* society: that of overcoming the egotisms and self-destructiveness of civil society.[66] The corporation entails "a limitation of the so-called *natural right* to practice one's skill," directing that skill to "a common end" (§ 254). The leap with respect to the logic of civil society consists in the fact that the members of a corporation have as their prime objective not individual interests but the *common* interests: education and vocational training, protection against contingencies, safeguarding the wealth earned through work.

In the corporation *ethical life manifests itself anew* and presents itself with the characteristics it had in the family. "The corporation has the right to assume the role of a *second family* for its members" (§ 252), Hegel writes, going on to say that, after the family, it is "the *second ethical root of the state*" (§ 255—my italics). In short: with the corporation *communal feelings and bonds* are reconstituted within *modern* civil society. But the corporation represents a decisive advance over the primitive ethical life of the family: while in the family the moments of particularity and universality were joined in an immediate manner ('in *substantial* unity'), now they are "inwardly united" (§ 255)—that is, they are explicitly known and willed.

It is the corporation, then, that lays the foundations on which the limits of civil society are overcome: in it, the individuals come to be versed in reciprocal relations and are given responsibility in determining common and universal interests. It is the corporation that prepares the *transition to the sphere of the state*: in the state, the universal is not "limited and finite" as it was in the corporation (where it is limited to its members), but is the "*universal end* in and for itself" (§ 256).[67] Nevertheless, in this transition to a sphere in which the universal ends up coinciding with the state as such, it remains to be seen whether Hegel's promise of an interweaving of individual freedom, relational freedom, and universality will be kept.[68] This is the question I shall tackle in the next chapter.

Chapter 3

Actualization of Ethical Life
The Sphere of the State

With the idea of a *modern ethical life* that solves the problems posed by the *advent of freedom as the sole ground of normativity* Hegel certainly did not intend to call this ground into question. His position does not represent a return to the ancient ontological constellation in which ethics and politics were grounded in *nature* and in *tradition*, were bound up with the specificity of a clear-cut context, and were based on belonging to particular historical *roots*. Hegel does not intend to call into question the *achievements of modernity*: the release of the good from nature and its apprehension in terms of freedom; the connection between the good, freedom, and individual subjectivity; and the superiority of the viewpoint of universality over the particularity of ethical traditions. But, if this is the case, what are we to make of his reproposal of the concept of ethical life as a corrective to the modern viewpoint of morality?

In Hegel, the *origins of the concept of ethical life* are intimately connected with the formative process of his thought: they stem from his lifelong intellectual fascination with the ethical life of the Greeks. In his earliest works he was already intent on criticizing the subjectivist paradigm of modernity not only in theoretical but also in ethico-political terms. Against the Kantian conception characterized by the universality of freedom and by political "constructivism" he pitted the "beautiful ethical life" of the Greeks—for Hegel, a concept in which the oppositions—typical of modernity—between individual and state, freedom and nature, morality and right, are reconciled.

In his Jena period Hegel's rereading of Aristotle's *Politics* was crucial to the development of this project.[1] In Aristotle's fundamental principles

83

(naturalness of the *polis*, priority of the state over the individual, communal characterization of social relations, unity of ethics and politics), Hegel found the ideal he could set against the diremptions of modernity. Of no less importance in this phase was his rediscovery of Spinoza's metaphysics, in which individuals stem from a single substance as its modes. Hegel transformed this into the ontological background of Aristotelian politics, in which individuals stem from the state as their true ground. Thus, he based his critique of modern politics on a revival of the ancient unity of ethics and nature. In his essay "On the Scientific Ways of Treating Natural Law," published in the *Kritisches Journal der Philosophie* between 1802 and 1803, he pitted against the modern cleavage of nature and positive right precisely the ontological nexus that connected them in antiquity, while grounding right not in a nature characterized in the empiricist sense (as in Locke) but understanding it in an Aristotelian manner as the "essence of man." The "ethical nature" that Hegel, in this essay, posits as the true foundation on which to build the state, against the modern notion of an "artificial" pact contracted between isolated individuals dominated by natural arbitrariness, is once again based on an ontological and not merely empiricist concept of nature.

But this profound link with the Greek conception of ethical life was radically transformed as Hegel's thinking evolved. Beginning with the second phase of his Jena period and, even more explicitly, with the *Phenomenology of Spirit*, Hegel abandons the ontological model of Spinoza and Schelling and—in a celebrated passage from the Preface to the *Phenomenology*—posits the true "not as *substance*, but equally as *subject* [*nicht als* Substanz, *sondern eben so sehr als* Subjekt]"* (PhG 18/PS 10). This has precise consequences for the ethico-political sphere as well: at this point Hegel begins to accept the viewpoint of modernity, which *no longer posits the ground of right, ethics, and politics in nature but, rather, in the subject and in his freedom.*[2] This induces Hegel to distance himself from the very notion of "natural law" [*Naturrecht*], which he now considers acceptable only on the condition that "naturalness" be understood as "the *nature of the thing* [Sache] postulated by natural law, that is, as *concept.*"[3]

The notion of "concept," which from this time forth becomes one of the keystones of Hegelian philosophy, has an exact meaning also with regard to the politico-juridical sphere. As Manfred Riedel wrote, "the dialectical movement of the 'concept' [. . .] is not just an empty abstract formula;

---

*The syntax here is—indeed—problematic. Grammatically, the phrase may be considered a non sequitur, which I have respected. Hegel—*alas*, for his translators—does *not* write "not only . . . but also [equally]. . . ."

instead, the content of this movement is the absolute 'freedom' of the will, which has been elevated to the principle of all law following Rousseau, Kant, and Fichte."[4] But Hegel's acceptance of the modern paradigm is not without conditions: as we have seen, he understands this subject-concept not as the moderns do, as the opposite of being, but rather as the essence of the whole. This means that instead of seeing freedom as Kant did, in opposition to nature, Hegel sees it as the ultimate truth of nature itself. This rearticulation of the relations between freedom and nature allows him to retain his youthful ideal of ethical life and the unity it entailed between ethics and "nature." But there has been a radical change in his perspective: nature is now thought of as "concept"—which means in the modern terms of *freedom*.

3.1. Characteristics of Hegelian Ethical Life

3.1.1. Unity of Freedom and Nature

On the one hand, Hegel reverses his early approach, in which he saw the metaphysical concept of nature as a corrective to the notion of modern freedom and practical subjectivity, and now posits freedom as the ground of the ethical. *On the other hand*, however, he remains faithful to his youthful ideal. In fact he continues to think—*versus* Kant—that the state and the ethical must be grounded in the nature of the whole, and he does so precisely because he no longer understands this nature in an ontological sense as the ancients did but—*like* Kant and Fichte—as subject, that is, as freedom. This allows him to accept the antimetaphysical *turn* of modernity that posits the ground of the political in the subject. Hegel's favorable remarks on Hobbes in the *Lectures on the History of Philosophy* is a testament to this. These remarks almost completely reverse the judgment he expressed during his first years in Jena:

> Before this, ideals were set before us, or Holy Scripture or positive law was quoted as authoritative. *Hobbes*, on the contrary, sought to derive the bond that holds the state together, that which gives the state its power, from principles that lie within us, which we recognize as our own. (GPh2 XV 395/HP III 316)

Although he accepts the Kantian advance that posits the ground of right in the free self-determination of the will, Hegel does not see this will as opposed to nature—that is, to being—but as its deepest essence.

> The expression *nature* has a double significance: in the first place the nature of man signifies his spiritual and rational being; but his natural condition indicates quite another condition, wherein man conducts himself according to his natural impulses. (GPh2 XV 397/HP III 318)

While the natural-law tradition saw nature as natural immediacy and made it the ground of right, Hegel sees nature as essence. But this essence is now comprehended not ontologically as substance but idealistically as spirit and reason. Nature, when thought in its ultimate truth, proves to be other than itself, just as essence in its actualization lies beyond its ontological self-comprehension.

For this reason the *ground of right* is not to be sought in objective nature but in *freedom*, in the autonomy of the subject, in the free self-determination of the will.

> The expression *natural law* or *natural right*, in current use to designate the philosophical doctrine of right, contains the ambiguity between right as something *immediately existing in nature*, or right as determined through the nature of the thing [*Sache*], i.e. through the *concept*. (ENC § 502)

In the *first* sense, right stems from the state of nature and the immediate instincts that distinguish it; in the *second*, it stems from the rational will.

> In fact right and all its determinations are grounded in *free personality* alone: in a *self-determination*, which is the very contrary of *determination by nature*. (ENC § 502)

If it is not rooted in freedom, natural right degenerates into the "existence of force" and the "perpetration of violence." The result is a state of nature as a "state of violence and injustice, of which nothing truer can be said than that *it must be left behind*" (ENC § 502).

But we still have to consider Hegel's early polemic against modern natural right in its "empiricist" variant (Grotius, Hobbes, Locke), against which he pitted an "essentialist" concept of nature. What changes is the conception of this essence, now no longer seen ontologically but in terms of freedom, reason, and concept.

The thesis advanced by Manfred Riedel in his work of the early 1970s, thus needs to be corrected. On the one hand, he is right when he says that "Hegel too distinguished between nature and freedom, law of nature and law of justice" and that he "categorically puts aside the traditional notion that the 'law of nature' can be a 'model' of law for human beings to the extent that they simply recognize and comply with it; the sole law that sustains historical human existence is the law of freedom that is given not by 'nature' but rather by the 'concept' itself."[5] But, on the other hand, *by not adding that this freedom is the true nature*, he fails to convey the completeness of Hegel's viewpoint: freedom is not something opposed to nature but is its ultimate truth.

Hegel's rethinking of ontology shows us, then, *a first fundamental meaning* of his concept of ethical life and the first real reason for its connection with the *ethos* of the ancients: in Hegelian ethical life *the ancient unity of ethos and physis* is reestablished, even if in a radically new sense.

On this basis it becomes possible for Hegel *to rethink the concept of social order*. It is no longer to be understood as an objectivity already given to which the individual is forced to adapt, but as the institution of historical and social structures *grounded in freedom*, that is, in the subject's self-determination. In this regard, Charles Taylor wrote:

> [Hegel] will reconstruct the notion of a greater order to which man belongs, but on an entirely new basis. Hence he fully endorses the modern rejection of the meaningful order of nature, as seen in the Middle Ages and early Renaissance. These visions of order saw it as ultimately just given by God. [. . .] But the Hegelian notion of Spirit as freedom cannot accommodate anything merely given.[6]

The order of which Hegel is thinking is grounded not in nature but in freedom—in the capacity of spirit to determine itself as universal will.

> Hegel sees the modern affirmation of a self-defining subject as a necessary stage. And he sees its necessary culmination in the radical Kantian notion of autonomy. Autonomy expresses the demand of Spirit to deduce its whole content out of itself, not to accept as binding anything that is merely taken up from outside.[7]

Unlike the old order, which resulted from an already given—already imposed—structure, the new order is determined by spirit: it is a free order, an order in which freedom has been objectified.

Analogously, Hegel recovers the old metaphysical concept of the *good*—it, too, is grounded in freedom: "The good is *realized freedom, the absolute and ultimate end of the world*" (PR § 129). Understood as the realization of freedom, for Hegel the good regains its status as the *leading principle of ethics*—*not* as objectivity pitted against individual conscience but as the complete unfolding of freedom. In this context we can well understand the first words of the section "Ethical Life": "Ethical life is the *Idea of freedom* as the living good" (§ 142). In ethical life freedom has made itself "Idea": it is no longer a subjective concept but has become a historical reality.[8] But it is not exclusively an *objective* good either: Hegel refers to it as "living" because this objectivity is no longer separated from the "life" of self-consciousness but has acquired a subjective dimension as well.

> The living good has its knowledge and volition in self-consciousness, and its actuality [*Wirklichkeit*] through self-conscious action. Similarly, it is in ethical being that self-consciousness has its motivating end [*bewegende Zweck*] and a foundation that has being in and for itself. (§ 142)

The objective good has united with subjective self-consciousness, that is, with the subject's self-determination, and has done so both in the sense that it is *known and willed* by this self-consciousness and in the sense that it has become *actuality* thanks to the action of the subject. Hence for there to be living good it is necessary that freedom recognize itself in the objectivity it has itself produced. This explains the *difference* between Kant's and Hegel's solution to the problem of the relation between freedom and history: for Hegel, freedom is not located outside history but becomes possible only within historical conditions.

3.1.2. Unity of Freedom and History

We can interpret Hegel's rethinking of Kant's conception of freedom not only as its de-subjectification but also as its *de-formalization*. Hegel insists that freedom must not be understood as a form without contents and determinations but as a "substance." This substance, however, does not present "metaphysical" characteristics that transcend history. As we have seen, in Hegel there is no ontological conception of the good from which the individual's moral duties can be deduced. As Taylor wrote, Hegelian ethics "has some affinities with Plato, since it does involve the idea of a cosmic order";[9] but this order has not been deduced from a transcendent idea—on the contrary, it has been historically constructed out of the progressive objectifications of freedom. Attributing a substantial nature to freedom must therefore be understood in the sense of its *historicization*: it is from history that we will discover the "contents" of freedom that were missing in Kant's formal theory; it is within social practices, in the functioning of institutions, in the constitutional orders, that we will find the ways in which it is exercised. Outside of these practices, institutions, and orders freedom ceases to exist: it is nothing but an empty idea. This is why freedom is possible only within historical conditions: far from limiting its exercise, history offers it the concrete modalities of its operation without which it literally disappears. Ethical life is this historical realization: it is freedom's making itself concrete substance and practical exercise.

"Ethical life is the *concept of freedom that has become the existing world* [*vorhandene Welt*] *and the nature of self-consciousness*" (PR § 142). This is the most precise definition of ethical life Hegel has given us. In it we find all its fundamental determinations. Here we have the two sides that are indispensable to the order of freedom: *self-consciousness*—that is, the subjective awareness of freedom; and its *realization* in a historical, existing, objective world. Both these components are necessary: only if freedom is put into practice in a world that its subjects recognize as the order of freedom can it be truly realized. For Hegel, this condition is concretized in the *modern state*: for him, it is in the state of his historical age that freedom became aware of itself, and individuals know themselves to be free and independent.

This is why Hegel holds the modern state to be not something simply existing, mere givenness or a de facto reality, but the *actuality* [*Wirklichkeit*] of the concept of freedom. "The state is the actuality of the ethical Idea" (§ 257) and as "the actuality of the substantial *will* [. . .] is the *rational* [*das Vernünftige*] in and for itself" (§ 258).[10] If, then, the category that distinguishes civil society is *appearance* (in its double sense of *Schein* and *Erscheinung*), the state's category par excellence is *actuality*, in which the cleavage between essence and appearance is reabsorbed in a concept that contains them both.

But the central idea of section 258 is unquestionably the forceful reassertion of the *unity of the rational* [*vernünftig*] *and of the actual* [*wirklich*], already asserted in the Preface to the *Philosophy of Right*.[11] This unity is one of the hallmarks of Hegel's entire philosophy—which, indeed, has often been harshly criticized for its absolutization of the existing historical reality allegedly produced by the rationality he championed. However, as Riedel quite rightly noted, "actuality" here is to be understood "in the speculative sense of the *Logic*, as the unity—immediate and the result of becoming—of inner essence and external existence."[12] In this sense, *Wirklichkeit* for Hegel does not signify mere givenness or de facto existence, but something similar to the Aristotelian notion of *energeia*, which is to say *reality in act*, reality insofar as it has developed all its immanent possibilities, the real insofar as it has been completely fulfilled. This is what Hegel means by the *actual* and *actuality*. Hegel, properly understood, is claiming that it is possible to distinguish true rational actuality from what is not rational (and therefore not genuinely actual either). As Bubner wrote, since philosophy has the task of "comprehending what is" it must also have the capacity to "separate what in actuality is rational from the irrationality of its accompanying phenomena."[13] Hence it will have the task "of distinguishing the fundamental tendency of historical situations from transitory phenomena or of asserting the substance against the prevalence of ephemeral and superficial things."[14]

If this is the general context of the Hegelian unity of the rational and the actual, we must also note that in section 258 this unity is explicitly referred to the state, described as "the rational in and for itself" as "the actuality of the substantial will." But there is another point we have to note: here, Hegel is not referring to the state of a specific nation (the Prussian state, for example, which he does not mention) but to the state *in general*, as he makes clear in the Addition to the same paragraph:

> In considering the Idea of the state, we must not have any particular states or particular institutions in mind; instead, we should consider the Idea, this actual God, in its own right [*für sich*]. (RZ 403/PR § 258 A)

The comparison between the state and God should not astonish us, because in the state the absolute and its actualization is at stake[15] (but, as we have seen, the absolute is freedom and the state is its historical actualization). In the same Addition, a few lines earlier, Hegel was even more explicit when he wrote that "the state is the march of God in the world [*es ist der Gang Gottes in der Welt, dass der Staat ist*]": the existence of the state is the result of the processual actualization of the absolute—that is, of freedom's journey in the modern world.

Manfred Riedel made an interesting observation in this regard. While insisting that the unity of rational and actual cannot be referred to the Prussian state, he maintains that it is in fact directly addressed to a specific model of state—namely, the *modern* state. This unity means "that in the modern state the concept of right has attained existence, that the rational—the idea of freedom—has become actual, and the actual—the state in the modern world—has become rational."[16] We can consider the actuality of the modern states to be *rational* because in them the idea of right—that is, the idea of the freedom and autonomy of the individual—has found its embodiment.

Analogously, the concept of freedom has been able to make itself *actual* because it has found a home in the political orders of these states.

This is the basic idea that underlies the very notion of "objective spirit," which—for Axel Honneth—is designed to represent an *objective reality in which a rational structure is embodied and enclosed.*[17] Hence "an offence against those rational grounds with which our social practices are interlinked at any given moment will cause damage or injury in social reality."[18]

In other words: *the universality* of reason in the modern world is not confined to the abstract world of ideas but becomes actuality, *makes itself history*, and is concretely practiced. Freedom has finally become an "existing world," realizing itself in political institutions. Hegel attests to this, declaring that "the objective ethos"—*das objektive Sittlichkeit*—"takes the place of the abstract good," adding that *substance*, finally "made *concrete*," "posits *distinctions* within itself" that "give the ethical a fixed *content*" (§ 144). Making itself actual, freedom can no longer permit itself to remain indeterminate and negative: it is realized in *differentiated contents*, which give it stability precisely because they are not changeable opinions but, indeed, *"laws and institutions that have being in and for themselves"* (§ 144).

Freedom has become so concrete that it articulates itself in the institutional and juridical world of the state. Its content is now those "various aspects of the organism of the state" which are nothing other than "the various powers" (§ 269). Once again, Hegel insists on the strict connection between *logic* and the sphere of *objective spirit*: the plural articulation of the organism of the state is in fact "the development of the Idea in its differences and their objective actuality" (§ 269). In other words, precisely because the Idea is articulation and movement in its *logical aspect*, it manifests this differentiation also in its *actual aspect.*[19]

This internal articulation of the state is what Hegel calls the *"political constitution"* (§ 269) or *"the internal constitution for itself"* (§ 272). It makes provision for a particular type of *division of powers* that—unlike in liberal theory—is not based on reciprocal independence (what Hegel calls *"absolute autonomy"**) but on a sort of *connection in difference*.

> The principle of the division of powers contains the essential moment of *difference*, of *real* rationality; but such is the view of the abstract understanding that, on the one hand, it attributes to this principle the false determination of the *absolute autonomy*

*In Nisbet's translation, "absolute self-sufficiency."

[*absolute Selbstständigkeit*] of each power in relation to the others, and on the other hand, it one-sidedly interprets the relation of these powers to one another as negative, as one of mutual *limitation*. (§ 272 R)

Here we have a recurrent theme in Hegel's exposition of the state, namely his constant *distancing himself from the liberal political conception*. In his theory of freedom (in particular in the critique of negative freedom) his dispute with liberalism had been evident all along. At this point in the *Philosophy of Right* that basic idea gives rise to important consequences also in terms of constitutional construction. Hegel's *critique of negative freedom*— that is, his criticism of the idea of an independence obtained by keeping others at a distance and limiting their action—is the root of his critique of the separation of powers. Indeed, his real dispute is with "mutual limitation" and with the idea that the relation between powers be interpreted as "negative."

In this view, the reaction of each power to the other is one of hostility and fear, as if to an evil, and their determination is such that they oppose one another and produce, by means of this counterpoise, a general equilibrium rather than a living unity. (§ 272 R)

The liberal conception applies the governing principle of civil society to politics: just as in civil society mutual limitation of the latitude of egotisms produced a general equilibrium, so in the political sphere the mutual limitation of powers will prevent the despotic predominance of any given part of the state. Hegel's dispute is precisely with this logic: no "living unity" can arise on the basis of negative freedom.

If the powers—e.g. what have been called the *executive* and *legislative* powers—attain *self-sufficiency* [autonomy], the destruction of the state, as has been witnessed on a grand scale [in our times], is immediately posited. (§ 272 R)

In order to avoid what he sees as nothing less than the self-destruction of the state, Hegel proposes a *difference* of powers without division, an *articulation* of the state without absolute autonomies. What he proposes is that each power be seen as an institution capable of *containing the other in itself*, according to the model of relational freedom: "*each* of the *powers* in question is in itself the *totality*, since each contains the other moments and has them active within it" (§ 272). This, once again, is the idea of *independence through the other* and in virtue of an *inclusive* (rather than exclusive and negative) relation with the other. Hegel concludes by saying that, in this way, those powers—far from losing their independence and autonomous capacity for action—will have constituted "*a single individual whole*" (§ 272)—an individuality constituted not by pitting itself against other institutional individualities but in virtue of their relation.

In Hegel's own time, when the liberal conception of the state was still far from widespread in Europe, his unquestionably striking idea could well have made a real contribution to the ongoing debate on the constitutional form of the modern state. In an age such as ours, in which the liberal-democratic constitution has virtually become the only model, it is far more difficult to accept Hegel's proposal. Nevertheless, a nonideological approach is duty-bound to meet the challenge represented by Hegel's constitutional model. Clearly, the real problem is to understand how his idea of replacing an *exclusive* equilibrium with an *inclusive* relation could be concretely realized. In any event, a practical realization that entails the abusive intrusion of one power on another is to be avoided, since it would end up endangering the freedom of all. As we shall see, this is precisely the risk Hegel's constitutional construction runs.

3.1.3. Reconciliation of Universality and Ethos

Hegelian ethical life corrects the Kantian conception of the political in three essential points. *First*, it overcomes the conception of the sphere of right as a coercive dimension, making it possible to rethink it as a sphere of objective freedom. *Second*, it opposes the "constructivist" conception of the political, in which the institutions and the entire sphere of the state are seen as a product of the subjective wills of individuals, replacing it with the idea that political institutions are grounded in "nature"—albeit in a sense radically different from that of the ontological tradition, since "nature" in Hegel coincides with freedom and reason. *Third*, Hegel puts an end to the conflict between the universality of the moral law and the particularity of the subjective dispositions of historical individuals: instead of seeing moral universality as an "ought," opposed to concrete historical being, it is now to be seen as the already realized historical reality and as the ensemble of practices we have always actually followed. The source of normativity is in these actual practices, not in a metaphysical moral law within us. With this solution Hegel reproposes that *ancient conception of ethos* in which the world of institutions and traditions was seen to be the true dwelling place of the individual and the root of his practical dispositions.

But in this latest rehabilitation of antiquity Hegel broaches a *fundamental difference*. Now, this dwelling to which the individual belongs is *not* his specific context of traditions, habits, and customs but is the *universal* in its realization: it is the idea of the free will that has made itself into historical institutions. Hegelian *Sittlichkeit* differs from the ancient *ethos* in its conception of a *universal ethical life*. The individual's dwelling is no longer his specific tradition but is the dimension of universality. Family and social institutions, but above all *political institutions*, have become the true dwelling of modern man.

The Hegelian concept of ethical life, then, rests on the idea of *the universal as the dwelling, the homeland, of modern man*. "Ethical life"—he writes—is "the *Idea* in its <u>universal</u> existence in and for itself" (PR § 33, my underlining). The ethos of the moderns is no longer constituted by traditions, historical and cultural belonging, or ethnicity, but by the political institutions in which the universality of freedom has been condensed—a reality that by definition surpasses any possible context. *Abstract freedom has become a dwelling and a world*: this is our new belonging, and on it we depend.

This, moreover, is Hegel's conception of *modernity* as the definitive fulfillment of the Idea, its making itself history and existing institutions. Universality ceases to be merely an object of philosophical speculation and becomes concrete reality: it is our world, our ethos. In this perspective, modernity represents the *actualization of metaphysics*. Hence, the task Hegel assigns to philosophy is that of comprehending and recognizing *in history* the fulfilled objectification of universality. Hegel's celebrated claim that "philosophy is *its own time comprehended in thoughts*" (PR 15/21) is not a banal historicist observation indicating the dependence of philosophy on its time but, as Ritter remarked, indicates the change in the object of philosophy after the advent of modernity: metaphysics no longer needs to abstract from the present historical time to think the absolute Idea. Now, as it thinks the present it thinks the structures of the eternal embodied in it. By elevating the historical fact to the level of thought, metaphysics manifests the universal structures—the truth and the freedom—objectified in historical institutions.[20] It is not thought that depends on the time but the time that depends on the structures of thinking and representing historical expression. At this point philosophy steps in, at the end, when the process of formation has been definitively completed. Its task is the hermeneutic one of elevating the historical fact to the level of thought—that is, to think its own time in earnest, displaying its universality and truth.

Thus, the elements of continuity between ancient *ethos* and Hegelian *Sittlichkeit* mingle with elements of discontinuity. Both are a "dwelling" for the human being, the habitual place of his living; just as both are the expression of an essential link with the structures of being. Yet, as we have seen, they are *different* in their ways of understanding this ontological nature; but—above all—they are different in their ways of understanding this *dwelling*. While for the ancients it is the specificity of a context made up of traditional manners and customs, for Hegel it is *universality* embodied in laws and institutions.

The fundamental concept for comprehending this "ethical" character of universality is an expression that Hegel uses a number of times in the course of the *Philosophy of Right*. I refer to the expression "*second nature*," which gives us a very precise idea of this embodiment of universality and of its becoming a "world"—that is, the place where the existence of objective spirit unfolds.

3.1.4. Ethos as "Second Nature"

In Hegel the *first meaning* of "second nature" indicates the *objective side of ethical life*—that is, the fact that the universal (i.e., freedom) has become existence and, indeed, "nature."

> The basis [*Boden*] of right is the *realm of spirit* [*das* Geistige] in general and its precise location and point of departure is the *will*; the will is *free*, so that freedom constitutes its substance and destiny and the system of right is the realm of actualized freedom, the world of spirit produced from within itself <u>as a second nature</u>. (PR § 4, my underlining)

Here, "second nature" tells us that the realm of objective spirit has the same objectivity and substantiality as nature. But it tells us something more: this objectivity is not merely "given" by "first nature," but is "produced" by spirit. In addition to the ontological substantiality of that first world, spirit has something more: it has *freedom*, whose actualization it is. Nature is totally unaware of this freedom, and therefore without it.

Hegel uses ontological connotations to indicate the character of institutions that set themselves up as objective and independent of subjects: "In relation to the subject, the ethical substance and its laws and powers are on the one hand an object, inasmuch as *they are* [*haben das Verhältnis, daß sie sind*], in the supreme sense of autonomy [self-sufficiency]" (§ 146). Their

primary legitimacy resides in the fact that they exist, just as the existence
of natural beings has authority for consciousness:

> The sun, moon, mountains, rivers, and all natural objects around
> us *are*. They have, in relation to consciousness, the authority not
> only of *being* in the first place, but also of having a particular
> nature [. . .]. The authority of ethical laws is infinitely higher,
> because natural things display rationality only in a completely
> *external* and *fragmented* manner and conceal it under the guise
> of contingency. (§ 146 R)

In short, this second nature is a product of spirit and therefore has
within it, in addition to its substantiality, the superiority of spirit over physical nature.[21] This, then, is the first meaning of "second nature" for Hegel.

The *other meaning* of "second nature" is of even greater importance for
our discourse. It is closely connected with the function of *dwelling* represented by *ethos*. As the original locus of the subject's freedom, ethical life is,
for the subject, a *locus of education and formation*. The universal, rather than
manifesting itself as an alien duty, becomes the *condition of the shaping of
free subjects*. It pervades their character, their mode of behavior, their habits,
to the point that they experience the universal laws as their own "nature."

> But if it is simply *identical* with the actuality of individuals,
> the ethical [*das Sittliche*], as their universal mode of behavior,
> appears as *custom* [*Sitte*]; and the *habit* of the ethical appears
> as *second nature* that takes the place of the original and purely
> natural will and is the all-pervading soul, significance, and
> actuality of individual existence. It is *spirit* living and present
> as a world, and only thus does the substance of spirit begin to
> exist as spirit. (§ 151)

Universality (the "universal mode of behavior" of individuals) has
become *Sitte*, manners and customs, habit, taking the place of natural
inclinations and transforming *itself* into the nature of the individual. Spirit
has become substance ("it is spirit living and present as a world"), but this
substance appears for the first time with spiritual characteristics ("only thus
does the substance of spirit begin to exist as spirit").

This marks *the end of the alienness between moral universality and the
individual*, between the "ought" and the existing substance, between the
inner and the external world. At last, modern man can feel "at home." What

he *must* do is what his second nature *makes* him do. For Bubner *this is the very core of the Hegelian theory of ethical life*:

> We want to live where we can feel *at home*. Just as the institutions in which we live and that oriented our socialization long before any of us could make mature decisions must be ours and belong to us, so must the intimate lifeworld, from which we do not take our leave willingly or as a rule. All other kinds of relations are under the dominant sign of estrangement. I have sought to express in simple words what I consider to be the core of the Hegelian theory on right and politics.[22]

It is on this basis that Hegel can ground the *priority of ethics over morality*. He does so less in the superficial sense that ethical life includes morality as its moment and therefore constitutes its supersession than, above all, in the sense that the validity of the individual's behavior—his morality—resides in his conformity and adequacy to the existent ethos—that is, to the realized universal.

Individual virtue is not grounded in the conformity to a moral principle or an abstract right but in its free and conscious adequacy to the existing universal. This is its *rectitude*: "Insofar as virtue represents nothing more than the simple adequacy of the individual to the duties of the circumstances to which he belongs, it is *rectitude*" (§ 150).

Hegel, here, follows Aristotle almost to the letter. Also for Aristotle virtue is the adequacy to good existing practices; that is, the individual absorption—interiorization—of the objective ethos.

> In an ethical community, it is easy to say *what* someone must do and *what* the duties are that he has to fulfill in order to be virtuous. He must simply do what is prescribed, expressly stated, and known to him within his situation. (§ 150 R)

Unlike the particularism of the ancient *ethos*, however, this rectitude is not related to any specific belonging but to the universal alone: "Rectitude is the universal quality that may be required [of the individual], partly by right and partly by ethics" (§ 150 R).

Hegel, here, *ethically "reverses"* morality, transforming it from an "ought" that is independent of history into an acting that is in conformity with the structure of objective spirit. Here, the laws and institutions of the state show their intrinsically ethical face. They not only have historical existence but are a reality that contains a *normative core*. In this sense morality comes to depend on ethics, since the content of the moral norms is embodied in institutions—that is, in the existing institutional practices. For this reason, it is not the institutions that depend on the moral point of view—on the contrary, it is the moral point of view that depends on the institutions.

Morality, then, instead of pursuing an abstract and unrealizable "ought," must take the content of its duties from existing ethical life—that is, from what is already being done. Its task is to strengthen and develop the normativity already in force.

> The crucial characteristic of *Sittlichkeit* is that it enjoins us to bring about what already is. This is a paradoxical way of putting it, but in fact the common life that is the basis of my *sittlich* obligation is already there in existence. It is in virtue of its being an ongoing affair that I have these obligations; and my fulfillment of these obligations is what sustains it and keeps it in being. Hence in *Sittlichkeit* there is no gap between what ought to be and what is, between *Sollen* and *Sein*.[23]

In this framework we can well understand Hegel's statement that what is obtained by the individual who acts ethically is an end that he "*brings about* by his *action*, but he does so as something that nevertheless simply *is*" (ENC § 514).[24]

However, this reversal of the relations between ethics and morals, which posits political institutions as the true ground of morality, entails neither a *moralization of politics* nor a *politicization of morality*. Not a moralization of politics, because the state is not made subject to moral imperatives. Its ethical finalities stem from its own operations—from its legal and constitutional procedures. It is not the state institutions that depend on morality—on the contrary, it is politics and morality that depend on the normative core contained in the institutions. For Hegel any moralization of the ethical would end up by dissolving its objectivity—hence his continual opposition to any such perspective. As Ritter expressed it, when subjectivity "makes itself the ground and master of what is ethical, and so renders objectivity something insubstantial and unreal, the danger exists that the moral will will dissolve the institutions giving it reality."[25] For Hegel the French Revolution is a graphic example of what the rule of moral subjectivity over historical objectivity can produce.

On the other hand, it is equally erroneous to think that Hegel's perspective entails a politicization of morality—that is, a dependence of morality on politics. There is no subjugation of individual morality to the imperatives of the state or to the functional necessities of the political system. Indeed, there is not the slightest trace in Hegel of a dependence of individual duties on the political necessities of the self-assertion of state power.

Thus, Hegel's operation eludes the usual categorizations of the relations between ethics and politics. His effort is to trace these two spheres back to their *common ground*—that is, to the normative core contained in the working of political institutions.

> Therefore, in Hegel's adoption of a practical philosophy encom-   ~~the below~~
> passing ethics and politics, he has at the same time annulled the   ~~turning only~~
> Kantian separation of virtue and right. He has incorporated moral-   ~~tried!~~
> ity and ethical life within the framework of the system of right
> and conceived this as the ground and condition of ethical life.[26]

On this basis, can it be said that Hegel's political conception goes in the direction of an *"ethical state"*? Yes and no. Certainly not in the sense of the term in common use today. For Hegel the ethical life of the state consists solely in the thesis that its institutions and laws contain a normative core that constitutes the fundamental direction of individual action. In this normative core individuals find the indispensable reference also for their individual morality, since it is precisely this ethical context that has educated them in the use of their freedom. Hence it is certainly true that Hegel's conception is far indeed from an ethically neutral idea of the political. But this does not mean that Hegel's is an "ethical state" in our common sense of the term. His state dictates no specific moral conception with definite value contents. The ethical life it represents comes before all subjective morality, before any conception of life and of the good. Fundamentally, it educates us in the practice of freedom, individual autonomy, and responsibility, providing us with the normative framework within which we can develop our moral convictions.

Hence the subordination of the moral viewpoint to existing ethical life produces a *higher degree of freedom* than is the case in its subordination to abstract and formal duty. This ethical life not only preserves the universalist ideals of morality but, unlike morality, does not stand apart from the individual and his concrete existence. The normativity that the moral perspective externally imposes on the individual has here already been incorporated into institutionalized practices. This means that ethical action is not an imperative action, coercive of inner nature, but, rather, is a habitual action: it does no violence to the individual but is performed naturally and without constraint. At last, *freedom* emerges from the contradictory condition that had transformed it into constraint—into subordination to an alien obligation. At last, *freedom becomes our second nature*: that is, the habitual practice and historical action of individuals.

All this is possible because freedom and universality have been incorporated into our historical institutions, which, in their turn, have performed the same role of education and formation as the ancient *polis*:

> When a father asked him for advice about the best way of educating his son in ethical matters, a Pythagorean replied: 'Make him the *citizen of a state with good laws*.' (This saying has also been attributed to others.) (§ 153 R)

The laws of the state are its citizens' locus of education par excellence. And when the state is the modern state, in which universal freedom has found its way to concretization, the laws constitute the condition of possibility for the shaping of free citizens. As Charles Larmore wrote, "The important thesis in Hegel's notion of *Sittlichkeit* is, therefore, that institutions not only protect our moral achievements, they also foster moral development. Without socialization into the existing forms of life that embody moral values, individual character would be a thin affair."[27] Thus the sense of Hegel's effort consists *not*—as some have believed—in abandoning Kantian morality, but rather in *completing* it, by showing that "the moral point of view" is not a product of pure practical reason but a consequence of the correct working of political institutions—of their educational role, their capacity to make moral convictions *take root* in the individual: "We must see, Hegel urged, that the central importance of universal morality in our time is sustained and fostered by the institutions and practices characteristic of our society."[28] The great modern diremption between freedom and existence has, in the end, been healed.

3.1.5. Healing the Diremption of Modernity

For Hegel, the unity of individual freedom and objective historical reality put an end to the diremption that characterizes the modern world—that is, to the separation, typical of *Bildung*, between the real individual and his abstract objectifications. The externalizations of freedom—the world of right, the autonomy of morality, the political and social institutions—no longer present themselves with the features of an alien universe but, on the contrary, as the dwelling and the very nature of modern man. The dialectic of freedom that, within the *Phenomenology of Spirit*, seemed to find no solution, comes to a halt with the *Philosophy of Right*, dissolving in the reconciled world of ethical life.

Hegel works on this solution in particular in part 2, "Morality," and most specifically in the transition from section 2 to section 3. Here, we already find all the elements that will later prepare the conclusive transition to ethical life. But, first, it must be said that the structure of the entire part on Morality is characterized by apparently unsolvable conflicts and clashes: indeed, in all three of its sections we find two practical spheres in reciprocal opposition. In section 2, "Intention and Welfare" [*Die Absicht und das Wohl*], we have the clash of two conflicting dimensions of freedom: the *universality of right* (with its demands for universal justice that is equal for all) and *individual happiness*, self-realization, authenticity (which differs from one individual to another). The conflict here seems not only between two opposing philosophical conceptions of practical life (Kant versus Aristotle, let us say) but between two full-fledged *worlds*: on one hand, the idea that our practical life must be regulated by *rules of justice*, by right, by moral intention that prescinds from the concrete consequences on life and on existence; on the other, the ideal of the *good life* as the true end of our actions—self-realization, the pursuit of happiness and welfare. These two worlds appear irreconcilable: strict observation of the rules of justice can lead to profound damage and unhealable wounds in the concrete life of individuals, just as the pursuit of my own happiness and realization can prove to be profoundly unjust to others.

On the one hand we have the demands of justice, before which "my particularity, like that of others" unquestionably represents a lesser right that "cannot assert itself in contradiction to this substantial basis on which it rests." In other words: "an intention to promote my welfare and that of others [. . .] cannot justify an *action that is wrong*" (§ 126).

On the other hand we also have the concrete demands of individuals, and here an indiscriminate realization of right can give rise to even greater injustice. Hegel cites as an example the extreme case in which the application of property right exercised by a creditor can endanger the debtor's very life. If, for an unpaid debt, all the debtor's resources were to be confiscated (his tools, agricultural implements, clothes, home), the damage would be enormous: the deprivation not only of his welfare but, potentially, of his very life. In short, the indiscriminate application of the principles of justice can cause "an infinite injury to existence" and entail "the total lack of rights [*die totale Rechtlosigkeit*]" (§ 127). The suppression of a life is the suppression not only of an individual's rights but of his fundamental right to existence, and this is a far greater injustice than the failure to apply the rules of justice. Hegel is even more explicit in the Addition to the paragraph:

Life, as the totality of ends, has a right in opposition to abstract right. If, for example, it can be preserved by stealing a loaf, this certainly constitutes an infringement of someone's property, but it would be wrong to regard such an action as common theft. If someone whose life is in danger were not allowed to take measures to save himself, he would be destined to forfeit all his rights; and since he would be deprived of life, his entire freedom would be negated. (RZ 240–241/PR § 127 A)

Thus, the Kantian primacy of the just over the good not only does not resolve the conflict between the abstract-universal dimension of freedom and its concrete-individual dimension but, indeed, heightens it. This conflict, then, "reveals the finitude and hence the contingency of both right [*Recht*] and welfare [*Wohl*]." In short, asserting the "abstract existence of freedom" without considering "the existence of the particular person," on the one hand, and asserting "the particular will without the universality of right" on the other, are both "one-sided" (§ 128).

In the next section, "The Good and Conscience" [*Das Gute und das Gewissen*], we have Hegel's solution to this antinomy: universal right and individual welfare must be conjoined in the Idea of the "good"; that is, they must present themselves together as one single good.

Welfare is not a good without *right*. Similarly, right is not the good without welfare (*fiat iustitia* should not have *pereat mundus* as its consequence). (§ 130)

The Idea of the good asserts itself less as a meeting point than as a *new normative dimension*, with respect to which the two previous moments lose their autonomous existence.

The *good* is the *Idea*, as the unity of the *concept* of the will and the *particular* will, in which abstract right, welfare, the subjectivity of knowing, and the contingency of external existence, *as autonomous for themselves*, are superseded [*aufgehoben*]; but they are at the same time *essentially contained* and *preserved* [*enthalten und erhalten*] within it. (§ 129)

Grounded in the Idea of the good, normativity must be able to realize, simultaneously, the universality of right and the welfare of the single individual ("the contingency of [his] external existence"). In this sense the good "has an *absolute right* as distinct from the abstract right of property and the particular ends of welfare" (§ 130).

But, in this transition, *there is still one problem*: the good must not be understood as a moral end, as a duty for conscience, or as an aim of our desires. If this were the case it would do no more than replace the previous approaches to justice (pure intention) or to welfare with a new one, which would still be external to and beyond the subject. The diremption that characterizes morality would not be overcome in the least, and would present itself anew in the form of an opposition between conscience [*Gewissen*] and the good [*Gute*] itself. To avoid this umpteenth defeat of morality (in Hegel, morality taken entirely on its own is never able to realize itself fully) the good must be something new with respect to the moral conception of the world: it must be an *already realized good,* an *institutional historical reality*—in short: an *ethical good.* Only in ethical life does the good lose the subjective features of the moral point of view (in which conscience still showed its essential difference from its object) to manifest itself as the "living good" ["*lebendiges Gute*"]—that is, as a good that is at the same time willed by the subject and already actually existing, which has its "knowledge and volition in self-consciousness" and is "ethical being" (§ 142).[29]

Hegel distinguishes very carefully between two inflections of the good, the moral and the ethical. In the *moral inflection* the two moments—the good and conscience—while "integrated," are "initially still in a *relative* relation" (§ 128). In other words, they establish a relationship to one another that is, at the same time, also of opposition and exclusion, in which the individual with his subjective intentions maintains all his difference from ethical objectivity (even though his approach to it is moral).

> The subjective will is not yet posited as assimilated to [the good] and in conformity with it. It thus stands in a *relationship* to the good, a relationship whereby the good *ought* to be its substantial character, whereby it *ought* to make the good its end and fulfill it. (§ 131)

We find ourselves here at the exact moment of transition from morality to ethical life, but the point of view is still that of morality: the subject *resolves* to turn toward the good—that is, toward the reconciliation of welfare and justice—but his disposition is still a *moral* one. He has renounced the pursuit of moral purity and wants something in which this purity is in agreement with concrete existence. Yet this is still not ethical life, because ethical life does not ask the subject to consider it an object of his intentions but posits itself as *what is behind* all subjective orientation, resolution, intention. Ethical life does not ask to be realized but is already this reality.

It is only in the *ethical inflection* that the two moments, the good and conscience, are truly "integrated so as to attain their truth and identity" (§ 128). The subjects are not external to the ethical good but are part of it in every respect and recognize it as their good. Subjective disposition and objective reality are the same. This is the specificity of the "living good": in it not only is happiness immanent in justice and self-realization one with autonomy, but this identity posits itself as actually existing in the world, and in particular in the world of ethical institutions.

For the Hegel of the *Philosophy of Right*, with the attaining of ethical life—and in particular with the sphere of the state—*the dialectic of freedom and of the Enlightenment comes to an end*: authenticity and autonomy, happiness and right, finally attain their reconciliation.

Rüdiger Bubner confirmed this reading. He wrote that unless and until the modern process of rationalization gives way to "a broadly accepted form of life in which reason is visibly articulated as such for everyone"—that is, unless and until reason corrects its subjectivism and takes on the features of institutional ethical life—"the dialectic of the Enlightenment will be reinforced."[30] In other words, only the state in its modern form contains the concrete bases for putting an end to the estrangement produced by rationalization. Only the state makes it possible to realize a form of life that is free and habitualized at the same time.

Christoph Menke totally disagreed. For him, Hegel's "ethical" solution is in fact not capable of overcoming the "tragedy" of modernity but essentially entails a retreat to the *premodern and pretragic phase*. In other words, Hegel's solution is nothing other than a reproposal of the ideal of the *polis* as a remedy for the diremptions of modernity.

> Hegel understands the ethical figure of the good as the leading normative principle of a modernity *beyond* the tragic. But Hegel can paint this picture of a post-tragic modernity only by secretly following the model of a *pre*-tragic ethical life.[31]

Distancing himself from the main route Hegel follows in his theory of ethical life, Menke treads a path on which he accepts Hegel's solution only in part. He accepts Hegel's idea of the good as a reconciliation of justice and the good life but, at the same time, finds it acceptable only in its *moral inflection*. He claims that moving the synthesis of self-realization and right back to the subjective level would avoid the imposition of an objectivist model of ethical life, thereby leaving each individual free to find his own best solution, from case to case. The result would be a "pluralistic" solution to the conflicts of modernity, without anchoring it to an objective order. Of course, there is a price to be paid for renouncing Hegel's "master solution": there would be no *guaranteed solution* to these conflicts, but only the *possibility* of finding "a *correction* for their 'infinite lacerations.'"[32] Instead of presenting an idea of the "living good" *beyond* the tragic, Menke's proposal presents itself more modestly as merely *post*-tragic.

Can Hegel's ethical life be the solution to the conflicts of modernity? I shall come back to the question later in this book—and to the question of Menke's proposal for a "moral" solution to the problem. I must comment, however, on the insufficiency of Menke's interpretation when he takes Hegel's theory of the state to be no more than a "restoration" of the ancient *polis*. With good reason I have dwelled on the decisive differences between the Greek and the Hegelian model, focusing above all on what for Hegel is the new foundation of the state—namely, *freedom*. This confers on Hegelian *Sittlichkeit* not only a *universalism* unknown in antiquity, but above all brings the fundamental role of *subjectivity* back into play. Let us tackle, then, this question of subjectivity.

3.1.6. Practical Unity of Subject and Object

The importance of self-consciousness as a constitutive element of ethical life leads, for Hegel, to an idea of *Sittlichkeit* in which the role of subjectivity cannot be reduced to an uncritical conformity to what exists. Ethical life *needs* the individual's conscious and free acceptance of objectivity.

Indeed, Hegel distances himself from the spontaneous and unreflective ethical life of antiquity precisely because it did not give due consideration to individual subjectivity. The "ideal beauty and truth" of the ethical life presented by Plato's philosophy is greatly compromised—for Hegel—because it "cannot come to terms with the principle of autonomous particularity,* which had suddenly overtaken Greek ethical life." In the end, "excluding [this principle from the state] from its very beginnings in *private property* and the *family* to its subsequent development as the arbitrary will of individuals and their choice of social position" gave Plato's philosophy a bad name, and "also explains why the great *substantial* truth of his *Republic* is imperfectly understood, and why it is usually regarded as a dream of abstract thought,

---

*In Nisbet's translation: "self-sufficient particularity."

as what is indeed often called an *ideal*" (§ 185 R). Hegel disputes this ancient conception, insisting that the free adherence of conscious individuals is essential for ethical life. As Claudio Cesa confirmed, "conscience"—the "moral habit whose content is the laws and the spirit of the laws"—orients itself toward this content "by its own choice, not because it is a necessity to have it." This is "what is essential" in Hegel's theory of ethical life: indeed, "not only custom but also education are considered inadequate forms of freedom: the 'spontaneous' behavior they induce is [for Hegel] incompatible with the sense of the self" that characterizes "modern consciousness."[33] In other words: the self-determination of the subject, which—unlike in Kant—leads not to opposition to what exists but to recognition of its rationality, is the constitutive and essential element for the advent of *modern* ethical life. For Hegel this becomes possible when ethical life is conceived as the locus in which the *practical unity of subject and object* is realized—a unity in which the object is recognized as identical to self-consciousness.[34]

> [The ethical powers] are not something *alien* to the subject. On the contrary, the subject *bears spiritual witness* [*gibt das Zeugnis des Geistes*] to them as to *its own essence*, in which it has its *sense of self* [*Selbstgefühl*] and lives as in its element that is not distinct from itself—a relationship that is immediate and closer to identity than even [a relationship of] *faith* or *trust*. (§ 147)

The identity of the autonomous subject with the ethical institutions and the absolute absence of alienness between them is due to the fact that the subject feels for these institutions what he feels for himself: in them he has his "sense of himself." His attitude within ethical life is that of *bearing witness*, an expression Hegel borrows from Christian religion and which he often used in his *Lectures on the Philosophy of Religion* (in fact the atmosphere of section 147 in its entirety is vaguely religious). What is Hegel referring to? He speaks of bearing *spiritual* witness. In other words, the subject who lives within a recognized ethical life bears witness to the "presence" of the spirit in it: he recognizes it as a product of the very spirit that is in him, and thus recognizes *himself* in his identity with ethical life. Just as bearing witness to Christ gives rise to religious faith, so bearing witness to spirit produces *faith* and *trust* in the institutions. Bearing spiritual witness coincides here with recognizing its immediate presence, and it is this immediacy that gives rise to the faith in institutions. (Hegel adds that the relationship between citizens and institutions is even deeper than the relationship of faith, since it is clearly a rational relationship, in which subjective reason recognizes itself in the objective rationality of the ethical.)

Once again, Hegel emphasizes *the vital role of civil society*. It is in civil society that the subjects became aware of their individuality and autonomy, experiencing their own interests as an essential part of their identity. At the same time, in civil society this individuality had already found its own access to the universal. Now the state brings this relationship to its completion, actualizing what Hegel calls "*concrete freedom.*" It consists in the superposition of two relations.

> But *concrete freedom* requires that personal individuality and its particular interests should reach their full *development* and gain *recognition of their right* for itself (within the system of the family and of civil society), and also that they should, in part [*teils*], *pass over* of their own accord into the interest of the universal and, in part [*teils*], knowingly and willingly acknowledge this universal interest. (§ 260)

Although civil society did in fact achieve the "full development" of individuality, a full relationship with the universal had not yet been completed. Hegel expresses this with the double "in part," showing precisely the two different times in which this relationship unfolds. In civil society the subjects had only *passed over* "into the interest of the universal" without being aware of it, much less willing it. But now the universal is "knowingly and willingly acknowledged." With their full awareness, it becomes the end of their action: they recognize it "as their own *substantial spirit*, and *actively pursue it* as their *ultimate end*" (§ 260).

Here, it is important to note that the subject's particular interest, developed and pursued in civil society, is not set aside or suppressed in the political sphere, but finds its completion in the universal interest: "the universal does not attain validity or fulfillment without the interest, knowledge, and volition of the particular" (§ 260).[35]

With great clarity Bubner explained the type of relationship that is established here, interpreting the individual's recognition of the universal (and thus of political institutions) as a "*wieder-erkennen*"—that is, a "*knowing-again.*" This is not a banal act of "consent"—no, it is far more profound. A subject knows "again" only when he has already known, when he *finds himself* "*again*" in the apparently alien environment of state institutions. Here, this "finding again" is a rediscovering of *his own place of origin*.

The two parties that meet are not independent entities that confront one another like the subject and object of modern philosophy—no, they are two realities that belong to one another, since "the institutions are spirit of the same spirit as the subject."[36]

> *Wiedererkennen* means *negating an alienness* [*Fremdheit*] that was initially assumed to be so. What I know-again I already knew as what I am. What is known-again [*das Wiedererkannte*] thus belongs originally to my own life-sphere, from which it had only temporarily vanished.[37]

The consent of its members is the condition of an effective ethical life, just as the consent of its citizens is the condition of a solid state: Hegel knows very well that "no law has any real chance of commanding obedience unless it is intrinsically *accepted by those involved*."[38] And this acceptance cannot be extrinsic or occasional but must be realized in long-term historical continuity: that subjects "find themselves again" shows itself in the "prevailing and long-term stable loyalty of enlightened citizens."[39] Hegel's opposition to a contractualist legitimation of the state does not mean that he annuls the dimension of consent. Ethical life also means the assent of the subjects, but the point here is that Hegel understands this assent not according to the coordinates of contractualism but by designing a state grounded in the stability of attitudes and habits, and in the incorporation of institutional norms within the subjects' "nature." "Assent is the basis of the stability of the relationships. But living assent cannot be produced by a contractualist fiction."[40]

The unity of subject and object finds one of its highest expressions in the phenomenon of *patriotism*. Hegel defines it as the "political disposition" [*politische Gesinnung*] that stems from the action of institutions on subjects. Hence it constitutes the subjects' *response* to this action—a response that expresses the citizens' recognition of the state's universality. This feeling, too, has the form typical of ethical institutions—that is, it manifests itself in the form of habit; it is "a volition that has become *habitual*" (§ 268). Repeated acts of trust in political institutions at a certain point become a stable disposition, which at that moment turns into patriotism.

> As such, it is merely a consequence of the institutions within the state, a consequence in which rationality is *actually* present, just as rationality receives its practical application through action in conformity with the state's institutions.—This disposition

[*Gesinnung*] is in general one of *trust* (which must pass over into more or less educated insight), or the consciousness that my substantial and particular interest is preserved and contained in the interest and end of another (in this case, the state). (§ 268)

Patriotism is the highest expression of the citizens' trust: it is the tangible sign of their daily continual consent. Indeed, without consent there can be no patriotism. Thus, at the highest level and more than any verbal consent, it expresses the meeting of the citizens with the objectivity of the institutions. A patriot is one who believes that his own identity, values, and interests are guaranteed in his adherence to his own state. But believing that my "own" interest is guaranteed in the interest of an "other" is possible because this other "is immediately not an other" (§ 268). In short, in my disposition in favor of the interest of an "other" there is the conviction that it is actually "my" interest that is being realized: this movement is the inverse—the mirror image—of the one that takes place in civil society, where in pursuing my own interest it is the interest of an other (society as a whole) that is realized.

Here, within a political community, I come to the conclusion that only by working for the interests of all do I truly work for my own interests, and "in my consciousness of this, I am free" (§ 268). With patriotism the freedom of the individual is not lost: in adhering to the interests of the community the individual does not lose his own freedom but, on the contrary, reinforces the collective conditions that make it possible. Once again, *freedom* is obtained thanks to the *relation* to the other. But now the other has become even more abstract and universal: it is no longer another subject, a "you," but an objective sphere—that of the state institutions and of the political community as a whole.

Patriotism is not a "heroic" virtue and has little to do with "a willingness to perform *extraordinary* sacrifices and actions." It is the ordinary disposition of citizens who habitually consider "the community [*Gemeinwesen*] [to be] the substantial basis and end" (§ 268 R). In essence, the patriotic citizen is one who has come to a complete awareness of who he is and what his true interests are. He knows that self-realization is impossible outside his communal relationships and that it is in his interest to see himself as an essential member of a greater civil and legal community that pursues common ends. Hence his patriotism is built on the basis of his trust in communal relationships, for only there can he develop his autonomy and responsibility.[41]

"Patriotism," moreover, is not to be confused with "nationalism." Even if, as we shall see, Hegel does conceive of the state as a *nation* state, we must not forget that the foundation of the Hegelian state is neither "blood and earth" nor particularity of race, nor even national history. It is grounded in freedom, whose maximum expression is the political constitution capable of embodying it in laws and institutions. Patriotism, then, in Hegel's view, is—first of all—the loyalty of a people to these institutions, laws, and constitution, grounded in freedom. If patriotism means loyalty to and trust in my own common heritage, here what is "my own" coincides with the freedom of "all" and with the constitution that defends it. Hegel's "patriotism" is a *patriotism of freedom*. At the same time, however, it demands of its citizens not servile obedience but active support for their common institutions—in short, it demands *civic virtues*. Axel Honneth was absolutely right to use the celebrated Habermasian expression "constitutional patriotism" [*Verfassungspatriotismus*][42] to characterize this Hegelian conception of the relationship between state and citizen. Indeed, it is in the *loyalty to the institutions*, in the *political virtues* necessary to sustain the community represented in them, in the *identification of the citizens with the constitution*, that Hegel grounds his notion of patriotism.

This point also makes the meaning of that *recognition* of the universal of which Hegel spoke in section 260 perfectly clear. This is not an *intersubjective* recognition: indeed, the relation between subjects has been superseded by a relation between subjects on the one hand and the objective sphere of the state on the other. Speaking of a "recognition of the universal" in regard to the relation between citizens and the state makes it clear that at the political level intersubjective relations are *mediated by objective relations*. This means that the citizens do not recognize one another as such, do not attribute rights and duties to themselves directly, but do so *indirectly*, through the mediation of their universal recognition of the state. It is by recognizing the legitimacy of the state that every citizen implicitly recognizes the rights and duties of every other citizen: this is the specific dynamic of "political recognition."[43] Hegel describes with great precision what the relation of reciprocity between the citizens and the state must be in the Addition to section 432 of the *Encyclopaedia*.

> What dominates in the state is the spirit of the people, custom, and law. Here man is recognized and treated as a *rational* being, as *free*, as a *person*; and the individual, on his side, makes himself worthy of this recognition by [. . .] obeying a *universal*, the will that is existent [*seienden*] in and for itself, the *law*. He behaves, therefore, towards others in a manner that is *universally valid*

[*auf eine allgemeingültige Weise*], recognizing them—as he wishes others to recognize him—as free, as persons. (EZ 221–222/ ENC § 432 A)

The institution has an attitude of respect for the individual, treating him as a free person, and the individual responds to the state by obeying the laws thanks to which he is "recognized and treated" as a person. It is through this universalist attitude (in which the individual's interlocutor is the state, not the other citizens) that one individual comes to recognize all the others.

In this regard, Ludwig Siep spoke of a *"second-degree" recognition*,[44] distinguishing it from a first degree that is still fundamentally intersubjective. For Siep this new type of recognition—in which the interlocutor is no longer a "you" but, now, a "we": the general will, customs, laws, institutions—represents the specific advance of Hegel's theory of recognition over Fichte's, which was still only interpersonal. In this way Fichte's original theory becomes, with Hegel, a *theory of institutions and of their legitimation*. But the opening of this second dimension coincides with its *limitation*. In opening to the universal Hegel fails to bring into its sphere that *reciprocity* which, indeed, is the fundamental principle of recognition: while the individuals are to recognize the universal "knowingly and willingly" (§ 260), the universal does not *reciprocate*. Hegel had insisted ever since his Jena period—in the *Phenomenology* in particular—that recognizing someone involves at the same time a negative action toward oneself: the process of negation that our natural instinctuality directs against the other is here directed to oneself in order to recognize the "lordship" of the other. When the other performs the same action on himself, following my own movement *specularly*, we can say that we have recognized one another reciprocally: we are both "lords"—that is, self-conscious and autonomous subjects. But we find none of this in the relation between individuals and the state in the *Philosophy of Right*. The universal does not negate itself but, on the contrary, *asserts* itself as the individual's supreme truth.[45] There is no sign here of the typical reciprocal constitution of the validity of each, no sign of the reciprocal conferring of legitimacy, and thus no sign of a full and proper legitimation of institutions based on a process of recognition. The universal and the particular are not constituted by the process but preexist it with all their asymmetry. Indeed, for Hegel the universal is considered to have an absolute precedence, as an "absolute and unmoved end in itself" (§ 258) to which the will and the consciousness of individuals are subordinated.[46] Individuals here are not considered full and proper "ends" but only as means for the recognition of the universal.[47] But without the reciprocity of the relation bottom-up recognition is itself weakened and its constitutive value ultimately dissolves. It follows that, in the end, institutions are not grounded in the process of recognition but are "justified in an 'absolute' manner."[48]

We find analogous objections raised in the work of Vittorio Hösle, who dwelled in particular on this disequilibrium between the universal-objective side represented by the institutions and the individual-subjective side represented by the citizens. Hegel knows very well that the ethical life of the state must be composed of both moments. Indeed, in section 267 he subdivides the substantiality of the state into two different sides: the "*subjective* substantiality" represented by the "political disposition" [*politische Gesinnung*] and the "*objective* substantiality" represented by the "*organism* of the state"—that is, by its "*constitution*" [*Verfassung*]. Well—Hösle remarked—Hegel dedicates only one paragraph (§ 268) to the former, while to the latter he dedicates sixty-one of them! Instead of adequately developing the side of patriotism and of *politische Gesinnung*, investigating the educational role of the state,[49] Hegel focuses exclusively on its institutional-objective aspect. Hösle concluded: "It is evident here that Hegel wants to minimize the positive function of subjectivity within the state as much as possible. In this neglect of the subjective moment the aporetic position of morality continues to produce its effects."[50]

The problem of the sacrifice of individuality in the *Philosophy of Right* has been tackled by many critics and is unquestionably one of the points that have militated against a favorable reception of the book today. The question has been so heatedly debated precisely because Hegel, from start to finish, makes it clear that *in no way* does he wish to sacrifice the individual and the contribution of the citizens to the ethical life of the modern state. Yet these declarations of principles seem to be contradicted by the concrete exposition of his doctrine of the state. Emil Angehrn brought this circumstance into focus:

> The modern state must overcome the deficiency of civil society by maintaining its most distinctive principle: subjective freedom. Now, it is very much open to question whether the state delineated by Hegel actually does justice to this postulate. To be sure, there are a number of points in which Hegel emphasizes the inalienable character of subjective freedom, since it is the foundation of the state. Nevertheless, it can hardly be denied

that the claim of the modern state to bring the subjective principle to completion and, at the same time, to reconcile it with substantiality (§ 260) is, indeed, nothing more than a claim.[51]

But, for Angehrn, this insufficient consideration for individuality must be set in its proper context—that is, in the relation between finite and absolute subjectivity: since truth resides in the latter, the former is destined sooner or later to be sacrificed.

> In the symptomatic formulation of the philosophy of right the individuals are degraded to the level of "accidents" of the spirit (§ 145; § 156 A; § 163 R), and their relation with the whole is thus conceived as a relation of substantiality; this is the figure that is opposed to absolutized subjectivism. The dilemma of the concept of subjectivity is its oscillating between absoluteness and nothingness.[52]

Heimo E. M. Hofmeister's objections move along similar lines: "Since the reception of the Kantian morality has a constitutive function for Hegel's concept of ethical life," Hegel is clearly inconsistent in his "not doing justice to the finite individual and his demand for self-determination, since he views individuality merely as particularity, as accident that in respect to ethics has its truth *outside* of itself."[53] For Hofmeister the reason for this resides in an inopportune absolutization of the state, that is, in considering it not just *one* "historical" actualization of the ethical Idea but its *one and only* "absolute" actualization, thus eliminating the state's specific historicity and "neglecting the fact that ethical life is the completion of objective spirit and not of absolute spirit."[54] Hence the true problem of the *Philosophy of Right* consists in its "failure to distinguish between the objective spirit as actual in the state, and the absolute spirit"—a failure that induced Hegel to view "the particular state of a certain time" as "the objectification of the absolute spirit." This, then, for Hofmeister, is the basis of the Hegelian idea that individual ethical life "can only be actualized where it relinquishes its individual freedom."[55]

I shall return to the relations between objective spirit and absolute spirit at the end of this chapter. But first we have to do something of fundamental importance for this investigation: we have to look more closely at Hegel's *characterization of objectivity* within his theory of the state and test its weight, above all with respect to the subjectivity of the citizens.

3.2. Ethical Life as Primacy of the Object

3.2.1. Reconciliation of Individual and Universal

The theory that Hegel *intends* to support (and all his *explicit* declarations go in this direction) is not that of the primacy of objectivity over subjectivity but, rather, that of a reconciliation between individual subjectivity and substantial objectivity. Not by chance, he declares that "the principle of modern states" consists in maximizing individual freedom within the maintenance of the unity of the state.

> The principle of modern states has enormous strength and depth because it allows the principle of subjectivity to attain fulfillment in the *autonomous extreme* of personal particularity, while at the same time *bringing it back to substantial unity* and so preserving this unity in the principle of subjectivity itself. (§ 260)

The state does not confine itself to taking the helm of civil society, to receiving and defending individuals within it; rather, it *furthers* the development of their individuality and autonomy. It does not destroy the principle of individuality, dissolving it in substantial unity, but "preserves" it. Indeed, the state makes itself *guarantor* of the subject's full development, "in the autonomous extreme of personal particularity."[56]

The substantial unity of which Hegel speaks is thus the coincidence of individual and collective interests: only by pursuing the common interest (the "recognition of the universal" of § 260) is the safeguarding of the individual interest guaranteed. Once again, we have a *specular inversion* of what occurred in civil society: there, the individual pursued his own interest and obtained the welfare of all; here, the individual seeks the interest of all and obtains his own welfare.

> In the state, as an ethical entity and as the interpenetration of the substantial and the particular, my obligation towards the substantial is at the same time the existence of my particular freedom. (§ 261 R)

Doing my own duty as a citizen does not mean limiting my freedom; rather, it means creating the conditions in which this freedom can be safeguarded and guaranteed. For Hegel "duty and right are *united* within the state *in one and the same relation*" (§ 261 R): they are the two indistinguishable sides of freedom.[57] Thus, when the state appears to the individuals as an "*external* necessity" and "higher power" to which the demands of the family and civil society are subordinate, this is only an external appearance because in reality the state is "their *immanent* end" (§ 261) and the true guarantee for the respect of their freedom.[58]

While this reconciliation between subjectivity and objectivity entails the just recognition of individuality, it is also clear that the individual remains subordinate to the state. The state, then, can never be considered an *instrument for the realization of the individual.* It is in this context that Hegel describes the state as "an absolute and unmoved end in itself," which, as "ultimate end," "possesses the highest right in relation to individuals" (§ 258).

But, *here,* that *absence of reciprocity* which Siep criticized is palpable. While the state "possesses the highest right in relation to individuals," the individuals do not seem able to claim any right in relation to the state. There is, of course, something "highest" the individual *can* claim, but it is only a duty, not a right.

> This substantial unity is the absolute and unmoved end in itself, and in it freedom enters into its highest right, just as this ultimate end possesses the highest right in relation to individuals, whose *highest duty* is to be members of the state. (§ 258)

If individuals should set themselves up as "ends," for Hegel we would no longer be in the sphere of the state but in civil society:

> If the state is confused with civil society and its determination is equated with the security and protection of property and personal freedom, *the interest of individuals as such* becomes the ultimate end for which they are united; it also follows from this that membership of the state is an optional matter. (§ 258 R)

Hegel makes similar remarks in his *Lectures on the Philosophy of History*:

> The state does not exist for the sake of the citizens; it might rather be said that the state is the end, and the citizens are its instruments. But this relation of end and means is not at all appropriate in the present context. For the state is not an abstraction that stands in opposition to the citizens; on the contrary, they are distinct moments like those of organic life, in which no member is either a means or an end. (PhWg I 112/PH1 94–95)

Hegel, then, continues to insist that the prevalence of the universal element by no means entails a loss of individual freedom: "*Union* [*Vereinigung*] as such is itself the true content and end" (§ 258 R). By positing the end of individuals in *Vereinigung*, Hegel on the one hand opens a window on the *intersubjective characterization* of the life of the state: here, the state is not simply a preexisting substance but is the result of the unification of the many individuals of which it is composed. On the other hand, positing something as an end signifies, in Hegel's language, positing it as ground and origin. In this case, it means positing as original not the single subjects in their interaction but their always already accomplished mediation—which is to say, the *priority of the objective order* over any type of individual demand.

3.2.2. The Originariness* of Order

For Hegel it is *not* the dynamic of *intersubjectivity* but the *objective* unity of individuals [*Vereinigung*] that has the value of original position. We see this clearly in his radical opposition to the political conception that posits the *contract* as the origin and ground of the state. Such a contract presupposes individuals who are reciprocally isolated—whose only relationship is constituted by the external relations of the struggle for survival and for the appropriation of goods. The contract alone is capable of imposing this relationship, which at this point proves to be artificial and contrived. The scenario here is the diametrical opposite of Hegel's, in which it is *Vereinigung* that is conceived as original.

> But Rousseau considered the will only in the determinate form of the *individual* will (as Fichte subsequently also did) and regarded the universal will not as the will's rationality in and for itself, but only as the *common element* arising out of this individual will *as a conscious will*. The union of individuals within the state thus becomes a *contract*, which is accordingly based on their arbitrary will and opinions, and on their express consent given at their own discretion. (§ 258 R)

Earlier in his Remarks to section 258 Hegel makes a statement that clarifies the general sense of this criticism. He makes it clear that his object

---

*Although I have translated "*originario*" as *original* (rather than *originary*) throughout this book, *originality* would be a misleading translation of *originarietà*.

is the *Idea* of the state, and "as far as the Idea of the state itself is concerned, it makes no difference what is or was the *historical* origin of the
state in general" (§ 258 R). Therefore it is not the *historical plausibility* of
the contractualist hypothesis that Hegel calls into question. Hume had done
so earlier, judging the social pact to be a historically untenable fiction; and
Kant, in the wake of Hume's critique, reformulated and refounded contractualism, no longer as an illustration of the genesis of the state but as a
justification of its legitimacy. For Kant, it was basically a question of taking
the pact as a working hypothesis—as an "as if": we can consider our state
to be legitimate if and only if we can imagine that its order would have
been approved by the common will of its future citizens in a condition of
natural originariness.[59] Hegel's critique, then, addresses this "second" version
of contractualism: it is intended to refute the validity of the contractualist model not historically but *theoretically* (an operation that therefore, in
principle, calls in question the contemporary versions of contractualism as
well—Rawls's *A Theory of Justice*, for example).[60] Here, theoretical refutation
means calling into question the thesis that the individual and his subjective
will constitute the source of legitimacy of the order of the state.[61]

Hegel sets against the contractualist (i.e., individualist) legitimacy of
the state an *objective and supra-individual legitimacy*, which he calls the
"objective will," and which "in itself in its *concept* is rational" (§ 258 R).
He rules out the possibility that the objective will may be the product of
individual wills. The individual is the result of an existing ethical life and
therefore cannot take himself to be the original author of what contributed
decisively to constructing him. Indeed, the contractual capacity to stipulate
a contract and to have it be respected depends on the preexistence (and
legitimacy) of a legal system, or at least on the already operative validity of
the norm by which the contracts are to be respected.[62]

All of this stems from the preexistence of the ethical and its function
of legitimation with respect to all normative demands. As we have seen,
this preexisting ethos is not an abstract universal but is a universal that has
become an institutional system. We are its products, not its authors.

> It is not we who are the authors of an order that we have long
> needed in order to be authors in a sense that is rationally recon-
> structible. We do not begin with the order, since the order is
> itself what we need in order to be able to begin with our praxis.[63]

This order is the condition of the individual and of his freedom, and
is thus also the condition of his praxis. It cannot be "constructed" after we

have already begun to act but, on the contrary, precedes our every possible action. Without institutions this social acting would be impossible.[64] It is in this context that Hegel's famous "hyper-statist" expressions are to be interpreted: "Everything a man is he owes to the state; he has his essence in it alone. Whatever worth and spiritual reality he possesses are his solely by virtue of the state" (PhWg I 111/PH1 94). But, here too, we in fact find confirmation of what we have already discovered: the priority of the state entails not the disappearance of the individual but his promotion. Hegel himself confirms this in the *Encyclopaedia* when he says that the spirit of a people constitutes "the inner power and necessity [*die innere Macht und Notwendigkeit*] of the autonomy of the persons [*von deren Selbstständigkeit*]" (ENC § 514).

The type of freedom that is sustained here by a functioning ethical life is clearly not the *negative* defense of the individual will against external interference and conditioning but, rather, the *positive* capacity of self-determination and choice regarding what we really want. The priority of the ethical (and of order) must therefore be seen in the context of that *positive conception of freedom* which constitutes one of the fundamental traits of Hegel's political thought.

Charles Taylor has been one of the strongest contemporary exponents of the positive over the merely negative model of freedom. The limit he sees in the negative conception lies in its positing itself exclusively as a mere absence of impediments. Accordingly, I am free if I am not impeded in the exercise of my freedom by physical or legal obstacles. But we are told nothing at all about what this freedom is, apart from this independence. In fact, an individual's freedom also depends on other factors—first of all, on his capacity to achieve his own ends, to discriminate between primary and secondary ends, between good and bad finalities. If, despite my recognizing the importance of a given aim, I fail to achieve it because I am attracted by other desires, I am most certainly not free. This, for Taylor, make it necessary to broach a positive notion of freedom, in which it is not simply a faculty to "do what one wants" but, rather, is a capacity to "discriminate motivations" and to do "what we really want."[65]

Now, this capacity is not only the *practical capacity* to overcome the internal obstacles to my self-realization but is, above all, the *theoretical capacity* "to recognize adequately my most important purposes."[66] Precisely because "the subject can be wrong about what he truly wants,"[67] he needs to couple his individual freedom with an adequate vision of what his truly important purposes are. Hence, the importance of the *form of society* in which to make him grow and mature, in order to allow him to develop this type of faculty. Positive freedom is not a natural gift but is acquired and increasingly refined through use, exercise, and repetition. All this depends, on one side, on the individual, since it is I myself who have to develop my *capacity to decide and to recognize* the ends of my actions—that is, "the ability to fulfill my purposes." On the other side, the development of these faculties depends on *objective conditions*, since positive freedom is "fully realizable only within a certain form of society."[68]

Albrecht Wellmer focused on this second element. For him, it is the characteristic element of Hegel's conception of freedom, and consists in the effort "to show that the negative freedom of bourgeois legal subjects could not be coherently conceived if they were not integrated into a context of public, communal, 'rational' freedom. It is in the institutions of political society that rational freedom in the communalist sense of the word has its place."[69] For Wellmer, then, Hegel does not seek to replace negative freedom with the positive freedom made possible by political institutions but to transform the one into the other, to integrate them reciprocally. True individual freedom is guaranteed only in the context of ethical life, and: "political freedom can be real only as a form of concrete ethical life."[70]

Peter Schaber investigated the role of the ethical sphere in constructing the positive freedom of the individual. For him, *Sittlichkeit* is the condition not only of freedom but of many other components that constitute individual identity—in particular, the "need for attention and recognition."[71] It is not only a question of the "need to be valued as a person" (for which abstract right is sufficient) or as a "moral subject" (for which self-reflection suffices), but of the subject's need "to be esteemed and recognized in his cultural, religious, and social being or, expressed differently: in his interest in attaining his own image in the others."[72] Seeing myself mirrored in the attention others pay me, I gain a sense of my own individuality and dignity. In the Hegelian sphere of ethical institutions the individual can consolidate his own image and his sense of self-respect.

But this sphere *cannot be "constructed"*—it cannot be an object of planning and execution. The very idea of a "planned" ethos strips it of its primacy over the moral and reduces it to a simple product of morality.

> If the aim of the Hegelian philosophy of right were that of founding a new ethical life, it would be not an ethical but a moral plan. It would itself assume a moral point of view. Morality plans a common normative world; for morality, it is a question of finding the norms to which everyone ought to be able to adhere. But the ethical is not that which everyone ought to be

able to consider right but, rather, that which makes a rational life possible for the individual. Consequently, in aspiring to a new ethical life one is not acting within the ethos.[73]

Let me say it once again: ethical life means the priority of an objective order over the individual's practical reason and over his very freedom of self-determination. Therefore it is not the realization of a moral "ought," but is the already operative normative reality that makes the moral viewpoint possible. It does not *follow* the subject's self-determination but, on the contrary, *precedes* it and is its presupposition.

Hegel makes it clear that ethical life cannot simply be understood as *realized morality*. The self-determination of the individual is only a moment within ethical life. For the ethical individual institutional actuality [*Wirklichkeit*] is not the reality [*Realität*] of his self-determination, but first of all—in any case—a datum [*ein Gegebenes*].[74]

Consequently, the individual's relation to the ethical sphere is not that of a producer to his product but only one of *ex post* recognition of the objective validity of an already existing sphere.

This brings us back to the question raised at the end of the first part of this chapter, by Siep and by Hösle in particular: What room does Hegel leave for the *individual's* recognition of institutions? In what does this recognition consist? Does he entertain the possibility of the individual's denying this recognition when the conditions do not render it legitimate? And *if he does not*, based on his *own* premises in the *Philosophy of Right* what conceivable margins could there be for such a possibility? In short: Apart from Hegel's own declarations of principles, what room does the individual actually have within the life of Hegel's state?

3.2.3. A Subjectivity Deficit

The decisive element that reveals just how little Hegel is disposed to grant to individual subjectivity in the process of the legitimation of state institutions emerges with great clarity in his discussion of sovereignty. In keeping with the primacy of objectivity, Hegel attributes sovereignty to the state (see § 278); but, for him, this sovereignty cannot be rooted in the people. Yes, it may be said that sovereignty "lies with the *people*"—Hegel writes—"but only if we are speaking of the *whole* [state] in general, in keeping with the above demonstration that sovereignty belongs to the *state*" (§ 279 R). This concession, in which "popular sovereignty" is made to stem from state sovereignty and is made identical to it, does not mean, however, that the latter also stems from the former. Indeed, Hegel wants to differentiate his conception from "the usual sense in which the term 'popular sovereignty' [*Volkssouveränität*] has begun to be used in recent times [. . .] to denote *the opposite of that sovereignty which exists in the monarch* [*gegen die im Monarchen existierenden Souveränität*]" (§ 279 R). This, for Hegel, is based on "a *garbled* notion of the *people*":

> *Without* its monarch and that *articulation* of the whole which is necessarily and immediately associated with monarchy, *the* people is a formless mass that is no longer a state. (§ 279 R)

This, in a new form, is Hegel's classic objection to the liberal conception of the state: a people is sovereign only if it is already constituted as such—that is, if the institutions of the state have already been able to organize and articulate it. Once again, the initiative stands on the side of the object. In the final analysis, while Hegel's conception of the state may be reconcilable with a conservative form of liberalism it proves to be clearly irreconcilable with the theory of the democratic state.[75]

Radically opposed to any theory that makes legitimacy depend on *explicit consent*, Hegel ultimately reduces the legitimating action of the citizens to an *implicit* attitude of ex post recognition. It is quite true that "the capricious moods and variable tendencies of a public opinion in itself contradictory" cannot be the "standard by which the institutions are to be measured" and that "the reduction of reason to the granting or the withdrawal of the consent of a plurality of voters, who become the object of manipulation or of opinion polls, cannot be the last word."[76] But what is the alternative? Denying the "postulating" populace the right to political expression, the capacity to grant or withdraw consent, the right to vote? If the alternative glimpsed here is that of constructing, forming, and educating a people that is really prepared to express itself politically, who will its "educators" be? And if, following Hegel, we wish to entrust this work of education not to social subjects but to already existing institutions, what about that subjective contribution which Hegel himself tells us is necessary for the process of legitimation of these institutions? If we choose to follow Bubner, for whom, in Hegel, the "subjective side" of ethical life consists in instituting a process of "new recognition" of institutional objectivity on the part of the citizens, we are confronted with a series of unsolved problems.

The first problem regards the criteria on the basis of which the recognition is to be granted: excluding every type of abstract principle we come right back to the institutions themselves, which at this point would be both the judges and the judged. The second problem regards the validity-legitimacy of the educational process that made it possible to create the responsible citizens who carried out the recognition. But it is the third problem that is decisive: What value can the subjective recognition of an institutional objectivity have if it was this very objectivity that prepared the subjects and therefore transmitted the recognition? Where does this entire process lead if not to a *self*-recognition and thus, in the end, to a sort of self-*absolution*?

These questions are heightened if we follow Hegel on his way to the individuation of a subject capable of expressing the sovereignty of the state and of exercising sovereign power. First he refuses to attribute this sovereignty to a people without a sovereign, but then he ends up attributing it *to the monarch alone*—that is, to what he calls the "power of the sovereign" [*fürstliche Gewalt*]. In Hegel's tripartition of powers, this is the "ultimate" power, superior to the "legislative" and "executive" powers (§ 273).

The terms of this tripartition clearly do not correspond to that of classical liberalism: Hegel shuffles the deck. For him, "executive power" [*Regierungsgewalt*] comprises what for us is both executive and judiciary power, while the "power of the sovereign" includes a part of the executive power as well. However, what truly distinguishes his constitutional theory is the fact that the power of the sovereign ultimately represents all three powers put together—that is, the sovereignty of the state as such. The result is a dramatic weakening of this division of powers, if not its out-and-out liquidation.[77]

Even if, in Hegel, the monarch is still subject to the constitution,[78] which means that the truth of the Hegelian state cannot be restricted to a single power but must reside in the organism as such (i.e., in the constitution), the social subject in which he condenses the universality of the state is not the people but the *monarch*.

Hegel's argument against the attribution of sovereignty to the legislative power—that is, to popular representation—is based once again on what has been described as a "naturalistic" representation of the social body. For Hegel, popular representation leads to nothing but a plurality of conflicting interests of the social classes—that which he calls "the universal of the interests" (ENC § 544) and "the *empirical universality* of the views and thoughts of the *many*" (PR § 301). These interests—Hegel adds—"do not regard the action of the state as individual (as peace and war do) and therefore do not belong exclusively to the nature of the sovereign power" (ENC § 544).

True universality must therefore be concentrated in a subject that does not belong to civil society: it must be "saved from being dragged down into the sphere of *particularity* with its arbitrariness, ends, and attitudes" (PR § 281). If the power of the sovereign were to be expressed in the legislative power, the dimension of civil society would never really be overcome. Hegel, then, continues to view parliament from the premodern perspective of a mere chamber of representation of social classes and estates. It does not occur to him that representation—institutionalized representation—makes a mediation of the specific interests that emerge from the social body possible. The role of parliaments ought to be precisely that of institutionally transforming the immediate interests and, thanks to this work of mediation, of expressing the full-fledged general interest. But Hegel, in keeping with his basic premise, transfers sovereignty to a *single subject*, "abstracted" from the conditioning of civil society. This subject is the *monarch*.

> The monarch, therefore, is essentially determined as *this* individual, in abstraction from every other content, and this individual is destined in an immediate and natural way, i.e. by his natural *birth*, to hold the dignity of the monarch. (PR § 280)

Wishing to free the sovereign power from social conditioning (and thus from any electoral procedure, which would involve society), Hegel ends up by grounding sovereignty in *mere naturalness*: the monarch—clearly—*is such by birth*, not by election—that is, on the basis of a dynastic principle. In short: for Hegel the lottery of nature is preferable to the lottery of society (interpreted, in its turn, naturalistically), but it is a lottery nonetheless. This solution has astonished many Hegel scholars, especially since this power (which is such by nature) is, for Hegel, the embodiment of freedom and rationality in and for itself—that is, of the universal will freed from all conditioning. Quite rightly, Marcuse wrote that with this solution "reason terminates in an accident of birth."[79]

In conclusion: Hegel's critique of the liberal conceptions of the state—contractualism, a real separation of powers, the legitimation of state institutions—is based on the argument, developed in numerous directions, of the priority of the universal over the particular, of rational objectivity over the naturalistic interests of empirical individuals, of the ethical order over subjective freedom. This position, however, does not exempt him from the necessity of *interpreting* this universal, of *individuating* it, of establishing what laws and what institutions are in *conformity* with it: in short, it does not exempt him from *the problem of the recognition of the universal*. Wanting to avoid recourse to society and to the social capacity to determine this universality (through consent, electoral procedures, and chambers of representatives in which the social universal becomes true common will), in the end he confines it in a *natural individuality*, exposing his entire theory of ethical life to the risk of a naturalistic and—above all—an *authoritarian* degeneration.

But, now, we have to deal with *one last element*, which makes Hegel's concrete political translation of his conception of ethical life *even more problematic*: not only does he neglect the subjective side of *Sittlichkeit*—which he had intended to make an essential component—in order to make room for objective and universal structures, but he confines the very universality of the ethical within the particularity of the *nation state*. This subjects ethical life to a particular dialectic that will, in the end, reveal its structural *contingency*.

3.3. Contingency of the Ethical

3.3.1. Failure of Ethical Life

The greatness of ethical life consists in attaining the unity of individuality and universality, subjectivity and objectivity, freedom and historical reality, difference and unity. But, even for Hegel himself, this greatness has a limit: it characterizes only the internal relations of the state—that which he calls the "internal constitution." In its foreign relations the state does maintain the moment of individuality and of unity, but it loses the moment of universality and of unity in difference. When confronted with the relations with other states, the universality of the state turns into *reciprocal exclusion*—an exclusion that is not regulated by any higher universality.

> [The state] as a single individual is *exclusive* against *other* like individuals. In their reciprocal *relations*, arbitrariness and contingency have a place, since between them, due to the autonomistic totality of these persons, the *universality* of right only has the character of an "*ought*" [*soll*] but is not *actual* [*wirklich*]. This independence makes contention between them into a relation of violence, a *state* of *war*. (ENC § 545)[80]

If it is true that the negative relation toward other states consolidates the internal cohesion and individuality of each single state, it is also true that it places them all under a logic of the relations between states that is completely beyond their control. Reciprocal recognition and international treaties do not depend on a single will and their logic defies the internal control of the individual state.

The problematic of recognition as innate in all individuality—hence also that of the state—reemerges here. At this point, Hegel emphasizes one specific aspect: namely, the *demand to be recognized* that is the basis and causing factor of every process of recognizing. If I am not recognized by others I cannot be certain of my own reality either; but this inevitably exposes me to the dependence on others: "The state has a primary and absolute entitlement to be a sovereign and independent power *in the eyes of others*, i.e. *to be recognized* by them"—but, obviously, this recognition "depends on the perception and will of the other state" (PR § 331).

Yes, when states stipulate an international treaty it is clear that there is a sort of reciprocal recognition between them. But the relation is precarious: the treaties depend entirely on the will to respect them, since there is no third party to enforce this respect. "[States exist] in a state of nature in relation to one another, and their rights are *actualized* not in a universal will with constitutional powers over them, but in their own particular wills" (§ 333). The logic of recognition seems incapable of producing between states what it does in fact produce between subjects, where it forms a *third subject* between the two self-consciousnesses, raising the process of mediation generated on the basis of the dynamic of recognition to the level of independent and objective reality. Where states are concerned, this dynamic appears to produce no qualitative leap: the logic continues to be that of the conflict between powers in a condition of mere mechanical naturalness.

For Hegel, the same is true of the Kantian ideal of *perpetual peace and cosmopolitanism*: it "presupposes an *agreement* between states. But this agreement [. . .] would always be dependent on particular sovereign wills, and would therefore continue to be tainted with contingency" (§ 333 R).

In this way the existence of the ethos is exposed to the most radical form of precariousness—to *war*: "the ethical whole itself—the independence of the state—is exposed to contingency" (§ 340). What is more, in this exposure to contingency the individual (especially in the case of war) loses the essentiality that had been guaranteed by the universality of the state: he is exposed to total precariousness and to death itself, and no longer feels protected within the secure refuge of the ethos:

> In the state of war the substance of the state proceeds, in its individuality, towards abstract negativity. This substance shows itself here as the power in which the particular autonomy of the individuals, along with their absorption in the external existence

of possession and in natural life, feels its own *nothingness*. (ENC
§ 546)

That which presented itself as the individual's dwelling, his recognition of himself in universality, his being with himself in the other, dissolves in a world of wars, violence, mere naturalness, contingency, and mutually exclusive particularities.

But, for Hegel, there is a *higher universality* in which to comprehend what occurs in the relation between states. Reason does not terminate within ethical life: it regulates the *totality* of relationships, and therefore also war. Hegel calls this new universality *"the world spirit"* [*Weltgeist*].

In section 340 of the *Philosophy of Right* Hegel writes that "the manifest [*erscheinende*] dialectic of the finitude of these spirits" is governed by the "*universal* spirit." Through this dialectic it "produces itself in its freedom from all limits" and "exercises its right—which is the highest right of all—over finite spirits in *world history* as the *world's court of judgment* [*in der* Weltgeschichte, *als dem* Weltgericht]." In section 341 he writes of the *finitude* of the "spirits of nations [*Völkergeister*] in their multifarious actuality," referring to them "only as *ideal*" [*nur als ideelles*]—that is, as not truly actual compared to the actuality and unlimitedness of the *Weltgeist*.[81]

There is a *logic*, then, that is not only *beyond* individuals but also beyond peoples and states. Now, while this logic most certainly maintains the element of universality, it can by no means realize a synthesis with the individual. *In this logic the individual cannot recognize himself.* He finds the logic incomprehensible, since he cannot discover its immanent finality, its direction, the reason that regulates it. Hence this universality cannot fulfill the task of ethical universality and cannot be a dwelling for the individual. On the contrary, it presents itself to the individual as necessity and destiny.

> Justice and virtue, wrongdoing, violence, and vice, talents and their [expression in] deeds, the small passions and the great, guilt and innocence, the splendor of individual and national life, the independence, fortune, and misfortune of states and individuals—all of these have their determinate significance and value in the sphere of conscious actuality, in which judgment and justice—albeit imperfect justice—are meted out to them. World history falls outside these points of view. (§ 345)

Moral points of view, legal certainties, our usual judgments on fortune and misfortune, on feats and talents, *no longer count* outside the protected territory of ethical life. In the vast horizon of universal history all our usual points of reference dissolve and events appear in all their incomprehensibility and senselessness.

At the level of world history, then, the unity of individuality and universality, of subject and object, is not actualized—on the contrary, we witness a cleavage between subjective spirit and world spirit, between individual rationality and the objective rationality of history. In history, subjects do not recognize their ethos, the dwelling in which they feel free.[82] On the contrary, in history they see only an alien necessity. The freedom of the ethical is broken by the necessity of world history.[83]

Of course, from the viewpoint of the *Weltgeist* there is most certainly an actualization: the world spirit recognizes itself in its products and is fully capable of recognizing the higher rationality that guides history—the rationality that is beyond the control of the individual historical spirits. But the world spirit can hardly be considered a subject: it lives only in objective relationships, *it is only objective spirit*. The point of view of the *Weltgeist* is, in the strict sense, no "point of view" at all: it is only the objectivity of history. Hence it is impossible to speak of a self-recognition of freedom in the spirit of the world. The concept of self-recognition attains its full sense only in relation to actually existing self-consciousnesses—that is, in those subjects to which history remains totally alien and at times incomprehensible.

The result is a standstill in the journey of freedom: it stops at the borders of the nation state. On the other side, we enter the realm of necessity, contingency, opacity.

3.3.2. Nationalistic Closure of the Universality of Sittlichkeit and the Defeat of Freedom

At the origin of the failure of ethical life, of its dissolution in the particularistic and conflictual logic of world history, stands the Hegelian operation that, while grasping the universality of ethical institutions, fails to consolidate it institutionally at the international level, confining it within the borders of the *nation state* and subjecting it to an anti-universalist logic.[84]

Some have seen this operation as the *revenge of the logic of being* against the higher point of view—attained in the logic of essence and of the concept—that had guided Hegel in the course of the *Philosophy of Right*. Henning Ottmann rightly observed that "Hegel traces the reciprocal recognition of states back to that abstract right with which the *Philosophy of Right* began,"[85] since the underlying logic of their relations is only the *external* logic that regulates the relations between owners of property. In short, the book's conclusion ends up posing "the question of whether—against all expectations—the logic of being must not in fact be considered the ground of the *Philosophy of Right*."[86] But the question remains open, even for Ottmann himself. To be sure, it is possible to see the world spirit as nothing other than what Ottmann—paraphrasing Adorno's famous definition[87]—called "the ideologue of natural history," and thus to see its naturalistic conclusion as finally "unmasking as mere semblance the excess of reconciliation within the state."[88] In the end, for Ottmann, even Hegel throws off his mask, unwittingly revealing the ideological character of his entire construction of the ethical. Still, as Ottmann sees it, a *second possibility* remains open: namely, that "the family and the state are something like 'islands' in the stream of a world history whose natural violence Hegel does not conceal."[89]

On this point Vittorio Hösle followed a similar line of interpretation. He remarked that seeing individuality as exclusion of the other is typical of the logic of being, since the logic of the concept posits otherness not outside the individual but as his constitutive part. Hegel, then, falls into the logic of being after having conceived the internal relations of the state according to the logic of the concept. "*Fürsichsein, Dasein, Andersheit**are categories of the logic of being; the concept has nothing *outside* itself, but integrates otherness as a moment."[90] Hegel's construction, then, proves to be curious indeed: while in its internal relations individuality relates to what is other than itself as something that is with itself, in its external relations what is other than itself is totally alien and excluded from the self. In this context—for Hösle—we can well understand Hegel's endorsement of the logic of war as the ultimate regulator of the relation between states.

The reader who has followed the course of the *Philosophy of Right* to this point is faced with a paradoxical conclusion: Hegel reasserts and returns to the *state of nature*—that very "state of violence and injustice, of which nothing truer can be said than that *it must be left behind*" (ENC § 502 R).

> Hegel's philosophy of right ends at the very point he had wanted
> to get away from all along—the state of nature [. . .]. This holds
> for the state of nature between individuals, just as it does for that
> between states. The latter imperative is even more pressing since
> states, unlike the fictitious individuals of the state of nature, have
> already passed through the state of right; their external relation
> is thus in contradiction not only to what, rationally, right ought

---

*Being-for-self, determinate being, otherness.

to be, but also to their internal structure. For the citizens of a
state of law it is intolerable that the behavior of their homeland
toward other states be based on criteria of force.[91]

The point, here, is that states cannot deny outside their borders the
rights that they affirm within them, and they cannot shirk their responsibility to broaden the ethical sphere in force within their own borders—especially since an obstinate attachment to the purely naturalistic and mechanical
logic of exclusion ends up affecting their own citizens, exposed in their turn
to the logic of war.

Now, let us take stock of our results to this point. On the one hand,
ethical life realizes the unity of individuality and universality: in it the universal will (apart from the specific way in which Hegel intends to actualize
it, and apart from the problems this entails) no longer opposes the will of
individuals but is realized in institutions and concrete practices. On the
other hand, Hegel confines this historical universality that has been attained
within the borders of the nation state. The universal will now manifests
itself as particular, as the embodiment of a specific spirit of the people, and
therefore opposes other particular wills. It is at this point that a *new universality* appears, a universal plane that is beyond the ethical—a universality
represented by the universal history of the world (the *Weltgeschichte*). But
there can be no ethical relationship with the *Weltgeschichte*, no recognition
on the part of historical subjects. The naturalist-individualist paradigm that
Hegel criticized so adamantly in his theory of the state reemerges and is
reasserted in the international relations between states.

As we have seen, it is as if we were faced with the projection on an
international scale of the relations that are realized between individuals in
the Hobbesian state of nature. But there is an important difference. At
first blush it seemed that Hegel, here, refused to make use of what he had
obtained with the dialectic of recognition elaborated in his Jena period and
in the *Phenomenology of Spirit*, where in the relation between two subjects
(be they individuals, groups, or states) there was a *logic of recognition* that
regulated the relation. This is Hegel's important lesson on the objectivity
of mediation, of which the subjects generally are not aware but that acts
behind their backs as a full-fledged *third subject*. In the relation between
self-consciousnesses the "we" proved to be the true champion of reciprocal
recognition, a sort of anticipation—Hegel told us—of the "spirit" that was
later to manifest itself in the course of the *Phenomenology*.[92] Here, in international relations, it is precisely this third subject that seems to be missing,
since states can make no appeal to any legitimate "third-party" authority

that could lend legitimacy and force to international treaties. In short, it seemed that the only logic was the Hobbesian logic of *bellum omnium contra omnes*. But this is not the case. Here too, in fact, a third subject makes its appearance. This "third subject" is a logic that is higher than that of the individual states at war—a logic that precedes these individualities and makes the conflict possible. This subject is the *Weltgeschichte*, world history, and the spirit that animates it, the *Weltgeist*, which, once again, asserts itself as a third factor, and such an important one that Hegel refers to it as the "world's court of judgment"—the *Weltgericht*, which is not only the power but also the legitimating capacity of this new horizon. It is only from this point onward that we begin to see the difference between this "higher logic" and the logic of recognition that regulates the relations between self-consciousnesses. They, too, had not noticed the presence that stood behind their backs, but their process of formation progressively made them aware of the actuality of spirit as the condition—produced in part by their own activity—that proved to be the condition of their identity. Here nothing of the sort occurs. It cannot occur. In its designs and in its process the "logic of the world" remains wholly inscrutable for historical subjects, who cannot recognize themselves in it as an expression of their own conscious activity.

At this point the *real question* presents itself anew—the question Ottmann posed, and which he himself did not answer: Are we to think of ethical life as a sort of "Fortunate Isle" in the middle of the ocean of world history, or does this history end up calling into question ethical life itself, showing it to be a mere semblance under which, inexorable, the naturalistic logic of conflict and violence is concealed?

I think that Hegel would endorse the "Fortunate Isle" hypothesis. While, on the one hand, he is firmly convinced of the impossibility of an ethical life outside the institutions of the nation state, since the opacity of history for its subjects prevents them from seeing the world in its entirety as their own dwelling, on the other the impossibility of a worldwide ethical life is, for him, not a sufficient reason to call the ethical life of the nation state into question. For that matter, I believe that the *real reason* for the nationalistic confinement of the ethical is to be found precisely in this second impossibility: it is not the romantic theme of the nation and the identity of peoples that prevents ethical life from extending across national borders—rather, it is the impossibility of an identity between the historical subjects and the horizon of world events.

But Hegel's defense of the national character of ethical life meets with two objections. The *first* concerns the *universal nature of freedom*, which in this way is radically called into question. On the one hand, Hegel upholds the universalist claim of ethical life: he refers to ethos as "the universal mode of behavior of individuals" (PR § 151); the aim of ethical action is "the universal that, though itself unmoved, has developed [. . .] into actual rationality" (§ 152); ethical life itself is "the *Idea* in its universal existence in and for itself" (§ 33). On the other hand, this universal is actualized in an extremely particular context, precisely because at the worldwide level freedom cannot find itself—indeed, it *loses itself*. But this means that its process of self-recognition finds no actualization. The moment the barriers between states break down the coexistence between men is regulated no longer by freedom but by contingency and brute naturalness. In the end freedom does not recognize itself, and a freedom that does not recognize itself is not true freedom. As Hegel writes, "if the spirit knows that it is free, it is altogether different from what it would be without this knowledge. For if it does not know that it is free, it is in the position of a slave who is content with his slavery and does not know that his condition is an improper one" (PhWg I 56/PH1 48). If freedom does not recognize itself universally and is not actualized it is not freedom.

The second objection regards the *actualization of ethical life itself*, which at this point is seriously endangered. If history is intransparent, then the reconciliation of subject and object within the ethical becomes an *incomplete reconciliation*. Since the historical events surrounding the subjects effectively maintain a structural intransparency, it is impossible to think of ethos as a Fortunate Isle, indifferent to the intransparent logic that governs the history of the world. In fact, a careful analysis of Hegel's own exposition of ethical life reveals some elements of opacity and incomprehensibility within it. Let us take section 262 as an example. After repeating that the true subject active in ethical life is the actual Idea, which "sunders itself into the two ideal spheres of its concept—the family and civil society—as its finite mode" in order to affirm its infinity on the basis of these finite spheres, Hegel goes on to say:

> [The actual Idea] allocates the material of its finite actuality, i.e. individuals as a *mass*, to these two spheres, and in such a way that, in each individual case, this allocation appears to be *mediated* by circumstances, by the individual's arbitrary will and personal choice of vocation. (§ 262)

Here, the Idea appears as a subject that has "finite actuality" at its beck and call, acting behind the backs of individuals. Not only does Hegel say that it allocates to the finite spheres (family and civil society) their "material"—namely human beings—but it uses these historical subjects in such a way that they do not even realize they are the mere executors and instruments of its design. They think that what happens to them depends on "circumstances, arbitrary will and personal choice." They do not realize that circumstances, arbitrary will, and personal choice are only the "mediation" of the operation of the Idea. Even within ethical life the events that happen to individuals thus remain *totally inscrutable and intransparent*: only the Idea is aware of them, while the subjects themselves are totally excluded from their logic.

Karl Marx was quite right when he wrote apropos of this paragraph that "the entire mystery of the *Philosophy of Right* and of Hegelian philosophy in general is contained [in it]."[93] The Idea receives empirical reality as a material at its disposal only because in the end it wants to demonstrate its absoluteness: "The actual Idea reduces itself to the 'finiteness' of the family and civil society only in order to enjoy and to bring forth its infinity through their supersession [*Aufhebung*]."[94] But, in addition to this, that which will be the *real* conclusion of the entire *Philosophy of Right* is anticipated here: the resolution of historical objectivity in the higher truth of the Idea.

3.3.3. From Objective Spirit to Absolute Spirit

At this point we can draw three important conclusions:

1. freedom has not attained actualization;

2. individuals have been reduced to unconscious instruments of the Idea; and

3. the identity of subject and object in ethical life has proved to be an identity that is incomplete and deficient.

In all likelihood Hegel himself would not entirely agree with these conclusions. We could *summarize his hypothetical objection* in these terms: it is not true that there is no reconciliation between subject and object and that the self-recognition of freedom has not been attained. What is more, historical objectivity is rationally comprehended in the end, losing the opacity and inscrutability that had hitherto seemed insurmountable. However, this takes place not in *historical consciousness* (the consciousness of the finite subjects who are active within history) but in *philosophical consciousness*—that is, at the level of *absolute spirit*.

But we must be very careful when we speak of absolute spirit. It is not a macrosubject, a sort of world soul, that governs its destinies from the heights of its transcendence. There is no "supersensible world" in which Hegel locates the absolute spirit. Actually, it is nothing other than historico-empirical consciousness, which, however, by thinking itself and its true nature, discovers itself to be absolute—that is, gains an awareness that is not at the disposal of historical subjects. In fact, at the moment in which it gains this awareness it *is no longer* historical consciousness. But this means that the self-recognition of the *Weltgeist*, of the world spirit, takes place outside objective spirit—that is, "outside history." Absolute spirit is not historical activity: yes, it is the self-consciousness of history, the *truth* of objective spirit—but absolute self-consciousness is attained in it precisely because historical contingency is no more. There are two paragraphs in which Hegel explains the *transition from objective to absolute spirit*, and in both of them the decisive factor is the substantial *unity* of the two moments. Hence, for the reader and for the exegete of Hegel, the true problem is that of understanding the element of differentiation that constitutes the specificity of each moment. The first paragraph is in the *Philosophy of Right*:

> The concrete Ideas of national spirits [*Völkergeister*] have their truth and destiny in the concrete Idea as *absolute universality*, i.e. in the world spirit [*Weltgeist*], around whose throne they stand as the agents of its actualization and as witnesses and ornaments of its splendor. As spirit, it is simply the movement of its own activity in gaining absolute knowledge of itself and thereby freeing its consciousness from the form of natural immediacy and so coming to itself. (PR § 352)

Here, the object is once again the *Weltgeist*. We have already seen how it cannot be called a *subject*: history does not have a conscious subject that leads it. The *Weltgeist* is nothing other than historical objectivity—the objective logic of world events. But Hegel recognizes, first and foremost, the *absoluteness* of this logic: not only are the national spirits mere "ornaments of its splendor," mere executors of its will, but its own ultimate truth is in its absolute self-knowledge. It is precisely because the logic of history depends on nothing other than itself that it is absolute—released from any external conditioning. But, then, consistency with this absoluteness *in itself* demands that it also become *for itself*—demands that it become *aware*: only at that point can it be truly absolute and independent. In short, the world spirit has to actualize its nature and really make itself "spirit"—that is, become self-conscious. This is why the process it must undertake is "the movement of its own activity in gaining absolute knowledge of itself": it must not only "be" absolute but "know itself" to be absolute. On only one condition can it achieve this result: it must free itself from natural immediacy—that is, from the elements of naturalness that characterize history, which are the reason why the *Weltgeist* is still subject to contingency and unfreedom. Voilà—the transition has taken place! The world spirit has apprehended itself as "absolute"—released from historical contingencies! But it has been able to reach this condition because, now, it is *thought* alone, *knowledge* alone: it is the philosophical consciousness that thinks its own absoluteness.

The second paragraph I want to consider is in the *Encyclopaedia* and is even more explicit: I refer to section 552, with which Hegel concludes his treatment of objective spirit before going on to discuss absolute spirit. Here the transition takes place directly from the *Volksgeist* (national spirit) to the *absoluter Geist*, and the mediation constituted by the *Weltgeist* is only briefly mentioned. The entire first part of the paragraph focuses on describing the limits of the national spirit: it is subject to "nature-necessity" [*Natur-Notwendigkeit*], to the externality of its existence, to the particularity and limitedness of ethical substance (which, while "in itself infinite"—its truth goes beyond the historical contingencies in which it is actualized—is "for itself particular and limited"—that is, circumscribed to the context in which it finds itself), and to "contingency." But its true limit—Hegel writes—consists in the fact that the *consciousness* of the *Volksgeist* is not absolute; that is, it is always in relation with *something external* (it is "temporal" and "in relation towards an external nature and world"). This relation is at the same time a limitation, an impediment to its comprehension of itself as absolute. Nevertheless, insofar as it "suppresses within itself the finitude" that characterizes it in the institutions of ethical life, it overcomes these limitations and "rises to knowledge of itself in its essentiality." At this point it seems as if the transition to absolute spirit has already taken place. But in fact we still find ourselves within the spirit of a nation. The *Volksgeist* has freed itself of the entire external world but it is still the spirit of *a* nation, of *a* people: its knowledge "still has the immanent limitedness of the national spirit." This bond to finitude is then superseded:

> But the thinking spirit of world history [*der denkende Geist der Weltgeschichte*], having sloughed off [*abgestreift*] both those limitations of the particular national spirits and its own worldliness [*seine eigene Weltlichkeit*], lays hold of its concrete universality and rises to *knowledge of the absolute spirit*, as the eternally actual

truth in which knowing reason [*die wissende Vernunft*] is free for itself. (ENC § 552)

Rising to the viewpoint of world history, spirit overcomes both the limitedness of the national spirit and its own *Weltlichkeit*: it is no longer bound to a place, neither does it depend on worldly circumstances with all the contingencies they entail. At this point it has raised itself to "knowledge of the absolute spirit." Having gone beyond history it has finally attained its freedom, in which "reason is free for itself." The relation has been reversed: nature and history are no longer the conditions on which spirit depends but are the places of its worldly manifestation, the theater in which its absoluteness is performed: "necessity, nature, and history are only in the service of its revelation and vessels of its honor" (§ 522). In the end, natural and historical necessity has shown itself to be merely an instrument in the hand of freedom.

So, for Hegel, in the end we do witness *freedom's self-recognition*, but only in its overcoming of worldliness—that is, in the world of pure thought, in *extramundane philosophical consciousness*. This "theoretical" conclusion of freedom's journey, on the basis of which its self-recognition cannot take place within history, could have an ulterior explanation in what Herbert Marcuse called Hegel's "realism." As Marcuse explained, for Hegel a freedom within history would mean the "attainment of a 'state of the world' in which the individual persists in inseparable harmony with the whole, and in which the conditions and relations of the world 'possess no essential objectivity independent of the individual.' "[95] This radical concept of freedom would entail not only the end of the estrangement in the relations with other individuals but also the end of the objectivity of things, the actualization of a state of the world in which natural objects, too, would "participate" in freedom.

As to the prospect of attaining such a state, Hegel was pessimistic: the element of reconciliation with the established state of affairs, so strong in his work, seems to a great extent due to this pessimism—or, if one prefers, this realism. Freedom is relegated to the realm of pure thought, to the Absolute Idea. Idealism by default.[96]

Thus, for Marcuse, Hegel's limit was his failure to express historically the freedom thought in absolute knowing.[97] In my opinion, *Hegel's limit* is to be found in a concept of freedom *so emphatic* that it *must* recognize itself in history: confronted with the *impossibility* of doing so, it is forced to take shelter in the world of pure thought.

The task he has left us, therefore, is that of rethinking his concept of freedom and its actualization in terms of a modern ethical life, *outside* the emphatic coordinates of an idealism that demands the absolute reconciliation of subject and object and a self-recognition of freedom so radical that it is only thinkable outside history.

Chapter 4

Elements of a Postidealist Ethical Life
A Democratization of Hegel's Political Philosophy

We have seen that, assumed in the radicality of its consequences, the transition within objective spirit from ethical life to world history *calls ethical life into question* and produces a *fracture in the history of freedom*. Not finding itself in history, freedom ends up losing itself, not recognizing itself, and thus no longer being freedom. We have also seen, however, that these consequences stem from the assumption of an *emphatic* concept of freedom—freedom understood in terms of self-transparency, self-position, and absoluteness. Even though it is consistent with the universalist premises of his ethos, Hegel opposed the idea of a universal ethical life that goes beyond the barriers of nation states and therefore eschews war as a "normal" solution in international relations. But the real obstacle to this idea is the claim, inherent in this emphatic concept of freedom, that subject and object are completely reconciled within history.[1] Given these premises, we have three theoretical operations to perform:

1. We need to *reconstruct the logico-ontological foundations* underlying Hegel's concept of freedom (and thus his concept of ethical life)—to step back and reexamine the Hegelian identity of freedom and self-transparency, freedom and Idea, freedom and reconciliation, freedom and the unity of subject and object. This, however, does not mean abstractly pitting an alternative model against Hegel's but, rather, testing the different potentialities of development within his model itself. As we shall see, this operation is possible because Hegel's emphatically *idealist* conception of freedom is coupled with

137

a *dialectical thinking* that acts as a corrective to any form of identity and reconciliation. Indeed, thinking dialectically means exploding all self-identity and constantly exposing it to its *other*. Hence our reconstruction of the logico-theoretical foundation underlying the concept of ethical life will have to consider this alternative possibility, along with the opportunity it affords of a *different theoretical constellation* within which to locate and rethink the notion of ethical life.

2. The second operation is a direct consequence of the first and will consist in *reformulating and rethinking a concept of ethical life* that has been released from the imperative of self-transparency. For this operation too we can find the necessary resources within Hegel's own work. It is here that we find the essential features of a *logic of recognition*—a logic that, with its intrinsically intersubjective character, can be utilized as an alternative to the solipsistic and individualistic logic of transparent self-reflection. As we shall see, in the relation of recognition no complete identification between the subjects involved is possible. Positing such an identification would mean canceling their specific identities—and thus would mean the failure of recognition as such.

3. Our final task will be to delineate the elements of a *modern Sittlichkeit*, based on Hegel's indications but reformulated in the light of a *democratic ethos* released from the opposition between states, grounded in the critical and reflective autonomy of the individual citizens and made compatible with the irrepressible ethical pluralism of contemporary societies. Rendering Hegel's formalization and universalization of the ethical substance of the ancients consistent with his fundamental ideas will allow us to draw ultimate conclusions that reveal new implications of his political philosophy. In this light it will, in the end, be possible to see his doctrine of ethical life as a fundamental resource for the ethics of contemporary democracy.

4.1. Logico-ontological Presuppositions of Hegelian Ethical Life

Hegel *accepts* the Kantian viewpoint that sees universality as the ground of morality and abstract right. In Hegelian terminology we could say that the universal is the ground of "right" in the general sense (the sense that occupies the entire *Philosophy of Right*, comprising abstract right, morality, and ethical life): it is the ground of the legitimacy and validity of individual action and of political and social institutions.

At the same time, Hegel *rejects* Kant's grounding of normative universality in transcendental subjectivity, whose normativity—lacking historical objectivity—would boil down to an indeterminate abstraction, without contents and substantially useless for the concrete practices of the individuals living in a society.

Now, the fact that normativity cannot be grounded in a "transcendental" reflection does not mean that it must be justified in an "empirical" procedure—that is, by conceiving it as the result of an *agreement between subjects*. Hegel refuses to think of normativity (what he calls "right") as the result of a multiplicity of individual wills. If this were the case, not only would it be subject to moods and interests, passions and drives—in short, to nature and not to freedom—but the deliberating subjects themselves would not even have existed if there had not been an ethical context capable of forming them—that is, an ethos already in force and operative. In other words: normativity cannot be conceived as the result of individual wills, since these wills are themselves the product of an already existing sphere of "right."

Hence, Hegel's solution: think normative universality as already existing in history, incorporated in our practices, operating within our institutions. Not the willful and conscious product of historical subjects but the *result of historical development* in its entirety—a process to which individual wills have most certainly contributed, but that is never reducible to their conscious intentions.

But there are *problems* with this solution, as we have seen. Its *immediate consequence* is the admission of a sort of *historical justificationism*, which claims that whatever history produces has normative value. Since it is produced by history, at this point any and every institutional order ought to be assumed as an actualization of freedom. The result would be an inevitable pluralism of contexts, hardly in line with Hegel's thinking: since there are many and different institutional orders, every context would have its own normativity. But this would make it impossible for us to distinguish between orders and to judge which of them can truly constitute the actualization of freedom.

For Karl-Heinz Ilting this, in the end, is Hegel's position. He maintained that Hegel was not able to provide a criterion capable of distinguishing what is indissolubly linked to freedom from what appears to be fortuitous or even incompatible with it: "On the basis of the Idea of freedom Hegel demonstrates the necessity of the relations in the modern state in a way that does not distinguish the social relations that are historically contingent or even irreconcilable with the Idea of freedom from those that are necessary."[2] For Ilting, all the moral indications contained within the chapter on ethical life—such as the exhortation for a member of an ethical community to "do what is prescribed, expressly stated, and known to him within his situation" (PR § 150 R)—lead us to believe that Hegel considers present reality in its entirety to be the full actualization of the Idea.

> In a state that is not yet fully ethical it ought to be possible to distinguish between true and presumed ethical duties. But Hegel does not help us here, since the exhortation "to do what is prescribed in the situation" takes the reader back to a level of development of the concept of ethical life where custom [*Sitte*] and ethical life [*Sittlichkeit*] were not yet distinct, i.e., to the time preceding the Sophists and Socrates.[3]

This regression of conscience with respect not only to the advances of modernity but even to the "Greek Enlightenment" is, for Ilting, confirmed by the fact that the *Philosophy of Right* itself is not normative in character but is in fact nothing more than a "phenomenology of the consciousness of freedom"[4]—that is, a mere description of the institutional forms of freedom that makes no truly normative claims. As Becchi and Hoppe[5]—editors of Ilting's posthumous work *Grundfragen der praktischen Philosophie*—confirmed, Ilting on the one hand gave Hegel credit for having made possible a meeting between the modern natural right that is grounded in individual freedom and the classical political doctrine that understands society on the basis of the state as a whole; but, on the other, he registered the substantial failure of this attempt. Hegel—Ilting claimed—did no more than pit one model against the other, and in the sphere of his state the substantiality of ethical life prevails over the individual.

In fact Hegel never endorsed any historical justification of the sort,[6] above all because he knew perfectly well that history is also the realm of the contingent, of the particular, and of naturalness. It follows that not all political and social orders, even if in the modern age, can be considered rational and free. Hegel confirms this, admitting that there can be social orders devoid of ethical freedom and, in such cases, even justifying recourse to the subjective freedom of the "inner forum" that in the conditions of actualized ethical life is, for him, senseless.

> The tendency to look *inwards* into the self and to know and determine from within the self what is right and good appears

in epochs when what is recognized as right and good in actuality and custom [*Sitte*] is unable to satisfy the better will. When the existing world of freedom has become unfaithful to the better will, this will no longer finds itself in the duties recognized in this world and must seek to recover in ideal inwardness alone that harmony which it has lost in actuality. (PR § 138 R)

At this point, however, the first problem becomes *the individuation of a reliable criterion* (and, with it, the procedure for its *justification*) capable of distinguishing between rational and nonrational institutions, between true ethical life and sociopolitical orders that represent nothing other than an unfaithful translation of freedom.

Then, a second, more general problem arises: Why does the ground of normativity have to be found in existing institutions, in historical products, and not in principles or values that transcend what exists? In other words: Why do we have to adequate ourselves to the normativity embodied in practices instead of following abstract ideals? It is perfectly true that in Hegel we find an articulated refutation of the "ought" and of moral abstractness—but this critique does not *necessarily prescribe* our adequation to what exists. Still, as we shall see, we do find this *justification of the normative value of ethical life* in Hegel's thought—indeed, it is one of its pillars.

4.1.1. From Ethical Life to the Philosophy of History

Within Hegel's system the answer to the *first question* is quite simple: the criterion to establish the degree of rationality of existing ethical life is constituted by the philosophy of history. As Herbert Schnädelbach wrote, "that which in Hegel leads beyond the relativism of concretely existing ethical life is world history as the 'world's court of judgment' [*Weltgericht*]."[7] The philosophy of history is the true substitute for Kant's transcendental grounding of normative universality. It establishes the degrees of freedom's development and is thus capable of discovering when a state, institution, or law truly has universal value. World history has a dual capability that makes it an irreplaceable element of Hegel's system. It is endowed with a *comprehensive gaze* capable of revealing the meaning of the whole—that is, the comprehensive truth of historical development. But is it equally capable of a *particular gaze* on individual events and institutions? Yes, in the guise of *historical hermeneutics* it interprets the given, recognizes its hidden meaning, and discovers the universal whose embodiment the individual element becomes.[8]

In light of this answer the focus of the problem shifts again, and we are confronted with another decisive question: *Do we possess such a gaze on totality?* In order to gather historical events around an ultimate purpose, there must be a gaze capable of rising to the level of totality and of apprehending its comprehensive meaning. For Hegel this is possible, but only on one condition: that this be the gaze of totality itself—that it be *the self-reflection of the absolute*. Only the absolute is capable of revealing the meaning of history, because only the absolute is "capable of totality." This is the famous *Hegelian thesis of absolute knowing*: the condition for an absolute knowing—a knowing that manifests totality—is that the subject of this knowing be the absolute itself. Properly speaking, *the absolute consists in this knowing alone*. It is not a transcendent being, it is not a soul immanent in the world, it is *only* the self-knowing of totality. It exactly coincides with that consciousness of history which—as Hegel clearly states in section 552 of the *Encyclopaedia*, analyzed at the end of the previous chapter—has "sloughed off" naturalness, externality, contingency, and has become philosophical consciousness. The elevation of objective spirit to absolute spirit is thus the true condition for the construction of a philosophy of world history.

Hence, Hegel's theory of ethical life refers back to his *Logic* and in particular to his *doctrine of the concept* as the loci capable of giving a "final" answer to the question of the legitimacy of ethico-political institutions. Those pages make it clear that the ultimate meaning of totality resides in its self-reflecting, in its becoming aware of itself, and in that radical self-reflection which is at the same time self-position—positing of self as absolute autonomy and independence. Without this resolution of substance in concept—that is, in the subject's self-reflecting—there would be no absolute knowing and, therefore, no philosophy of world history either. But Hegel also needs to put this absolute knowing into circulation with our finite individual consciousness. If the two terms failed to touch, absolute knowing would remain separate and transcendent but we would know nothing of it and our sole resource would continue to be the historico-empirical knowledge that is structurally incapable of rising to the level of totality. Hence Hegel's *full thesis* is that finite spirit is *in truth* absolute spirit. It is only necessary that finite consciousness reflect on itself and comprehend its true nature: at that point it will be elevated to the self-reflection of the absolute and made identical to it.

When both these conditions have been satisfied (the absolute's self-determination as an absolute knowing of itself, and the identity with absolute spirit of the finite spirit that has fully attained self-awareness) the gaze on totality, a philosophy of history, and a justification of existing ethical life as the actualization of freedom are all, at last, possible.

4.1.2. From Philosophy of History to Logic

This reference from the theory of ethical life to logic as its ultimate ground also allows us to answer our *second question*, regarding the justification of Hegel's thesis that the ground of our normativity is to be found in history and in existing ethical life. The true superiority of the concrete universality of the ethical with respect to the abstract universality of the moral rests precisely on Hegel's thesis in the *Science of Logic* that actuality (what Hegel calls *Idea*) is absolute self-reflection. At this point history becomes the field in which this self-reflection takes place, the ground on which freedom recognizes itself. The historical structures in which all this comes about—the spheres of ethical life—are thus the true ground of normativity, because it is in these spheres that freedom has become actual, has completed its process, and has revealed itself in its fullest expression. Precisely because *actuality is Idea* (i.e., self-reflection) it demands its revelation in history, and it is in history that we find the essential references of normativity.

But this "ideal" nature of freedom—that is, its being inscribed within the coordinates of the "Idea"—is the root of the unsolvable problems that conclude the *Philosophy of Right*. For Hegel the work was to express absolute self-recognition—full reconciliation, without residue, of subject and object. The undertaking proved so radical that it could not be actualized in history but only in the *knowing* that is within absolute spirit. Hence this "ideal" concept of freedom gave rise to a conception of ethical life as a transparent dwelling in which the individual can recognize himself without residue. At this point it is clear just how difficult it is to actualize such a project. But the difficulty turns into radical impossibility when world history is brought into play—since, as we have seen, world history is totally impenetrable to the gaze of its own actors.

What is more, the logico-ontological structure sustaining the concept of freedom ends up by heavily conditioning the way in which the process of self-recognition takes place. Its effects are felt not only in Hegel's strongly "idealist" characterization of the notion of ethical life, conceived as the transparent reconciliation of subject and object, but also in the fact that this reconciliation is seen as *the work of a single protagonist*—namely, "*ethical substance.*" As an objective structure, to be truly itself "ethical substance" needs to *recognize* itself, so that *it* can become the subject that will produce self-recognition.

This structure is clearly revealed in Hegel's descriptions of ethical life. First, it is "the *Idea of freedom* as the living good" (PR § 142)—a clearly ontological characterization not only because it refers to the ontological notion of the good but also because—as we have seen—"Idea" in the *Philosophy of Right* signifies *actuality* in its full objectivity. Second, ethos (*das Sittliche*) is described as "substance made *concrete*" (§ 144), a further ontological-objectivistic characterization. Finally, this substance is "*sich wissend*"—a substance "that knows itself" and as such is "*actual self-consciousness*" and "an object of knowledge" (§ 146).

Note that in all these remarks there is but one single actor—substance—which is also the subject of recognition: this substance is the source of self-consciousness and knowing. Again, nota bene: the subjective side of ethical life—which is so important for Hegel—refers not to the self-consciousness of individuals, that is, to the civic consciousness of citizens, but rather to the self-knowing of substance. Which means: the role of subjectivity in constituting the ethical is nothing other than the self-recognition of spiritual substance. *The true subject is therefore objective spirit itself*, which, most assuredly, recognizes itself thanks to the self-consciousness of individuals[9] (for Hegel, on earth or in heaven there is no other self-consciousness but *individual* self-consciousness), but for which citizens are only the instruments of its own self-recognition.

As Michael Theunissen has shown,[10] this logico-ontological structure accounts for the substantial *elimination of intersubjectivity* from the *Philosophy of Right*. On the one hand, Hegel shows the genesis of universality based on the intersubjective overcoming of individuality. This takes place in the sphere of abstract right through the contract, which forces the individual to enter into a relationship with the other and to homogenize himself, since both he and the other are property owners. In civil society the process was analogous, in the relationship of "all-round interdependence," in virtue of which each individual is "assigned" to the other and completely depends on him. On the other hand, none of these are ever truly intersubjective relations, since the individualities that reciprocally enter into relationship are never valorized in their specificity. What prevails in these relationships is the individual's *becoming abstract*, his identifying with and making himself indistinguishable from the others. This produces a universality composed never of concrete but only of abstract relations, in which the individual alienates himself from his specific identity.

This situation is confirmed and strengthened in the theory of the state, within which—as we have seen—the subjects no longer have any active function or significant role. In Hegel's state the reconciliation between individual and universal or between subject and object concludes de facto in the *cancellation of the citizens' subjectivity*: in the end, subjectivity dissolves in the spiritual substance of the ethical and in its substantialist-objective relations.[11]

4.1.3. Two Competing Conceptions of the Idea of Freedom

The model of freedom and of ethical life that is proposed in the *Philosophy of Right* is grounded in the Hegelian conception of the *Idea* elaborated in the *Science of Logic*. In the *Logic* Hegel represents the Idea as constituted by a process of self-reflection without residue and without opacity, within which any presumed *immediacy* is incessantly resolved in the *mediation* of thought.[12] At the end of the *Logic* this process leads to an ultimate immediacy, not further reducible to mediation; but, in the end, Hegel shows us that this immediacy, consisting in the Idea's relation with itself (i.e., the identity of the "I" with itself), is nothing other than the totality of the process in its purest formality.

Hegel presents this thesis not as a presupposition of his system but as its conclusion—that is, as the consequence of a demonstration, the "result" of the logical process. But he can reach the conclusion that all immediacies are resolved without residue in mediation precisely because from the very beginning the immediacies have been thought logically—that is, resolved in logicity. In short: they are *already* mediations. They are not the *actually existing* totality but rather that totality which—from the very beginning—has been tamed and posited as reducible to the "I." On the other hand, the conclusive claim of the *Logic* to resolve the logical process of mediating in a *conclusive immediacy* (i.e., in the *identity* of the Idea with itself that leaves no residue—no other immediacy to mediate) reveals this immediacy to be a *false mediation*. Precisely because it has canceled otherness it has not mediated anything, it has never come out of itself, it only apparently referred to the other. A mediation is reference to a true other, but if this were truly so then this mediation would be an infinite mediating that could never be resolved in immediacy. In short, a "final summary" of the entire process represented by the ultimate immediacy of the absolute Idea would be impossible. If thought is engagement—mediation—with the other, with a *true* other, it can never claim to reduce the other to itself, and therefore there can never be a "final meaning" of this movement. The process of mediating cannot conclude in an ultimate immediacy, and the immediacies met with in the process cannot be resolved in mediation. In this way, the opening to the other explodes Hegel's identity of mediation and immediacy.

These two arguments, which give us the gist of the theoretical objections raised in the past two centuries against Hegel's claimed self-transparency of totality, radically call into question his notion of the subject, and his claim that subjectivity is absolute self-reference in which every relation to other entails the reduction of this other to the subject itself.[13] In the contemporary idea of a *decentered subject*, the subject is such *thanks to* the other: instead of Hegelianly resolving mediation with the other in mediation with the self, this idea shows how mediation with self leads the subject beyond itself, to the not-mediable extra-subjective conditions that have made it possible.

This critique of Hegel's notion of the Idea simultaneously calls into question his notion of *freedom as being-with-self*—the model of freedom that finally asserts itself in the doctrine of ethical life, and which is the root of the many problems I have been obliged to engage with. However, as we saw in the first chapter, this was not Hegel's only model of freedom. In the *Science of Logic* he elaborated an *alternative concept* of freedom that we described as "being-with-self-in-being-other-than-self." We find it in his definition of *concept* as a "relation of self to the different only as *to its own self*" (WL12 35/SL 603). It was Theunissen who put this *heterodox variant* of the concept of freedom into the proper perspective. Even though it constitutes a minority (and, ultimately, vanquished) current in Hegel's work, it is efficaciously present on several occasions in his writings. Theunissen defined it in his work on the *Science of Logic* as "communicative freedom," but later redefined it, with more precision, as "*communal freedom*" [*kommunale Freiheit*] in his work on the *Philosophy of Right*,[14] precisely because it locates the condition of being free in the relation of reciprocal communality.

Given the prevalence of the other model in the *Philosophy of Right*, the heterodox variant is adequately developed only in the section on "The Family" and is given no consideration in the other two sections of "Ethical Life," even though Hegel posits "union" [*Vereinigung*] as the "true content and end" of the state (PR § 258 R). Now, in Theunissen's opinion this resolution in favor of an idea of freedom as being "with itself" and as that which "has reference to nothing but itself" (PR § 23) does not correspond to the articulated exposition of freedom present in the *Science of Logic*. In his reading of the *Logic* he maintained that the *two alternative models* of freedom are *equally legitimate*. If it is true that the Idea as ultimate identity expresses the demand for a self-reflection without residue, it is also true that in the *Science of Logic* Hegel insists that identity with self entails reference to other—he insists that the other is a condition of the self and that difference is a condition of identity.

In my opinion, this thesis is meaningful *on one condition*: namely, if one admits that the other to which identity, subjectivity, and Idea refer *cannot be reduced to this identity, subjectivity, and Idea all over again*. The reduction of difference to identity (even "in the last instance") is a cancellation of difference and an admission that it was not true difference. For the other to be the condition of my identity it cannot be reduced to me but *must* retain its independence and irreducibility. If it is reduced to me it is no longer other and there is no more sense in insisting that I am constituted through the other.

The development of this thesis cannot but take us *outside the coordinates of Hegel's idealism.* And yet, once again, it is Hegel himself who provides us with a model by which we can give concreteness to the idea of communal freedom that passes like a *fil rouge* through his works—without ever having the last word. This model is represented by the *logic of recognition.*

4.2. Ethical Life and Logic of Recognition

For Hegel, the ethical and its institutions are legitimate because they are grounded in freedom and represent its highest historical manifestation. Therefore, to his mind, no explicit justification or any consent of the citizens is necessary. Freedom itself legitimates its manifestations and the entire normative sphere that derives from it and from them. As we have seen, this involves a rigorously monological justificatory procedure, grounded in that notion of the Idea as self-reflection which for Hegel is the same thing as freedom. Hence the only justification of the ethical institutions is to be found in the *absolute knowing* that is the manifestation in *actual* philosophical consciousness of the *logical* self-reflection of the Idea.

Hence normativity (what Hegel calls "right" in general) is not something that depends on individual subjectivities, or on their ideals, or—less still—on their interests or the intersubjective convergence of their moral convictions. Normativity depends on a single objective structure—the Idea; which is to say, freedom insofar as it recognizes itself.

Within Hegel's works, this conception—which could be summarized as *the primacy of normative objectivity*—is in fact not inconsistent with an intersubjective conception of the normative. In fact, Hegel often thought of objectivity as the result of work in common.[15] Along the route of the *Phenomenology of Spirit* we continually meet up with objective structures that stem precisely from the cooperation, meeting, and encounter of individual subjectivities. This was the idea Hegel followed in his early works, in Jena, where ethical and legal norms were seen precisely as the result of their *intersubjective recognition.* Then, little by little, he came to believe that the genesis of the objectivity stemming from intersubjective convergences was only apparently in subjects—rather, it *preexisted* subjects as an independent structure, which the subjects were only called on to recognize *ex post*. It is in this context that the Hegelian concept of *spirit* is consolidated: spirit is in fact the *product* of social cooperation of which, in truth, it is the *condition*.

But to demolish the objectivistic and solipsistic notion of the Idea that is the root of the many problems within the *Philosophy of Right* we have to retrace Hegel's path, return to the point where this objective structure was seen in its intersubjective genesis, separate the two moments, and attempt to call into question his reduction of intersubjectivity to the monological process of self-reflection. By freeing Hegel's theory of recognition from its "idealist" self-comprehension we will at last be able to find an alternative solution to the problem of the justification of normativity that, until now, has seemed to be unsolvable.

4.2.1. Logic of Recognition[16]

The best synthetic exposition of Hegel's theory of recognition, as it matured at the end of his Jena period, is in the *Phenomenology of Spirit*, right at the beginning of the celebrated passage known as the "dialectic of lordship and bondage." This is how Hegel expresses it: "Self-consciousness is *in* and *for itself*, in that and by the fact that it is in and for itself for another self-consciousness; i.e., it *is* only in being recognized" (PhG 109/PS 111). Let us look closely at this passage. Awareness of the self—that which makes it possible for me to know myself as myself and to give myself an identity ("self-consciousness in and for itself")—is not my product. It is neither a work of my biology nor a result of my capacity for reflection; it stems neither from nature nor from spirit. The "I" is not materialistically a product of the brain, neither is it to be understood idealistically as a product of the self-reflection of transcendental subjectivity. It is the result of a meeting with another subject ("in that and by the fact that it is in and for itself for another self-consciousness") and, in particular, is the result of *recognition* by this other. It is thanks to the gaze of the other on me that I learn to turn my gaze on myself. Inwardness is not discovered by the subject alone: it opens by virtue of the attention of the other. Yes, a capacity for individual introspection is necessary; but it is "wakened" by the interest of the other. As a subject I must "feel" myself recognized to know myself to be so; but to obtain this I necessarily have "need" of the intervention of another. This, however, is not a generic need for identity but, rather, the need to feel myself recognized in my humanity.

"Recognizing" another individual in this specific sense does not indicate a generic attention to her but implies an involvement with her personal sphere. And if the degrees of this involvement may differ—from respect to interest, to esteem, to caring, to love—the general attitude is the same: recognizing the other as a subject, seeing in her the same humanity I see in myself. Hence this relation is an affirmation of the equality of all human beings. At the same time, in the other I see something specific that is necessarily different from me. Recognizing someone means seeing her specificity, valorizing the difference between us. The other is a subject as I am, but is also an "other"—that is, is not simply a doubling of my own identity.

With great precision Hegel describes this process that within the *Phenomenology* marks the genesis of self-consciousness based on simple consciousness—based on simple experience of the external world, on an experience that is unaware of its inwardness. In this careful diagnosis he brings an essential element to light: being recognized by another means simultaneously recognizing this other. I can "feel" myself recognized only by someone I consider "worthy" to recognize me. This explains the *reciprocal nature of recognizing*: I cannot be recognized unless I recognize in my turn. This is the specific *logic* that regulates the recognitive relation.

> Thus the movement is simply the double movement of the two self-consciousness. Each sees the *other* do the same as *it* does; each does itself what it demands of the other, and therefore also does what it does *only* insofar as the other does the same. Action by one side would be useless because what is to happen can only be brought about by both. (PhG 110/PS 112)

The two self-consciousnesses are subject to an *objective logic* that both are obliged to follow if they want to be recognized. This, once again, is the great Hegelian theme of the objectivity of mediation. In a process of recognition there are never only *two* subjects: there is also a *third subject*—namely, the objective logic to which they must subjugate their individual wills. For Hegel this is *the truth* of recognition: what is *true* is not the two individual self-consciousnesses but the "middle term" that sets itself between them as their true lord. This middle term is spirit, which is introduced here in an anticipatory form and which is destined—in the course of the *Phenomenology*—to become the only true subject in this "experience of consciousness." In the end, the monological logic of the Idea wins out over the dialogical logic of recognition. Yes, spirit originates in the dialectic of self-consciousnesses, but what comes genetically *after* comes ontologically *before*. In the end, self-consciousness, as "different" from other self-consciousnesses, will have to recognize the fact that its truth is only a limited truth and that its true nature is beyond it, in *spirit*—that is, in the common element in which all individualities are resolved. And if spirit will, for a time, continue to present intersubjective features, at the end of the *Phenomenology* its truth will consist in its solitary self-recognition as the truth of the entire process.

The fact of the matter is this: the logic of recognition—which posits itself as an objective force between the two subjects and which Hegel interprets idealistically as a "spirit"—indicates the emergence not of the Idea but of an *ethical normativity*. Recognizing someone is not only an act of knowing—it means attributing a status, a value, a dignity to the other. When I *recognize* her I grant her the dignity of a *moral person*, and thus have obligations to her. I cannot recognize someone without recognizing and implicitly accepting the obligation to respect her. In short, what Hegel sees as "no more" than a *logic* is in fact an *ethic*—a series of norms that, with the act of recognition, we are obliged to accept. *This* is the genesis of normativity: our fundamental moral intuitions are not innate but are *learned* from the original relation that connects us with others. While—thanks to the other—our individual identity constitutes itself, our moral capacity constitutes itself at the same time.

Hence "behind our backs" there is an *ethical substance* that we cannot permit ourselves to deny, because its denial would raze the foundations of our very identity and humanity. In fact, our subjectivity is a product of our relations of recognition—*and* a product of the normativity embodied in these relations.

If, then, the basis of individual subjectivity is not self-reflective reference but intersubjective recognition, by the same token the basis of individual *freedom* is not the self-transparent relation of the subject that knows itself to be self-identical but—on the contrary—a reference to *other*. It is thanks to the recognition of the other that we have acquired the awareness of our autonomy and our independence. It is precisely the continual relations with others—the confirmation we receive of our value and our dignity—that strengthen our autonomy and independence. Freedom—like morality—is learned and consolidated within relations of recognition. As we have seen, this is another great Hegelian lesson: the thesis that independence consists, paradoxically, in the relation of dependence on the other. But it is only within a theory of recognition finally emancipated from idealist confinement that the thesis of freedom as "being-with-self-in-being-other-than-self" acquires its full validity, without the risk of being swallowed up by the thesis of freedom as a "being-with-itself" that excludes the other. Within a theory of recognition the relation with the other is not a logical mediation destined to resolve otherness in the process of the Idea—rather, it is a *practical, ethical, normative relation*, in which the other remains irreducible to the self. Only in this irreducibility can the other be constitutive of subjectivity, without reducing the process to mere fiction.

Here, freedom loses both the supersensible traits it had in Kant and the ontological characterization it acquired with Hegel, who made it an attribute of the absolute and of totality. It therefore manifests itself simply as a historical acquisition by empirical individuals who conquer it progressively through processes of socialization. Human beings become free the more they become social—the more they learn to use their autonomy thanks to their relations with others. Albeit in a postidealist context, this is a confirmation of Hegel's thesis of *relational freedom*. Being free does not mean keeping the other at a distance but, on the contrary, including the other within oneself and making her the fundamental resource of our autonomy.

In this context, in which freedom does not mean absolutistic self-reflection but intersubjective relation and recognition of an other, the theory of ethical life can finally abandon the imperative of transparency (4.2.2) and normativity can recover its foundation, grounded in a plural and intersubjective idea of freedom (4.2.3).

4.2.2. Ethical Life and Otherness

When freedom is based on intersubjective relations ethical life ceases to be a reconciliation between subject and object and becomes a meeting between subjects. Yes, this locus does retain its objective character, since it is composed precisely of recognitive relations that have assumed "institutional" forms—practices, traditions, habits, legal procedures, economic exchanges, political relations, and normative references. Institutionalized relations of recognition have thus become the *original locus of our dwelling*, in which subjects meet in the ways these "institutions" allow. But, here, *meeting* does not mean idealist reconciliation: a recognition that concludes with identification is a false recognition, because it reveals a posteriori that the other was not truly other but only a double of the first.

Subjects establish an analogous relation with the ethical ground that constitutes them and on which they live. There can never be full reconciliation because the different ethical spheres manifest themselves as *a continuous resource* of normative references, never exhausted by the recognition of subjects. In these spheres the *objectivity* of the normative tradition prevails over the subjectivistic appropriation of them. Hegel himself had shown how these ethical objectivizations, like many other objectivizations produced by the modern process of *Bildung*, necessarily retained a moment of alienness, of unrealized appropriation, of objectivity not reducible to the very subjects that produced it. Only the conception—dominant in Hegel—that freedom in its maximum actualization consists in the full resolution of every in-itself in a for-itself could view this unrealized appropriation as a defeat, a failure, as something to be combated. On the contrary, it is in this very distance that we recognize the richness—and the beauty—of ethos.

> Eichendorff's expression "Beautiful Alien" rises above the romantic,
> felt as world weariness and suffering for alienation. The recon-
> ciled condition would not be the philosophical imperialism of
> annexing the alien. Instead, its happiness would lie in the fact
> that the alien, in the proximity it is granted, remains what is
> distant and different, beyond the heterogeneous and beyond
> what is one's own.[17]

With these words Adorno definitively takes his leave of an idealisti-cally connoted theory of alienation.* The alien is not necessarily something that causes suffering, something I must free myself of in order to restore the dominion of the subject. The alien is something in which the subject can find enrichment and support, precisely in its remaining alien—in its keeping its distance and not being subdued.

Emancipated from the conception that alienness not only causes pain but also creates a need to annex the alien, modern ethical life no longer manifests itself as a locus of reconciliation but only as a *dwelling place*—as the objectivity that is our home precisely *because* it is not always reducible to our coordinates. On this ground it constitutes itself as the vital condition that makes our freedom, morality, and daily practices possible.

4.2.3. Normative Background of Recognition and Spheres of Ethical Life

Replacing the logic of Hegel's absolute Idea with the logic of recognition makes a different solution possible for the problem of the grounding of

---

Entfremdung: Although in chapter 2 I translated the term as *estrangement* (to distinguish it from *Entäußerung*, alienation), the context here is quite different.

ethical life. At this point we have all the elements needed to demonstrate that the *validity of the ethical spheres* is grounded in their constitution by the *logic of recognition as an inescapable normative background.*

But the keystone here is not the subjective recognition expressed every day by every member of these spheres. This, indeed, is an indispensable element of their existence. Hegel himself—by no means indulgent with the forms of subjective justification of normativity—explicitly introduces this component in the *Philosophy of Right.* But intersubjective recognition as the ground of ethos is broached by the Jena Hegel, not by the mature Hegel. In the *Phenomenology of Spirit* he has already left this perspective behind, showing the movement of spirit and its objective logic to be the true subject of recognition and the real ground of independent self-consciousness. But the *Philosophy of Right* turns the Jena perspective completely upside-down. Now, we no longer have an intersubjective grounding of the ethical institutions but an institutional—an *objective*—ground of intersubjective relations: it is thanks to the institutions of the family, of civil society, and of the state that we can establish relationships and become subjects. In short: the institutions of freedom are the true ground of subjectivity, of individual morality, and of intersubjectivity itself.

This acquisition is not a reversion to a subjectivist grounding of the ethical but, on the contrary, means viewing the validity of the *ethico-institutional substance* from a new perspective: instead of seeing it as the manifestation of a solipsistic self-recognition of freedom, it is now to be seen as an *objectification of recognitive relations and of the normative logic that sustains them.* The fundamental principle of respect for the other, of receiving her, of recognizing her dignity and autonomy, has been embodied in these ethical institutions and is the source of inspiration of their workings. Here, essentially, we have their validity and legitimacy.

We have no need of recourse to the philosophy of history (with its ontological presuppositions) to assess the rationality of ethical institutions: they are ethical insofar as their structures embody recognitive relationships, and insofar as they correspond to the fundamental principles of the normative background that constituted them. This is why we express our unconscious daily legitimation of these institutions, which consists in conforming our action to them (what Bubner called "*wieder-erkennen,*" renewed recognition, continuing to recognize): we do so because we feel the ethos that acts behinds our backs at work in them. If this trust in the institutions should break down, their very existence would begin to waver.

But the normative logic of recognition never manifests itself abstractly. We can always reconstruct the ethical principles that are behind our backs, formalizing *the ethics implicit in the ethos*[18] and showing its fundamental norm—that is, the moral imperative to recognize the other, to respect and receive her in her dignity and autonomy, and to articulate—on this basis— the general lines of an ethics of recognition. But this reconstruction does not constitute a grounding: it can only reconstruct that which is already valid. And that which is already valid and operative shows itself within concrete practices, habits, and historical institutions. This gives rise to what also in Hegel appears as a *plural characterization of ethos*, which never finds actualization in one sphere alone but in a *plurality of spheres*. Just as there are different ways of being free (legal, economic, political, or moral freedom), likewise there are different spheres in which freedom is actualized: in legal, socioeconomic, political, affective, or moral relations.

Opportunely, Axel Honneth elaborated a *plural articulation of the modalities of recognition* based on Hegel's own plural articulation of the ethical.[19] His first modality is what he terms *affective recognition*, characterizing relationships between family members, friends, and lovers. Here, the relationship is realized through the medium of affection, friendship, or love, and helps to develop a feeling of self-confidence. The second is *legal recognition*, in which individuals respect one another as legal persons, bearers of rights: in this modality the individual is recognized in his abstract universality, independently of his body, ideas, and history, and in his consciousness he develops a basic feeling of self-respect. The third modality is *social recognition*, characterized by esteem and appreciation for a person's specific qualities. The basis of social recognition is what Honneth terms "solidarity"—that is, a sharing of the same values, or objectives, or life plans. It is on these bases that reciprocal appreciation of one another's qualities becomes possible. This type of relation is of great importance because it helps the individual develop a fundamental feeling of self-esteem.

This tripartition of Honneth's is clearly inspired by Hegel's *Jena Lectures on the Philosophy of Spirit*, which, however, does not include Honneth's third type of recognition (in Hegel's work the third sphere, after the affective and the legal, is that of the state—as it will be in the *Philosophy of Right*). But, despite Honneth's strenuous efforts to show correspondences with Hegel's theory, no value-based recognition is possible in Hegel, precisely because his conception lacks the idea of a community built on specific values and life plans. There are affinities, then, between affective recognition and the Hegelian sphere of the family, or between legal recognition and the Hegelian sphere of civil society (regulated by abstract right and by property relations); but it is hardly possible to make the third modality of recognition correspond to the sphere of the state. And the difficulty is even greater in the case of the *Philosophy of Right*, in which—as we have seen—there is practically no trace of intersubjective relations of recognition.

But what is at stake here is not a more or less correct correspondence with Hegelian theory. The fundamental problem is this: when Honneth eliminates the sphere of the state from his theory he also eliminates any theory of *political* recognition in the literal sense—that is, the vertical and bidirectional recognition that is instituted between the citizens and the state.[20] The reason for this lies very probably in the fact that, as I said earlier, political recognition is not intersubjective recognition in the strict sense but, rather, a "second-degree" recognition (as Siep called it)—that is, a recognition of the other mediated by institutional recognition, which is a modality Honneth hardly appreciates. Quite rightly, Rainer Forst, in his study on the different "contexts of justice," broached an important distinction between "legal" and "political" recognition: in the former the subject is recognized as a *legal person* endowed with rights, while in the latter he is recognized as a *citizen*, endowed with both rights and responsibilities.[21] To this Forst added the important sphere of "moral" recognition, in which the subject is recognized as a person worthy of moral regard [*Achtung*], which is to be carefully distinguished from legal respect [*Respekt*].[22] In this type of recognition there is no sharing of values or of legal norms but, rather, a belonging to the same humanity: if, on the one hand, moral persons see themselves as strangers because they do not belong to the same family or community or nation, on the other they attribute the same human dignity to each another. Moral recognition goes beyond all borders and all differences of gender, nationality, status. In it, the universality of ethos that we have seen to be constitutive of all normative relations attains its maximum expression.

At this point we can correct both Hegel's tripartition and Honneth's as well, distinguishing between at least *five different spheres of ethical life*: the affective (family), the legal (civil society), the political (state), the sphere of values (community), and the moral (humanity). In all these spheres recognitive relations and the specific universal normativity that characterizes them have been institutionalized. From the workings of these ethical spheres we learn to love, to respect the rights of other subjects and follow the legal norms, to perform our duties and exercise our rights as citizens, to appreciate and esteem those to whom we are linked by common ideals, and to have moral regard for all humanity.

Hegel's merit, apart from the concrete modalities in which he articulated these spheres, resides in his avoiding the facile philosophical path of transcendental reflection on the normativity that "stands behind our backs," that is, in his turning *away* from theorization of the universal principles of the ethical background and turning *toward* an exposition of our ethical life in its concrete articulations—in its practices, traditions, and institutions. Hegel's ethical life is not formal but is historically embodied, because it is this *Sittlichkeit* alone that provides us with the standards for our practices at their different levels. While this approach does expose Hegel to inevitable elements of contingency it does not diminish his historical merit:

> He had not discarded the quasi-Aristotelian idea of his youth that the normative principles of communicative freedom in modern society must not be anchored in rues of external behavior or mere coercive laws but needed to be internalized by practical training in habitualized patterns of action and custom if they were to lose the last remnants of heteronomy.[23]

But, then, if the effort of the mature Hegel is to show how the logic of the Idea in its self-transparency is actualized in these ethical institutions, it is our task to demonstrate how a logic and an ethics of recognition has been objectified and embodied in them. At this point it becomes possible to rethink the political sphere of our modernity, the *democratic political sphere*, not only as a product of the ethos of recognition but *as ethos itself*—as the normative source of our public identity.

4.3. Democracy as Ethos

The *Philosophy of Right* invites us to rethink the meaning of the democratic political conception, in an effort to discover the ethical life Hegel attributed to the modern state within the contemporary form of the state as we know it. Instead of seeing democracy as a more refined technique for distributing power and obtaining consensus, our task is thus to rethink it as that *new community* which has risen from the ashes of the old traditional communities, tied to specific places, group memories, and manners and customs handed down by the forefathers. It is not true that contemporary man is without communal bonds: the dissolution of the old ethos was in fact followed by the constitution of a *new ethical life*, characterized by universal and impersonal rules, which—nevertheless—have represented a new order with which the democratic citizen can identify. Contemporary man has made the impersonal rules of the state of law into his new habitat, *his new home*. He has *accustomed himself to legality*, to legal responsibility, to active participation in a public sphere that goes far beyond the old borders of his house, his family, his village. This broad public sphere has effectively replaced his old habitat. The reiteration of legal, civil, and political practices—their becoming everyday tasks and habits—has made them a constitutive part of the democratic citizen's inner nature, no longer representing an element of *external coercion* and heteronomy. On the contrary, they increasingly become a factor of *inner motivation* for his behavior and for the planning of his action. Precisely because he sees these practices as a guarantee of his freedom he no longer considers them external commands to be obeyed but something in which to recognize his own autonomy. Indeed, the democratization of the state has accelerated that process of internalization of legal behavior which was the center of Hegel's ethical conception of the state. Many years ago, Guido Calogero intuited this very well:

> The more a situation is civil, the more a well distributed and well accustomed freedom prevails, and the less is it necessary to intervene with force: penal codes can be applied less frequently, punishments are less severe, the police make their rounds unarmed, while the citizens have so much civility they can take their rifles home with them from military service, as they do in Switzerland, without the risk of their being used for a civil war.[24]

In other words, as Bubner writes, the rule of law has become "absolutely preponderant" in our *Lebenswelt*. "Whatever position one may take on this current tendency, there is no doubt that in the modern era lifeworld and right converge."[25] There is an echo of Hegel here, who described freedom as "being-with-self-in-being-other-than-self." This "other" with which we feel no longer "alien" but "at home" is, precisely, legality: *Herrschaft des Rechts,* the rule of law. This is the new home of the moderns. Schnädelbach wrote:

> Legality [*Legalität*] concerns the conditions of freedom in the *outer* relationship between human beings. Precisely this moment of outwardness, which the traditionalist deplores, we subjectively experience as *the basic condition for our individual freedom in the modern lifeworld*; legality is the most important *non*-Aristotelian element of what we can comprehend as our ethos.[26]

While the traditional ethos (represented by the Aristotelian model) was based on personal communal bonds, on obligations handed down directly from father to son, on local traditions, the *ethos of modernity* is represented by the impersonal force of legality—a force no longer perceived as external constraint but as the condition of individual freedom. What distinguishes this impersonal force from the traditional ethos is precisely its *universalist features*: "A *Lebenswelt* in which universal principles guaranteeing individual freedom are institutionalized embodies not only a *historical-contingent* but a *rational-universal ethos*, with which one can be 'reconciled' also as a rational individual who reasserts his rational autonomy."[27]

The use of the compelling expression "*democratic ethical life*" takes on precise meaning in this context. As Albrecht Wellmer wrote, it "signifies a habitualization of liberal and democratic attitudes and ways of acting, which can only emerge with the support of appropriate institutions, traditions, and practices."[28] The so-called "republican virtues" are constituted by this internalization—in the citizens' motivational structure and behavior—of the legal procedures of the state of law and "are nothing but the expression of a habitualization of liberal and democratic attitudes and reflexes."[29] There is nothing heroic or extraordinary here, but precisely the everyday "loyalty" to state institutions that Hegel called "patriotism." Without these institutions we lose the substance of what Habermas calls "deliberative democracy"—a model of participation in political life whose functioning and legitimation is based on the formation of public opinion and on the processes of a free and discursive formation of consensus.

4.3.1. Fundamental Characteristics of a Democratic Ethical Life

Habermas's thesis is that a liberal culture, associations of citizens, and participation in the *res publica* are essential preconditions for deliberative politics. It is in this sphere that we must stabilize the attitudes, practices, and habits that render the observance of laws prescribed by the political sphere less precarious. Such laws and prescriptions are accepted by the citizenry thanks not only to the "discursive filter" (on the basis of which only what is argumentatively justified in a public forum is legitimate), or even only to the coercive force of law. To stabilize legal behavior the intermediate sphere constituted by democratic habits is necessary: not precarious (albeit indispensable) rational justification or the fear of sanctions, but inner motivation. In short: democracy functions not only in the presence of "formal" democratic procedures but thanks to an ethical and cultural "substance" that makes it possible for these procedures to be "motivationally" accepted.

> It is precisely the deliberatively filtered political communications that depend on lifeworld resources—on a liberal political

culture and an enlightened political socialization, above all on the initiatives of opinion-building associations. To a large extent, these resources form and regenerate spontaneously, and in any case they are not readily accessible to direct interventions of the political apparatus.[30]

This sphere does not depend on political power—on the contrary, it is political power that depends on the workings of this sphere. The principles of the democratic state must be "anchored" in the citizens' motivations—an anchoring that manifests itself in the *habit* of behaving according to the logic of freedom; that is, according to the logic of rights and duties, of autonomy and responsibility. It is this habit of exercising freedom that Habermas refers to as a "democratic ethos."[31]

But contemporary ethical life is important not only for its legitimating function: it also plays a fundamental role in the *education* of citizens. If democracy demands freedom of judgment and the exercise of autonomy as its precondition, this precondition increasingly depends on the goodness of the ethical background in which its subjects are formed. We can no longer presuppose an autonomous constitution of the individual independently of the social and cultural processes that contribute to its formation. The conception of an individual who is "free and rational" in his isolation from society is now nothing more than an ideological representation of early modernity.

Therewith the burden of proof shifts from the morality of citizens to the conduciveness of specific processes of the democratic formation of opinion and will, presumed to have the potential for generating rational outcomes.[32]

As Ceppa expressed it, "a citizen's autonomy no longer lies in his aprioristic moral virtue à la Rousseau or Kant but is the *result* of political socialization: it is *the effect* of the procedures by which collective opinion and will is structurally formed."[33] In other words: individual autonomy does not risk being suffocated by democratic ethical life but, on the contrary, is strengthened and, indeed, constituted by it. Michael Walzer reasserts this: for him, the "liberal self" is not a "presocial self" (as the classical liberal tradition would have it) but, rather, a *"postsocial self"*[34]—an individuality that does not exist prior to society but is its specific product. From this perspective, contemporary society continues to perform its "ethical" function in the etymological sense of "dwelling": it now constitutes a veritable "cradle" for modern autonomous individuality.

Walzer, then, acknowledges the validity of the communitarians' point of view when he insists on the "situated" condition of the self, its dependence on context, the persistence of its location "within" a community. But when this is a liberal community the individual it produces is no longer a subject incapable of autonomy and critical reflection on the traditional ethos but, rather, one who has been formed by the culture of individual rights.

> If we really are situated selves, as the second communitarian critique holds, then our situation is largely captured by that vocabulary [constituted by] the language of individual rights— voluntary association, pluralism, toleration, separation, privacy, free speech, the career open to talents, and so on.[35]

Democratic ethical life represents a "new community" precisely because it "constitutes" individuals capable of reflecting critically and distancing themselves from the very ethical life that has constituted them. When this result has been attained it means that this ethical life has played its role fully and achieved its purpose.[36]

But along with the formation of autonomous individuals the sphere of public ethical life creates, above all, loyal and responsible citizens who are capable of civility. This task, however, must not be left entirely to the state: the other ethical spheres—the family and, above all, society—must do their part. "The production and reproduction of loyalty, civility, political competence, and trust in authority are never the work of the state alone"[37] but are made possible by the network of citizen associations that take root within civil society. It is clear that Walzer's "civil society" is not the same as Hegel's *bürgerliche Gesellschaft*, at least not in its more economistic and naturalistic aspect, expressed by the "system of needs." It can, however, be referred to the associational component Hegel himself identified within that sphere when he theorized the role and function of the corporations. It is in this soil that the ethical nature of civil society—its capacity to form and educate citizens—can take root.

> Only a democratic state can create a democratic civil society; only a democratic civil society can sustain a democratic state. The civility that makes democratic politics possible can only be learned in the associational networks; the roughly equal and widely dispersed capabilities that sustain the networks have to be fostered by the democratic state.[38]

This ethico-formative character of civil society and of the democratic state is further accentuated in Wellmer's version of the contemporary ethos. The full actualization of Hegel's demands within our age ought in fact to consist in the concretization at a political level of the idea of a *relational freedom*. Ethos should not limit itself to developing the independent judgment and critical capability of the individual citizens but must also teach them to promote the freedom of all. In this way *negative* freedom would be actualized as *communal* freedom [*kommunale Freiheit*]. Everyone must be given the opportunity to be free; for this, the precondition is that freedom become an objective of the political institutions.

> Communal freedom is freedom that—through the institutions and practices of a society, through the self-understanding, concern, and habits of its citizens—has become a common *objective*. Negative freedom changes its character when it becomes a common concern. For then it is not only our own freedom we want, but a maximum of self-determination for each individual and collective.[39]

Hence communal freedom is nothing other than a negative freedom that, no longer the right of an individual, has become the common objective of an entire society. Here Hegel's demands are pursued not only in the democratic state but in the very structures of the social state itself—that state whose objective it is to empower "each individual and collective" to exercise their rights of freedom.

At the same time, however, the contemporary pursuit of the political project contained in Hegel's theory of ethical life becomes fully possible only if new elements are introduced that represent *a break with the coordinates of Hegel's theory of the state*. In concluding this book, *democratization* is the expression I shall use to delineate this "break."

4.3.2. A Democratization of Hegel

The fundamental breaking point between the idea of a democratic ethos and Hegel's conception of the state regards the *substantialist* characterization of the ethical sphere that in Hegel plays such a key role. In a democratic political configuration the institutions cannot be immune from possible criticism and modification by the citizens. As Wellmer wrote, the concept of a posttraditional form of democratic ethical life means thinking the habitual forms of democratic behavior *as compatible with* "the absence of any ethical 'substance' that is beyond criticism." The fact that "ethical tolerance, critical rationality, and democratic self-determination" have become *tradition* must not preclude a *reflective distancing* from the institutions that make this form of life possible. Hence "a democratic ethical life would be *an ethical life of the second degree,* an ethical life beyond the standpoint of ethical life."[40]

Peter Schaber confirmed this when he remarked that modern ethical life is no longer a quasi-natural given that cannot be transformed by human action. It is not an invariant that can only be noted and accepted, just as one accepts the existence of the sun, moon, and stars. The new ethos, which arose from the ashes of the traditional—naturalistic and substantial—ethos, is a *posttraditional* ethos: an ethos "constructed" and *artificial,* which means that it "constitutes itself ever more frequently through the cultural processes of formation [*Bildungsprozesse*]."[41] In the condition of modernity *Bildung* is the constitutive subject of ethical life and becomes a "construction" of human freedom. This means that the essential part of modern ethical life constituted by right can no longer be understood as grounded in the nature of things: "Natural right is now understood as what it is in itself: as something posited."[42]

As Wellmer sees it, this postsubstantialist conception of ethos was in fact already proposed by Hegel,[43] since for him ethical life represented the historical actualization of the modern idea of freedom and would therefore fully qualify as an ethical life of the second degree. Yet, as we shall see, in Hegel there is an evident attempt to immunize the institutions against subjective criticism, along with an equally evident underestimation of the citizens' active contribution, which he reduced to a mere exercise of assenting to the state. It is thus incumbent on us to render Hegel's conception of the modern state consistent with his fundamental ideas, distinguished by his demands for freedom and universality. This means delineating a posttraditional ethical life characterized by: (1) formality; (2) pluralism; (3) universality; and (4) deflation of the political and the state.

1. *A formal ethical life.* What does it mean to conceive of a postsubstantial and artificial ethos? It means renouncing the idea that it constitute a form of identitarian life that excludes alternative conceptions. Its only substance is constituted by *formal rules* whose function is to discipline the coexistence of different "substances." *In contemporary democracies it is the rules that constitute the form of life*: "For there is no ethical substance beyond that of the democratic discourse itself that could be made obligatory—be it philosophically, theologically, or politically—for all members of society."[44] Hegel's idea that modern ethical life consists in freedom's making itself substance could be translated here into the new idea that, for the contemporary

democratic citizen, the rules themselves have become the only substance. To be sure, contemporary democracy itself rests on habitualized behaviors and traditions. But now they are constituted by our "procedures" alone—by the basic idea that conflicts are to be resolved through discourse; which is to say, through democratic engagement.

> We might, then, elucidate the term "procedural" as follows: it means a way of dealing with dissent or conflict, in which orientation by the normative conditions of democratic discourse defines not the only standard of judgment but the only ultimately inescapable standard of judgment.[45]

Conflicts are not resolved by excluding those who have different values, but by requiring everyone to utilize democratic procedures to settle their disputes. A democratic ethical life does not ask its citizens to accept a specific form of life but only to be loyal to the legal system of freedom.

As Habermas wrote regarding the assimilation of non-European immigrants in Western countries, the democratic style in the solution of the problem must not be based on imposing "the way of life, the practices, and customs of the local culture," but, rather, on fundamental assent to "the principles of the constitution." Instead of pursuing an "ethical-cultural integration" that would take us back to an ethnic and premodern conception of ethical life and would have "a deeper impact on the collective identity of the immigrants' culture of origin," we need to take a path inspired by the basic idea of posttraditional ethical life. It, too, is a community, and "nothing, including immigration, can be permitted to encroach upon" its identity. But this identity is not constituted by discriminatory values or by absolutized forms of life. On the contrary, "that identity is founded on the constitutional principles anchored in the political culture and not on the basic ethical orientations of the cultural form of life predominant in that country."[46]

Hence it is only on the basis of a formal—a *procedural*—ethos that otherwise incompatible forms of life have the possibility of living together. This, however, does not entail the reconciliation of differences, according to an idealist model that is no longer feasible in the contemporary condition. Ethical life does not "dissolve" social and political conflict but limits itself to "regulating" it, and to furnishing the instruments for its different and progressive solutions.

2. *A pluralist ethical life.* Is the metaphysical category of the good still meaningful within a posttraditional ethical life? Can we still speak of

a "common good" when our societies are characterized by an—at times conflictual—multiplicity of conceptions of the good? It is for these very reasons that political Neo-Kantianism has proposed to replace the substantial category of the "good" with the formal category of the "right." The "good" is associated with specific views of the world and of life while the "right" prescinds from substantial views, asserting only the universal norms at which subjects—even with different philosophies of life—can converge. But this "right" is nothing other than the "good" that is the basis of posttraditional ethical life, which is pervaded by a sole common good consisting in the intersection and meeting of different ideas of the good. Or, more precisely, the good is constituted by the normative and institutional condition that makes this plurality possible.

> The concept of a democratic ethical life does not yet define
> a specific content of a good life, but rather only the *form* of
> an egalitarian and communicative coexistence of a plurality of
> competing conceptions of the good.[47]

Democracy's true common good is the *defense* of the plurality of "goods" that pervade it. Instead of reducing cultural differences to a sole common identity it constitutes the only true defense of their irreducible *nonidentity*.

> The sole common good (in the sense of a good that is binding
> on all) can only reside in the realization and defense of those
> liberal and democratic principles which afford the only possible
> protection against the violent destruction of the *particular* tradi-
> tions and cultural identities of individual societies.[48]

Posttraditional ethical life not only defends pluralism but is a veritable *school* of pluralism. In other words, in this school the pluralism of options and forms of life has become tradition, habit, everyday socialization. The new community in which we live has this fundamental character: it is *plural*.

> Any definition of community that is meaningful in the modern
> context has to settle accounts with the "fact of pluralism." "Com-
> munity" for us cannot but mean a community that contains
> diversity—one that is not entirely amalgamated by consensus.[49]

It is evident, then, that within this plurality of orientations the legitimation of common norms and rules of socialization can only come from

intersubjective processes of the formation of political will: this is the irrefut-
able core of Habermas's proposal of a deliberative democracy. But—and here
Habermas disagrees—the existence of a democratic ethical life is itself this
proposal's condition of possibility: it is possible that citizens accept argu-
mentative-discursive procedures as the source of legitimation of norms only
if they share and accept the ethical background, embodied in the practices,
procedures, and institutions that make democratic engagement possible.

3. *A universal ethical life*. What does it mean to extend globally the
model of ethical life that Hegel limited to the nation state? Does making
the ethos of modernity consistent with Hegel's universalist inspiration mean
imagining a World State? Not necessarily. Universal ethical life is not the
universal state but is the constitution, on a global scale, of international
institutions and of a common praxis modeled on the tradition of freedom
and of rights. This process got underway some time ago and, despite resis-
tances and counterthrusts, has been growing stronger. The European Union
is an example of this construction of supranational institutions that do
not entail the cancellation of nation states, neither do they intend to take
their place. The very process of globalization, with all its perverse effects, is
introducing—with difficulty, and in a distant horizon—*the idea of a common world*, in which not only commodities or financial "products" but also
human beings—their ideas and cultures, the respect for human rights—have
to be able to travel without limitations and barriers. Here, strengthening
a universal ethical life would mean the birth of a global culture of tolerance, of pluralism, of socialization between those who are different. The
consolidation of this ethos at the institutional level would make it possible
to increment globally not only a culture of rights but also their effective
practice and institutionalization in international norms and procedures.

Here too, however, rendering the perspective of ethical life universal
does not mean imposing the Western model of culture on the world. Universalism is not ethnocentrism, it is not the globalized extension of Western
"values"—on the contrary, it is the condition that, thanks to the advent
of the tradition of freedom, makes a world characterized by a plurality of
values possible. Universalism does not mean a sole culture but shared rules
that make different and multiple cultures possible.[50]

4. *Deflation of the political and the state*. From the perspective of a
posttraditional ethical life does maintaining the Hegelian primacy of the
state over the other domains of common life still have any meaning? On
the one hand, the very structure of the *Philosophy of Right*—subdivided into
three different spheres, each with its specific character that is not delegable

to the others—seems to suggest a recognition of their autonomous validity. On the other hand, Hegel clearly gives the state not only primacy over the other spheres but also the specific functions of resolving within itself the conflicts and contradictions of its subordinate domains. As a result, the political sphere is assigned tasks that regard the social, family, and individual domains. In other words, politics has the task of reconciling not only subjective freedom with the freedom objectively embodied in the institutions, but also happiness (welfare) with justice (right), authenticity with autonomy, and self-realization with universality.

At this point, Hegel's critics who insist that the task is unrealizable have a field day. Adorno, in particular, acknowledged the honesty with which Hegel sharply delineates the relation of reciprocal estrangement that arises between the institutional embodiments of modern freedom and the concreteness of the individual; but he also duly noted how this conflict is, in the end, unrealistically resolved within the sphere of the state. In other words, for Adorno, Hegel sees that it is impossible for subjective feeling to recognize the objectively existing institutions, but in the end he glosses this over "assuringly" [*beteuernd*].

> If the individual conscience actually regarded "the real world of
> right and of ethos" as hostile because it does not recognize itself
> in it, one should not gloss this over assuringly; for it is the point
> of Hegelian dialectics that conscience cannot act differently, that
> it cannot recognize itself in it.[51]

Christoph Menke returned to this question more recently, as we have seen (3.1.5). His thesis is that Hegelian ethical life is structurally incapable of resolving the conflict between individual authenticity and universal justice. For him, there is "no dialectical solution"[52] for the modern tragedy of the ethical. While it is true that the modern state, grounded in subjective freedom, is able to harmonize the freedom of individual citizens with the rights of the collectivity represented by political power (reconciliation of autonomy and justice), it is not able to reconcile the individual demand for self-realization with the sphere of legality (reconciliation of authenticity and right): "the primacy of justice over the other political values comes about *in the name* of subjective freedom, and yet it can also mean *a loss* of freedom."[53]

Wellmer himself, who agrees with the Hegelian solution on many points and defends it against the proceduralist perspectives à la Kant, on this question emphasizes the necessary incompleteness of Hegel's idea: the primacy of the universal over the particular broached by the advent of a democratic ethical life inevitably produces a *conflict with the specificities* of the traditions that *cannot be resolved* by a state of law expanded on a global scale.

> It cannot be denied that such a supersession [*Aufhebung*] of the particular in the universal is hardly conceivable without moral violations; all the indications are that, with the transition to a cosmopolitan state of law, Hegel's "tragedy in ethical life" [. . .] will repeat itself on a global scale, since the *relativization* of the particular cultural traditions also means their transformation and partial disempowerment.[34]

From this perspective modernity proves to be structurally incomplete and constitutively irreconcilable: "The 'project of modernity'—this is the truth in Hegel's critique—has no utopian telos."[55] Modernity—for Habermas an "unfinished project"[56]—is destined, for Wellmer, to remain so. Whatever project modernity had in mind will never be completely actualized. Utopia becomes, once again, wishful thinking, since its completion—*any* completion—is structurally impossible.

> The open-ended character of the project of modernity implies the end of utopia, if utopia means "completion" in the sense of a definitive actualization of an ideal or a telos of history.[57]

All these critiques have one feature in common: they continue, Hegelianly, to assign politics the *exclusive* task of finding a definitive *solution* for the problems of modernity. But it is not the task of politics to resolve the conflict between happiness and justice, precisely because neither happiness, nor the individual's self-realization, nor his authenticity, are political tasks. The only political task is to resolve the conflict between the autonomy of the individual and the freedom of all.

The political unquestionably maintains its primacy over the other spheres, but only in the sense that it must guarantee the *preconditions for the realization of the self.* But only the preconditions. The self will have to find its realization in another sphere—in that of private relationships, in the family, in friendship, in affection, in the community, in work, in civil society. From this perspective *there is no conflict between happiness and justice*, precisely because they are two dimensions of freedom that find their realization in two different spheres.

Then again, posttraditional ethical life, far from impeding or clashing with the ideal of authenticity, must be able to make it possible. As the ground on which the autonomy of the individual is built, it creates the conditions for him to find the way to self-realization. As Axel Honneth wrote,

> Subjects are equally in a position to determine their life-goals without external influence only to the extent to which the establishment of civil law gives them all, in principle, individual freedom to make decisions. In short, self-realization is dependent on the social prerequisite of legally guaranteed autonomy, because only with its help can subjects come to conceive of themselves as persons who can deliberate about their own desires.[58]

Self-realization is not in conflict with autonomy but is its further development. The only conflict that can arise between autonomy and authenticity is the one that regards individual moral choices. Here Menke is quite right when he says that such conflict must be resolved in a plural and differentiated manner, individually assuming the "moral" idea of the good as the criterion of orientation for such choices.[59] Indeed, in the idea of the good it is possible to conceive of the coexistence and combination of happiness and justice.

Hence as regards the ideal of authenticity the political has only indirect tasks. It must limit itself to guaranteeing *the independence* of all the *extra-political spheres* in which subjects can realize the relations of solidarity and reciprocal esteem that are necessary for the (inescapably individual and plural) realization of happiness. In this context it becomes possible to rehabilitate the premodern concept of *community*, precisely in order to define the domains in which the *care for one's own realization* can develop.

Honneth, with this in mind, broached the expression *formal concept of ethical life.* By this he does not mean the political notion of "democratic ethical life" but, rather, the conditions of communication and reciprocal recognition "that can be shown to serve as necessary preconditions for individual self-realization."[60] It is clear that these conditions apply only to *communal relations*, since, for Honneth, a *community* is distinguished from a *society* by the fact that in a community the intersubjective relationship does not consist simply in "respect" for the other's space of freedom but, rather, in "esteem" for specific individuals based on their particular characteristics. "But reciprocal esteem means entertaining relations of solidarity."[61] The prime feature of the communal relationship is thus *reciprocal solidarity*, whereas in social relations the basic characteristic was tolerance. But by "solidarity" Honneth does not mean helping one another but, simply, recognizing the value of the other—that is, appreciating and admiring his qualities. He is referring, then, to relations that imply a personal relationship with the other—that personal relationship which is lacking in the broader social sphere: "relations of this type are to be called 'solidary' since they give rise not only to passive tolerance for one another but to affective participation in the individual particularity of the other person."[62]

But for this to come about the subjects involved must share the same values: such values represent the normative standard in the light of which individuals are esteemed. A community is therefore necessarily a *community of values*, a "*Wertgemeinschaft*." I refer here, of course, to posttraditional communities grounded in the freedom of individuals: access to them is free, as is the choice of values and of life plans.

For Honneth, the advent of modernity does not make it impossible to constitute relationships of this type. What has changed compared to traditional communities is the freedom of access and, above all, the scale of values in light of which to build up esteem of the other. In modernity values lose any vestige of rigid and preordained hierarchy: intelligence can prevail over morality, but so can money, force, or power. Hence, if the institution of these relations remains unchanged, what are changed are the values: it is the single individuals who choose them and, on the basis of their choices, who institute the posttraditional communal relations that characterize our world.

Hence the ethos of modernity coincides not only with *legality*, with the state of law, and with the culture of universal rights. Here we must grasp Hegel's legacy in its *wholeness*. What Hegel attributed to the *family* must be extended to all affective relations, including relations with friends and with the most "extended" of families. By the same token, what he attributed to *civil society* must be rethought as the domain of communal relations, of work and of social exchange. It is in these spheres that we can realize the relations of solidarity, affection, and esteem that are inevitably precluded in the political domain. Hence it is outside the political that we must seek to cultivate our realization and to discover our authenticity.

Notes

Introduction

1. The ethical is that which belongs to the *ethos*, whose first and original meaning is "customary place of living for humans and animals"—the stable and the pasture for the horse, water for the fish, the city for the Greeks. Later, however, in a linguistic usage that was still absolutely in force for Aristotle and his time, it came to mean the traditional and customary order of life. Those who dwell in the *ethos* inhabit it as the world that forms their life: *ethos* as practices, customs, and everything in which life has its proper order, but also the "habitual" institutions grounded in tradition and practice, home and family, the cult of the gods worshipped by the city, the multiplicity of communities, associations, friends, neighbors, societies for the burial of the dead and for celebrations—*ethos* as the institutional lifeworld [*Lebenswelt*] of those who inhabit it as citizens that, thanks to the city, has become customary. (Ritter, 1960, p. 486)

2. Aristotle, *Hist. An.* VIII, 1, 588a 18.
3. See *Nic. Eth.* II, 1, 1103a 17–18.
4. Reaffirmed in the *Philosophy of Right*: "When we speak of the opposition between morality or ethics and *right*, the right in question is merely the initial and formal right of abstract personality" (§ 30 R).
5. The *Philosophy of Right* must therefore be considered Hegel's most detailed and complete exposition of objective spirit. The other two discussions of objective spirit in his mature work are the second section of the *Philosophy of Spirit* (part 3 of the *Encyclopaedia*) titled "Objective Spirit" (particularly §§ 483–552) and the important anticipation of the different themes of objective spirit in the "Spirit" section of the *Phenomenology of Spirit*.
6. It is important to note the particular meaning Hegel attaches to the notion of "Idea" in the *Philosophy of Right*—a strongly objectivistic meaning, contrasted with the notion of "concept," used in a subjective sense. He writes in the

first paragraph of the work that "the subject-matter of *the philosophical science of right* is the *Idea of right*—the concept of right and its actualization" (§ 1), where, then, the "Idea" is characterized as the "actualization" of the "concept." In his Remarks on this paragraph Hegel reaffirms his thesis, writing that "the other essential moment of the Idea"—the moment expressing its actualization—"is different from its *form* of being purely as concept"—different from its simply subjective form. Vittorio Hösle has rightly observed that this distinction, in which the "Idea" is taken in an objectivist sense, "is not in agreement with the use of the corresponding categories in the *Science of Logic*" (Hösle 1987a, p. 43), since in the *Logic* the category of the *Idea* signifies a mediation between the subjective and the objective side of the concept—a mediation that is articulated in its self-reflective characterization. We find none of this in the *Philosophy of Right*, where "*Idea of free will*" means that freedom is no longer merely a subjective concept but has become reality.

7. Honneth 2001, trans. p. 17.

8. Ibid., p. 17.

9. "A person, in distinguishing himself from himself, relates himself to *another person*, and indeed it is only as owners of property that the two have existence for each other" (PR § 40).

10. Aristotle, *Nic. Eth.* I, 1, 1094a 3.

11. Aristotle, *Pol.* I, 2, 1253a 3.

12. Kant 1788, trans. p. 33.

13. Kant 1796–97, trans. p. 34.

14. Kant's philosophy is based precisely on "those two characteristically modern phenomena—the pluralism of ideals of the good life and the existence of reasonable disagreement about which ideals are preferable—that stand at the center of liberal political thought. Neutral principles of justice are the solution that liberals (such as Hume and, even more so, Kant) have urged for the political problems that these competing ideals produce" (Larmore 1987, p. 73).

Chapter 1

1. Marcuse 1941 (1960), pp. viii–ix.

2. "It was seen that being inwardizes itself [*sich erinnert*] through its own nature, and through this movement into itself [*Insichgehen*] becomes essence." (WL11 241/SL 389).

3. WL21 57/SL 71.

4. "The genuine refutation must penetrate the opponent's stronghold and meet him on his own ground; no advantage is gained by attacking him somewhere else and defeating him where he is not. The only possible refutation of Spinozism must therefore consist, in the first place, in recognizing its standpoint as essential and necessary and then going on to raise that standpoint to the higher one through its own immanent dialectic" (WL12 15/SL 581).

5. If the condition for being absolute substance is that of being *causa sui*, then being mere substance is an insufficient determination. Mere substantiality is only the effect of the cause, and is therefore not true substance: it is, as Hegel says, "superseded substantiality, that which is merely posited, or *effect*" (WL11 396/SL 558). The true substance proves to be the cause.

6. The resolution of ontology into logic corresponds, at the same time, to a resolution of logic into self-reflective logic. The truth of logic is not the exposition of ideal conceptual structures but, rather, the reflectivity of these structures on themselves. It is in virtue of this reflectivity that they posit themselves and thus manifest themselves as absolute. The true specificity of Hegel's *Logic* consists less in its being the exposition of the ultimate logical structure of the real (in a sort of reproposal of the Platonic noetic cosmos) than in its having this structure reflect in itself and in its rooting the condition of the structure's absoluteness in this reflectivity. The true meaning of the Hegelian notion of *concept* is its self-reflectivity.

7. "The pure concept, or infinity as the abyss of nothingness in which all being is engulfed [*versinkt*], must signify the infinite pain [of the finite]" (GuW 413/FK 190).

8. Ritter 1974, p. 30. Aristotle in fact defined the slave as "a human being belonging by nature not to himself but to another" (*Politics* I, 4, 1254a 16).

9. Kant 1785, trans. p. 114.

10. Ibid., p. 114.

11. "The indeterminate will is to this extent just as one-sided as that which exists in mere determinacy" (RZ 54/PR § 6 A).

12. Many Hegel scholars have emphasized the importance of sections 5–7, not only for Hegel's synthetic statement of the three essential dimensions of freedom, but also because they represent a sort of programmatic exposition of the entire *Philosophy of Right*. As Manfred Riedel (1970) has remarked, section 5 is a foretaste of the first part of the work, *abstract right*; section 6 of the second part, *morality*; and section 7 of the third part, *ethical life* (as the unification of the first two):

> Thus *absolute right* corresponds to the first moment of the concept, its empty universality and indeterminacy with respect to the "person as such," to "property as such," etc. The level of *morality* represents the second moment, i.e. particularity, the limitation of the will effected by an external world, on the one hand, and by subjective principles and ends on the other, as well as by the demand to realize them. Finally, in the sphere of *ethical life* the two moments are unified by the fact that the will finds its contents and particular ends not merely as tasks opposing it but—in the existing institutions, in socio-historical actuality—now finds itself, [finds] freedom as its substance and determination. (p. 16)

13. In this regard, Theunissen (1978) speaks of "communicative freedom." Honneth (2001) picked up on this concept, relating it precisely to section 7 of

the *Philosophy of Right*, and in particular to the Addition, which we have examined in detail.

14. The exact reference here is to the category of *opposition*, in which the opposing terms belong to one another—indeed, they are the more *opposed*, the more they *belong* to each other. Dependence on an other thus becomes the condition of their opposition and, therefore, of their independence: "The positive and the negative are thus the sides of the opposition that have become independent. They are independent or self-subsistent" but "on account of their independence they constitute the opposition determined in itself," and therefore, "each is itself and its other" and "each refers to itself only insofar as it refers to its other" (WL11 273/SL 425).

Chapter 2

1. Michael Theunissen (1982) introduced, in this regard, the concept of "*Veranderung*," used to indicate the process of becoming-other, of changing oneself in making oneself identical to the other (pp. 361–363).

2. Hegel later confirms that the legal relation does *not* "have a *positive* reference to the will of others" (PR § 113 R).

3. "Diremption is for him the fundamental condition of the modern age" (Ritter 1957, trans. p. 63), and "the diremption is understood by Hegel as the form of the modern world and its consciousness" (ibid., p. 64).

4. Ritter 1969, p. 351.

5. Ibid., p. 351.

6. Ritter 1957, trans. p. 65.

7. See Ritter 1957, pp. 56–67.

8. Taylor 1979a, p. 7.

9. Ibid., p. 8.

10. For greater details see the illustration of the three figures of the self (the legal person, absolute freedom as the conclusion of modern *Bildung*, and moral consciousness certain of itself) at the beginning of the section on *Gewissen* (moral certainty, conscience) in PhG 341–342/PS 384.

11. "A person, in distinguishing himself from himself, relates himself to *another person*, and indeed it is only as owners of property that the two have existence for each other" (PR § 40).

12. Ritter 1969, trans. p. 132.

13. Ibid., p. 130.

14. Ibid., p. 134.

15. Ibid., p. 139.

16. Ibid., p. 141.

17. Hegel treats estrangement [*Entfremdung*] as the consequence and result of alienation [*Entäußerung*]. It is the process of externalization that produces an estranged world in which the product of this externalization is no longer recognized

by the one who created it. On the relation between these two terms see Massolo 1973, pp. 198–211.

18. "Substance is in this way *spirit*, the self-conscious unity of the self and essence; but each has for the other the significance of estrangement [*Entfremdung*]. Spirit is the *consciousness* of an objective actuality freely existing on its own account; but this consciousness is confronted by the unity of the self and essence, *actual* consciousness by *pure* consciousness" (PhG 265/PS 295). In the world of culture substance is not a natural entity but is "spirit"—that is, a product of the individual and of his "cultural" activity, and thus something that is in intimate unity with the self. But this unity is in fact inwardly broken. This unity of the self and its estranged essence is confronted by what Hegel, here, calls "consciousness"—namely, awareness of the distinction between the self and the objective world.

19. Rüdiger Bubner (1989) sees the roots of this "dialectic of the Enlightenment" in "reflection," which Hegel had criticized ever since the time of his *Differenzschrift*. In *Faith and Knowledge*, Bubner writes, reflection produces autonomy but, at the same time, also diremption and estrangement, a diremption to be healed through the use of reflection itself: "the wounds of reflection as something that can only be healed through reflection itself is a constant theme throughout Hegel's work" (trans. p. 152). Also in the *Phenomenology of Spirit* the doubling of actuality created by *Bildung* can be ascribed to reflection: it "posits, over against the original one, a second actuality in which the cultured individual disappears amongst his fellow cultured individuals" (p. 153), but this is only a "semblance" [*Schein*] "with which a specific social product of culture [*Bildung*] is presented as actuality itself" (p. 153).

20. See Menke 1996. The title of Menke's book—*Tragedy in the Ethical*—refers to a celebrated expression used by Hegel in his Jena essay *On the Scientific Ways of Treating Natural Law*: "This is nothing other than the enactment, in the ethical realm, of the tragedy that the absolute eternally plays out within itself—by eternally giving birth to itself in objectivity, thereby surrendering itself in this shape to suffering and death, and rising up to glory from its own ashes" (NR 458/NL 151).

21. For a detailed analysis of Hegel's criticisms of Kantian "morality" in the context of the *Phenomenology of Spirit*, see Cortella 2002, in particular pp. 218–230.

22. Jürgen Habermas (1986), in an essay specifically dedicated to Hegel's objections to Kant, focuses on four key points: tautological formalism; incapacity to arrive at concrete and plural contents; the opposition of existing reality and the "ought"; the terrorism of pure intention. But the last of the four regards more the moralism of the Jacobin revolutionaries than it does Kantian morality. The later statement of these objections in Habermas 1999 (pp. 224–225) omits the first and the fourth criticism of the 1986 essay and, while it confirms the third, divides the second into two distinct criticisms (the incapacity of the universal moral law to attain concrete contents can be seen both as its capacity of revision in relation to the consequences, and as its incapacity of application in relation to the concrete case).

23. This is the fundamental objection we find in the subsection "The Moral View of the World" (in section C of chapter VI of the *Phenomenology*), articulated in the critique of the three Kantian postulates (see PhG 324–328/PS 364–369).

24. Habermas 1986, p. 25.

25. For Hegel, the failure of "reason as lawgiver" inevitably induces Kant to devise a reason that is only a "tester of laws" (see PhG 228–232/PS 252–256).

26. This is the second objection to Kant raised by Hegel in the subsection "The Moral View of the World" (in particular PhG 329–329/PS 369–371), taken up again in the subsections to follow, dealing with *Verstellung*, moral dissemblance (PhG 339/PS 381), and *Gewissen*, conscience or moral certainty (PhG 342/PS 385–386).

27. "In modern societies the more particular interests and values are differentiated, the more the morally justified norms regulating the freedom of action of individuals in the general interest are general and abstract" (Habermas 1986, p. 23).

28. On the role of the faculty of judgment in the field of morality, see Ferrara 1998 and 2008.

29. On Hegel's treatment of "reason as testing laws," see PhG 232–237/PS 256–262.

30. "Kant's further form—the capacity of an action to be represented as a *universal* maxim—does yield a *more concrete* representation of the situation in question, but it does not in itself [*für sich*] contain any principle apart from formal identity and that absence of contradiction already referred to" (PR § 135 R).

31. On this point both Wildt 1982 (pp. 44–84) and Habermas 1986 (p. 21) have come to Kant's defense.

32. Honneth 2001, trans. p. 39.

33. Ritter 1974, pp. 33–34. Hegel criticizes the French Revolution for analogous reasons: it too failed to recognize the freedom already existing, and its intention to "realize" freedom is nothing but the unwitting expression of a freedom already at work within modern civil society. "The political revolution itself and with it its central idea of freedom belong historically to the emergence of the new society" (Ritter 1957, trans. p. 72). Civil society, in its mechanisms, is already geared to freedom for all human beings, "insofar as it has for its subject individuals in the equality of their needful nature, and thus extricated from all institutions limiting them politically or legally" (ibid., p. 72). The "original equality" supposed by modern political theory is itself rooted in the homogenization process of civil society, in its systematic destruction of the old inequalities of class and status. "The French attained, historically, equality of conditions as a result of their particular history, but theory makes them know, and they know theoretically, that they are absolutely equal" (Biral 1991, p. 311). The combined mechanism of political absolutism and the development of civil society sweeps away the ancient aristocratic world and empties all social conditions "of their specific, compact ethos, to fill them with a new uniform ethos that makes them all equal" (ibid., p. 313). But the French revolutionaries are completely unaware of this: they think they are equal on the basis of a political theory that posits their original equality and proclaims the political necessity of constructing an equality under sovereignty. This theory "will *make* them ignore the fact that this 'revolutionary' transition had already taken place; consequently, they will take it to be a project still to be realized, a goal that must be reached, and in whose name there is no battle that can be refused" (ibid., p.

313). Biral's analysis, sharply individuating the singular modern unawareness of the objective, historical, and social nature of freedom, fits in perfectly with the Hegelian critique of modernity. For Hegel this lack of awareness will prove to be the original sin of the French Revolution, the root of its emphasis on a revolutionary subjectivism that *wants* to realize freedom, but ends up by obtaining just the opposite. On the Hegelian critique of the French Revolution, see Cortella 2002, in particular pp. 205–217.

34. Marquard 1964–65, p. 42. For an analogous line of interpretation that sees Hegelian ethical life not as an abolition of Kantian morality but as its completion, see Hofmeister 1974.

35. Ibid., p. 44.

36. Ibid., p. 47.

37. The conception of freedom as an inner property of the subject finds its constitutive theoretical context in the modern opposition of thought and being. In modernity, Hegel writes, "the concrete form of thought, which we have here to consider on its own account, essentially appears as subjective with the reflection of being-in-itself [*Insichsein*], so that it stands in opposition to being [*Seiendes*]" (GPh2 XV 242/HP III 160).

38. Ritter 1957, trans. p. 75.

39. Ibid., p. 77.

40. Ibid., p. 78.

41. Taylor 1979a, pp. 131–132.

42. Ritter 1957, trans. p. 73.

43. As Albrecht Wellmer (1993) notes, the process of education implemented by civil society makes it possible to attain "the intersubjectivity of *universal* points of view and standards" (trans. p. 114), which is to say the universality of right, of philosophy, and of morality itself. Obviously this form of universality is not yet the actuality of the ethical idea, "but it is the precondition for that actuality" (ibid., p. 114).

44. Marini 1978–90, p. 82. On the same page, Marini acutely noted that with this type of judgment it is evident that Hegel has come to see *Bildung* somewhat differently from the way in which he saw it in the *Phenomenology*: it now appears as the realm of freedom, not of estrangement. In short, "the negative and pessimistic tones are less strong and frequent in the Berlin period than in the Jena period" (ibid., p. 82).

45. Wellmer 1993, trans. p. 25.

46. On this point—for Wellmer—Hegel differs sharply from the romantic critics of modernity: he opposes the conciliatory utopias of romanticism precisely by exalting the role of the "individualist" institutions of the modern world. Hegel's defense of the emancipatory function of these institutions and of their role as a guarantee of the reconstitution of communal relations "can also be read retrospectively as a metacritique of Marx's critique of bourgeois individualism" (ibid., pp. 24 and 36).

47. It is evident here that Hegel has taken up the standpoint of classical political economy. Indeed, in these lines we seem to hear Adam Smith's famous

pronouncement: "It is not from the benevolence of the butcher, the brewer, or the baker, that we expect our dinner, but from their regard to their own interest. We address ourselves, not to humanity but to their self-love, and never talk to them of our necessities but of their advantages" (Smith 1776 [1963], vol. 2, pp. 21–22). However, it must also be said that Hegel's perspective does not fully coincide with Smith's. As we shall see, Hegel maintains that the universal produced by subjective selfishness must be considered only a *universal of the understanding* in which the true reconciliation of individual and totality is not achieved, just as the thinking of political economy must be judged no less "of the understanding" (see PR § 189 R). What is more, the unconscious character of this universality ends up by making it altogether contingent and fortuitous. Consequently, a different universality is called for (one that, as we shall see, will be represented by the corporation).

48. "For Hegel modern civil society, by structuring itself as nature does, guarantees that which no society of the ancient or medieval world had been able to achieve: it allows the greatest possible development of individual subjectivity and prevents, at the same time, that this intensification of freedom corrupt the organic unity of the whole." In short, that which for the young Hegel had been the locus par excellence of diremption becomes in the Hegel of Berlin 'the locus of maximum naturalistic harmony" (Finelli 1990, p. 77).

49. Indeed, Hegel places the entire sphere of the administration of justice within civil society (in the *Philosophy of Right*, the entire second part of the section on "Civil Society" is devoted to it) and not within the state, since the purpose of such administration is to regulate the natural needs and empirical interests of individuals as they manifest themselves in society. This led Giuliano Marini (1978–90) to equate Hegelian civil society and its judicial system with the Kantian and liberal state of law: civil society, too, is nothing other than the instrument necessary to guarantee the development and security of individual economic interests.

50. Here is the entire passage from section 184: "It is the system of ethical life, lost in its extremes, which constitutes the abstract moment of the *reality* of the Idea, which is present here only as the *relative totality* and *inner necessity* of this external *appearance* [*Erscheinung*]."

51. Here is the entire passage: "To put it first in abstract terms, this [stage] gives the determination of *particularity* that is related to *universality*, but in such a way that the latter is its fundamental—though still only *inner* and formal—basis; consequently, this universality is present only *seemingly* in the particular" (PR § 181).

52. Quite rightly, Giorgio Cesarale (2009) emphasizes that *Schein* is "manifestative" and refers to an "other": the concept of *scheinen* "expresses the process by means of which essence comes to shine *through* its determinacies" (p. 106). In other words, the universal of civil society—the system of all-round interdependence—manifests itself in the "particularity of economic individuals, who, in their turn, assuming a self-negating demeanor, become the immediate position of a complex and articulated totality. Here, as with the *Scheinen* of the *Logic*, what we have is a play of reciprocal mirrorings" (p. 107).

53. Cesarale was right to call into question Marini's claim that Hegel made no distinction between *Schein* and *Erscheinung* (Marini 1978–90, pp. 229–252). Nonetheless, while his own claim does have its merits—namely, that the "seeming" character should be referred to the first part of "Civil Society" ("The System of Needs") and the "appearing" character to the second and third parts ("The Administration of Justice" and "The Police and the Corporation"), in which the existence of a tissue of concrete relations concretely shows the ethical universal (see in particular Cesarale 2009, p. 109)—it is not explicitly confirmed by Hegel's text.

54. In the *Science of Logic* Hegel refers to *Schein* as the "being-superseded of being [*Aufgehobensein des Seins*]" and "its nothingness" (WL11 246/SL 395), and to *Erscheinung* as "*realer* Schein" (WL11 341/SL 498–499), that is, as a semblance that has real consistency: "Essence *appears* [*erscheint*], so that it is now *real* semblance [*realer Schein*], since the moments of semblance have existence [*Existenz*]."

55. It is clear that other correspondences of the three moments of ethical life are possible: with the three sections of the logic of essence itself (*essence, appearance, actuality*)—but also with the three sections of the logic of the concept (*subjectivity, objectivity, Idea*). Giuliano Marini (1978–90, pp. 11–42) endorsed the latter correspondence, based on Hegel's statement that civil society was to be understood as the sphere of "*Realität*" (§ 181) in which the moments of particularity and universality (compactly united in the family—i.e., present in it only as *concepts*) become independent reality (*selbstständige Realität*). In this reading, civil society represents a sort of "objectivity" of the "subjective concept" in which the family consists. Each of these correspondences is plausible to a certain extent, also in light of the paucity of Hegel's indications on the subject, but above all if we consider the fact that the Hegelian system is characterized by a *multiple* interweaving of its moments.

56. Here we clearly see the limit of Joachim Ritter's interpretation, with his unreserved endorsement of the viewpoint of civil society and of the juridical sphere. He fails to see the insufficiency of this sphere—specifically, its failure to go beyond the viewpoint of the understanding. As Rüdiger Bubner observed: "Ritter's important and influential essay on 'Subjectivity and Industrial Society' has the merit of highlighting the modernity of the Hegelian conception against the suspicion of its being reactionary. This occurs, however, at the cost of completely referring modern subjectivity to the organization of society, while according to the Hegelian philosophy of right this subjectivity comes to itself completely only in the state" (Bubner 1996, pp. 150–151n32).

57. Theunissen, too, is in disaccord with Ritter's idea that the Hegelian philosophy of right is an affirmative exposition of the freedom of the moderns, revealing the "truth of bourgeois abstract right." Theunissen, by contrast, sees it as a "critical exposition of modern natural right and, through this, of social reality" (Theunissen 1982, p. 318). His line of interpretation here is consonant with that of his celebrated reading of the *Science of Logic* (see Theunissen 1978): just as in the *Logic* the critical side manifests itself in the doctrine of being and of essence, then becoming affirmative in the doctrine of the concept, so in the *Philosophy of*

Right the critique is in the first two parts (abstract right and morality), becoming positive exposition in the doctrine of ethical life: "The philosophy of ethical life secures Hegel's affirmative viewpoint. For Hegel himself it constitutes the beginning in the proper sense. Abstract right and morality are, by contrast, the addressees of his critique" (Theunissen 1982, p. 321). I discussed the plausibility of this double register in the *Science of Logic* (see Cortella 1995, pp. 265–266n56, and pp. 346–347), substantially agreeing with Fulda's and Horstmann's criticisms of Theunissen (see Fulda, Horstmann, and Theunissen 1980) regarding the impossibility of such a sharp separation between exposition and critique purely on the basis of the how the parts of the book are arranged. I have to make an analogous criticism of this reading of the *Philosophy of Right*, which keeps the doctrine of ethical life outside the classical Hegelian paradigm of the unity of exposition and critique. For that matter, Theunissen himself was obliged to correct himself, admitting soon afterward that in the theory of civil society the unity of exposition and critique re-presents itself.

58. Theunissen 1982, p. 339.

59. Emil Angehrn (1977) follows Theunissen's line of interpretation. For him, the unity of exposition and critique finds, in the *Philosophy of Right*, a historical root-edness in the intrinsically twofold structure of the entire reality of objective spirit—a reality characterized by the unity of "factuality" and "normativity," of "being" and "validity." For Angehrn, this real unity—that is, the normative nature of historical reality—is the ground that makes the theoretical unity of exposition and critique possible. Since the object of the philosophy of objective spirit is freedom—that is, a normative object—it constitutes itself as theory that is *descriptive* and *normative* at the same time. Freedom "is per se a critique of all the partial concepts of freedom, of all the concepts fixed in particular determinate moments, such as freedom as a juridical determination or as moral autonomy" (pp. 178–179).

60. My point of reference continues to be Theunissen 1982.

61. This can also be seen as a sort of *transition from nature to spirit*. The individuals in civil society continue to be natural beings, driven by impulses and needs, who form only external, mechanical relationships with one another. By contrast, in the transition to the state it is necessary "that the individual develop an intimate adhesion to the prescriptions of the universal and, consequently, cast off his original chaotic and rebellious nature, ruled by drives. In short, the individual himself *must* transform his *nature* into *spirit*" (Cesarale 2009, p. 60).

62. Hegel refers to it as "the *objective* right of particularity" (PR § 200 R, my italics).

63. On this point see Riedel 1970, p. 22.

64. Bubner 1996, pp. 151–152.

65. As Michael Theunissen (1982) acutely noted, the real elevation of the individual to universality consists less in the mechanism individuated by political economy, on the basis of which the individual, working for himself, works at the same time for the universal, than it does in the becoming-abstract—and therefore universal, and therefore self-estranged—of the individual himself. In civil society intersubjectivity is possible only as abstraction and estrangement (see pp. 373–377).

66. In this regard, Manfred Riedel wrote: "For him 'corporations' are not the communities, cities, or estates in their political constitution ('corporations of the bourgeoisie or the nobility'), neither are they all the 'communities' and 'associations' up to the state and the church; rather, they are forms of organization of the 'work performed by civil society' (§ 251) whose task is to overcome the individual's isolation in himself and in his particular ends" (Riedel 1970, p. 65).

67. Giorgio Cesarale (2009) is critical of Hegel's argument in support of the transition from the corporation (and thus from the sphere of civil society) to the state. For Cesarale, the existence of a multiplicity of "universals" in competition with one another does not give rise to the necessity of a *single* universal that includes all of them together. The mediation (i.e., the process) that leads to the state is not "superseded" in the immediacy of the state—a remnant of it remains: "the mediation jams, it no longer 'vanishes' in that which ought to ground it" (p. 19). As I see it, yes, it is true that Hegel shows the *demand* for a universal without conflicts with other universals but does not show its *necessity*. But this is not to say that the argument is not plausible—especially if we keep it in mind that Hegel shows the universality of the state to be the *ground* (this is his true argument on the supersession of the mediation) and *primary* factor of the particular and formal universalities of civil society, positing them as its moments.

68. Axel Honneth (2001) criticizes Hegel's decision to place the universalist institution of the corporation within civil society rather than within state ("that way he would at least have been spared the embarrassment of having to accommodate in the same sphere two completely different forms of recognition, the first linked to transactions mediated by the market and the second to value-oriented interactions," trans. p. 77). For Honneth, Hegel failed to do so because of his tendency to exclude the dimension of the intersubjective relation from the sphere of the state, favoring instead the vertical dimension of the relation between individual and universal. I shall discuss the intersubjective relations within the sphere of the state in the next chapter, but I bring up Honneth's objection here because it poses the key question of the role of individuality in Hegel's theory of the state—the question of its freedom, and of its relations with other individualities—and thus alerts us to the possible limits of this theory.

Chapter 3

1. For a detailed analysis of Hegel's development during his years in Jena see Ruggiu 2009.

2. On this question see Manfred Riedel (1969), in particular his brilliant essay "Criticism of Natural Law Theory" (trans. pp. 76–104).

3. Riedel 1971, p. 121.

4. Riedel 1969, trans. p. 100.

5. Ibid., trans. p, 103. We find similar considerations in his 1970 essay: "Hegel decidedly rejects this representation of a theological-metahistorical 'law of

nature.' The necessity, for example, that is attributed to the existence of the state in relation to the being of the individual means nothing more than that for the individual it is a law of nature that he must live in the state; but the necessity of the state is based on the law of freedom, which is not an immutable nature but the historical concept itself in its movement, and which gives itself the form of self-conscious will" (Riedel 1970, p. 11). There is no natural law that causes individuals to live together and to constitute a state: Hegel decidedly rejects any such teleology, just as he rejects the pessimistic representation of a state of nature that is a war of all against all. The basis of the state is neither natural association nor the flight from natural war—rather, it is freedom and its actualization.

6. Taylor 1979a, p. 76.

7. Ibid., p. 76.

8. In the Introduction (note 6) I remarked that the Hegelian notion of "Idea" takes on a strongly objectivistic meaning in the *Philosophy of Right*.

9. Taylor 1979a, p. 82.

10. The category of *Wirklichkeit* is, for Hegel, the fundamental attribute of the state, as he emphasizes repeatedly throughout the first paragraphs dedicated to his political conception. See, for example, section 260: "The state is the actuality of concrete freedom."

11. "What is rational is actual; and what is actual is rational" (PR 14/20).

12. Riedel 1970, p. 13.

13. Bubner 1996, p. 137.

14. Ibid., p. 138. "A philosophy that comprehends its time in thoughts does not conform to the *journalistic* task of reporting on the facts of the day or on what from one time to the next is believed to be so. Here no faithful description of the existing order is pursued, since the existing order is evidently not the same as thought. [. . .] Philosophy must come to terms with a *difference between surface and substance*, between fundamental tendency and mere current events, or between what seems actual and that whose existence can be rationally legitimated" (Bubner 2002, p. 158). In other words: "What is comprehended in thoughts is thus historically structured actuality without the constantly accompanying appearance constituted by contingency" (ibid., p. 159).

15. For Michael Theunissen (1970) the theological background is the true key for interpreting the unity of the rational and the actual, since it presupposes the Christian figure of the *incarnation*: "only after the actualization of reason through Christ can actuality come to be known as rational" (p. 440). At the same time, however, this theological root contains, for Theunissen, all the ambiguities of this unity and its inevitably *double result*. On the one hand, it is possible to interpret this actuality, "after Christ brought it to completion," "as *what has to be actualized*, rather than as an object of knowledge" (p. 441). On the other hand, the announcement by the Church "that the *eschaton*, still to come in its completion, already everywhere exists thanks to its anticipation through Christ" (p. 442) makes it possible for Hegel to project "the factuality of the divine reconciliation onto the plane of the social realities of his time." In this way he ends up by eliminating "the gap that separates

the level of the subjective process of reconciliation currently attained from the future actualization of the kingdom of God in a world that presses beyond itself"; which is to say, he eliminates the qualitative difference between "absolute-objective and merely subjective-objective reconciliation" (p. 441). For Theunissen, it is this absolutization of the Christological event that led to the separation of Christian eschatology from that of the Jews, allowing Hegel to ground his absolutization of the existent theologically. As I see it, Theunissen's reading stems from an excessively unilateral interpretation of the Christian *eschaton*: it is not clear why he favors the "already" over the "not yet" when their equilibrium is in fact an essential element of Christian theology. This distortion has a series of consequences for the interpretation of Hegelian philosophy. It must never be forgotten that Hegel's undeniable favoring of the present over the future dimension is coupled with a *normative* conception of the actual that prevents identification of the actual [*wirklich*] with the factual [*real, faktisch*]. On this question, apart from the present remarks I refer the reader to section 2.2 above, on the relation in Hegel between being and the "ought."

16. Riedel 1970, p. 13.

17. The notion of objective spirit "leaving aside its interconnection with the whole of the Hegelian system, seems to me to contain the thesis that all social reality has a rational structure" (Honneth 2001, trans. p. 6).

18. Ibid., p. 6.

19. Hegel confirms this in a passage from his Remarks on section 272: "How the *concept* and subsequently, in concrete fashion, the Idea, become determined in themselves [. . .] can be learned from logic (though not, of course, from the logic commonly in use)." Taylor comments: "[The] content [of universal will, the will 'not of man alone but of *Geist*'] is the Idea that produces a differentiated world out of itself. So that there is no longer a lack of determining grounds of action. To put this less succinctly, Hegel's free rational will escapes vacuity because unlike Kant's it does not remain merely universal but produces a particular content out of itself" (Taylor 1979a, p. 80).

20. "Hegel equates traditional metaphysical theory directly as such with knowledge of the age and the present. Philosophy as knowledge of being is at the same time 'its own time comprehended in thoughts'" (Ritter 1957, trans. pp. 39–40).

21. Rossella Bonito Oliva (2000) particularly emphasized the "spiritual" essence of second nature, which "contains traces and testimony of the work of the spirit" (p. 139). By the same token the *character* of modern human beings, in which freedom has taken root, makes them no longer reducible to mere naturalness. In other words, they "can assert themselves only through their no longer being merely natural because there is, or there was, a concrete exercise—an act—of freedom in the synchronic and diachronic dimension of the formation of human beings" (p. 163).

22. Bubner 2002, p. 165.

23. Taylor 1979a, p. 83.

24. Claudio Cesa (1981) wrote, in this regard, that freedom and necessity find their reconciliation in the modern world when the individual makes his own

"that which at first had appeared to be destiny" (p. 67). On the reconciliation of freedom and necessity in Hegel see Laska 1974.

25. Ritter 1969, trans. p. 172.

26. Ibid., p. 177.

27. Larmore 1987, p. 101.

28. Ibid., pp. 102–103. In recognizing the validity of Hegel's project, Larmore distances himself at the same time. He maintains that Hegel posited his conception of ethical life in an organic model of society in which there is no real distinction between the individual and the political level—that is, in which the state "must have an institutional order that reflects our full self-understanding" (ibid., p. 103), by which he means a people's specific conception of the good. But in fact, as we have seen, Hegel says nothing of the sort. His conception of the good is not particularistic, linked to traditions, nations, or peoples. For Hegel the good is identical with freedom and therefore maintains all the universal validity of Kantian freedom, which thus re-presents itself also in the condition of ethical life.

29. In this context the first words of the first paragraph on "Ethical Life" take on even broader meaning: "Ethical life is the *Idea of freedom* as the <u>living good</u>" (§ 142, my underlining). Posited as "living good," ethical life collects the entire precipitate of the dynamic of morality within itself. It is that good which posits itself as the synthesis of justice and happiness, but it is also that good which posits itself as the synthesis of moral subjectivity and ethical objectivity.

30. Bubner 1989, trans. p. 161 (translation modified: see Bubner 1989, p. 109). Bubner maintains that, for Hegel, the process of *Bildung* will not be completed as long as it continues to be administered by subjective reason—that is, by the understanding. Hence, in his interpretation, Hegel proposes to replace the intellectualistic regulation of cultural and social processes with a regime of objective reason. The modern state, albeit a product of *Bildung*, realizes this very transition from the understanding to reason, and this entails the end of the dialectic.

31. Menke 1996, p. 304.

32. Ibid., p. 305.

33. Cesa 1981, p. 177.

34. Hegel's ambitious project consists in rendering the modern principle of autonomy *compatible* with its contrary principle, namely, with the ancient idea of the primacy of the community. His fundamental challenge thus consists in "drawing the borders of a *new community* capable of 'tolerating' the subjective principle of freedom" and in finding the connection "between subjective freedom and objective freedom, between morality and ethical life" (Bonito Oliva 2000, p. 11, my italics).

35. Hegel makes this even more explicit in his Remarks to the following paragraph, where he refers to the reconciliation between particular and universal as a *relation between interest and duty*: "The moment of particularity is also essential, and its satisfaction is therefore entirely necessary; in the process of fulfilling his duty, the individual must somehow attain his own interest and satisfaction or settle his own account, and from his situation within the state a right must accrue to him whereby the universal cause [*Sache*] becomes *his own particular* cause" (§ 261 R).

36. Bubner 1996, p. 160.

37. Ibid., p. 162.

38. Bubner 1995, trans. p. 96.

39. Ibid. (On p. 97 of the translation the sentence is omitted; see pp. 82–83 of the German text.)

40. Bubner 2002, p. 165. I consider these observations of Bubner's the best reply to criticisms—such as Ernst Tugendhat's—that basically arise from a misunderstanding of the essential function of subjectivity within Hegel's theory of ethical life: "The possibility of an independent and critical relation to the community or the state is not admitted by Hegel. Rather, we hear the following set of claims: The existing laws have an absolute authority; what the individual has to do is firmly established in a community; the private conscience of the individual must disappear; trust takes the place of reflection. This is what Hegel means by the overcoming of *Moralität* in ethical life" (Tugendhat 1979, trans. pp. 315–316). As we have just seen, trust, far from being irrational adherence, emerges precisely from autonomous and self-responsible subjectivity. By the same token, what Tugendhat calls "community" ["*Gemeinwesen*"] by no means connotes an "indistinct mass" in Hegel; rather, it is composed of the autonomous individuals, jealous of their own interests, who have grown up and become aware of themselves within civil society.

41. As Ludwig Siep made clear (1992), the "trust" Hegel refers to is not blind obedience to *every* act of state authority but, rather, a fundamental attitude that precedes assent and dissent regarding *specific acts* of state authority. This "trust" is a disposition that stems from an awareness of the "accordance of my 'substantial and particular interest' with the interest and end of the state" (p. 234). This basic trust is thus not to be confused with the explicit assent to *specific* orientations of individual states—an assent with which Hegel does not deal. Neither does he deal with the question of the proper attitude of citizens who live in a state that is not the product of a free will, and who therefore do not recognize themselves in it. Siep concludes: "Hegel evades the question of determining the relationship between the citizen and such states" (p. 235).

42. Even though Habermas (1987, p. 173) had broached the expression "constitutional patriotism" in a very different context from Hegel's, Honneth chose to refer it to section 268 of the *Philosophy of Right* (Honneth 2001, trans. p. 79).

43. I traced the basic lines of the notion of recognition in the political sphere in Cortella 2008b, where I also distinguished between a bottom-up recognition by the citizens (legal recognition) and a top-down recognition by the institutions (full-fledged political recognition). It seems, however, that Honneth did not grasp the full importance of this objectivist aspect of recognition in Hegel. He complains that, in the *Philosophy of Right*, "at the point at which Hegel starts to speak about the corresponding relationship of recognition in the chapter on 'the state,' a horizontal relationship has suddenly been replaced by a vertical one. [. . .] Here the subjects do not relate to each other in a spirit of recognition in order to achieve the universal through common activities, but the universal seems to be given as something substantial, so that the recognition acquires the sense of a confirmation from below of

what is above [*von unten nach oben*]" (Honneth 2001, trans. pp. 78–79). But this is the only recognition possible for the other citizens in a macrodimension such as the state: it is impossible to imagine a public life in which recognition of the rights of others should come about directly, through the reciprocal exchange of rights and duties. It is by recognizing the legitimacy of the laws capable of guaranteeing these rights and duties that each individual citizen obtains recognition.

44. Siep 1979.

45. Ibid., p. 278 ff. and p. 284.

46. Ibid., pp. 125–126.

47. If Hegel had been consistent with the premises of his theory of recognition he would also have had to consider the recognition of singularity as an "end" of the process—as an end of "second-degree" recognition (ibid., pp. 144–145).

48. Ibid., p. 293.

49. Hösle 1987b, pp. 190–195.

50. Ibid., p. 190.

51. Angehrn 1991, p. 27.

52. Ibid., p. 32.

53. Hofmeister 1974, p. 156 and p. 154.

54. Ibid., p. 154.

55. Ibid., p. 157 and p. 154.

56. In light of its exemplary clarity, I quote Bubner's comment on this passage in its entirety: "Individuals can develop *only in the states* of a modern type, but not on behalf of their autonomous subjectivity. They need the free space guaranteed by institutions to test their personal particularity in its extreme ramifications. Without this framework they would ultimately find themselves in a sort of competitive struggle, which the doctrine of the *status naturae* artificially projects to the origin when, on the contrary, it constantly lurks in the shoals of everyday social life. Without the support of institutions individuals would end up entangled in conflicts where they have neither strength nor time to care for their personalities. In this respect Hegel's thesis is in accordance with the credo of liberalism," which from Humboldt to Mill "appointed the state as guarantor of the personal rights of freedom" (Bubner 1996, pp. 156–157).

57. Bubner remarks: "Only as a citizen in the framework of existing right is the human being free" (Bubner 2002, p. 173).

58. As Franco Chiereghin emphasized, this solution of the relation between individual and state, duty and right, individual freedom and substantiality of the universal is evidence of Spinoza's influence on Hegel—an influence that endured from his early works in Jena on into his mature work. It was Spinoza who insisted that the individual not only maintains his rights in the state but, more radically, that it is thanks to the state that he is recognized as a legally responsible subject. Paradoxically, then, Hegel obtained "from the metaphysics that delineated the most radical model of immanence in our speculative tradition his principle of the incoercible freedom of the subject" (Chiereghin 1980, p. 107). Hence "the individuality of the person, whom Spinoza presents as the subject of right not in the unsustain-

able state of nature but within that concrete organization of freedom which is the state, constitutes, at the same time, the starting point of the Hegelian philosophy of right" (ibid., p. 108).

59. "It is by no means necessary that this contract, as a coalition of every particular and private will within a people into a common and public will [. . .], be presupposed as a *fact* (as a fact it is indeed not possible) [. . .] This contract is instead *only an idea* of reason, which, however, has its undoubted practical reality, namely to bind every legislator to give his laws in such a way that they *could* have arisen from the united will of a whole people and to regard each subject, insofar as he wants to be a citizen, as if he has joined in voting for such a will. For this is the touchstone of any public law's conformity with right" (Kant 1793, trans. pp. 296–297).

60. "In justice as fairness the original position of equality corresponds to the state of nature in the traditional theory of the social contract. This original position is not, of course, thought of as an actual historical state of affairs, much less as a primitive condition of culture. It is understood as a purely hypothetical situation characterized so as to lead to a certain conception of justice" (Rawls 1971, p. 12). Hence this hypothetical assumption only serves to establish that "our social situation is just if it is such that by this sequence of hypothetical agreements we would have contracted into the general system of rules that defines it" (ibid. p. 13).

61. Manfred Riedel (1970) noted the importance of the antinaturalist argument in Hegel's opposition to contractualism. While it is quite true that the contractual theory postulates a break with the natural state, it is also true that when a multitude of individuals deliberate on the constitution of a state it is their interests, needs, and drives that determine their decision. In Kant, in Fichte, in Rousseau, the state, though grounded not in nature but in freedom, ultimately turns out to depend on nature. "But in Kant and Fichte (and in Rousseau before them) the principle that they make the basis of the doctrine of right comes into contradiction with the implementation they give it. Nature, which, on the one hand, the principle of the state excludes [. . .] on the other is introduced once again by the fact that they exalt the will only in the determinate form of the 'individual will,' as 'particular individual'" (pp. 40–41).

62. As Bubner acutely observed, taking an original contract as the condition of the state and of right is contradictory: the contract is regulated by right, but such a contract would have to precede the institution of right. A contract that has the value of right *before right even exists* is a total fiction. In other words, right, the institutional order, order in general, have to precede any contract between individuals (see Bubner 1995, p. 78; 1996, p. 170).

63. Bubner 1996, p. 171.

64. Robert Pippin forcefully emphasized the *priority* of this objective normativity over the subject's individual reasons. At the same time, however—this is his thesis—institutional restriction precedes the individual but does not limit him. On the contrary, it is *the true condition of his free agency*: "Hegel is clearly stressing another dimension of the rationality claim, its objective side. Individual

reflection and deliberation may be institution-bound, ruled, or governed by institutional rules [. . .], but such dependence is not a qualification or restriction on
freedom, understood as an individual's exercise of rational agency, because such
institutions themselves can be said to be objectively rational" (Pippin 2008, pp. 241–
242).

65. Taylor 1979b, p. 217.

66. Ibid., p. 228.

67. Ibid., p. 223.

68. Ibid., p. 229.

69. Wellmer 1993, trans. p. 10.

70. Ibid., p. 10.

71. Schaber 1989, p. 7.

72. Ibid., p. 7.

73. Ibid., p. 144.

74. Ibid., p. 5.

75. As Hermann Lübbe wrote, Hegelian philosophy is not "a theory of political restoration" but "a progressive theory of constitutional monarchy. As such it is
a theory that comprises the postulates of liberalism. But it is polemical against a
liberalism whose subject is the postulating people [*das postulierende Volk*]" (Lübbe
1963, pp. 50–51).

76. Bubner 1996, pp. 158 and 159.

77. For Ludwig Siep (1992) there are two reasons for the weakening of this
division. The first is ontotheological and stems from Hegel's thesis that the power
of the state is the incarnation of the absolute and the politico-historical representation of the incarnation of the Christian God (a thesis that, for Siep, can no longer
be reasonably defended); the second stems from Hegel's singular repression of the
spiritual (and, in the highest sense, *free*) character of the subjects' action in society.
In the *Philosophy of Right* the individuals are described in a way that is "surpris-
ingly restricted to concepts of the philosophy of nature" (p. 321); consequently,
entrusting them with the sovereignty of the state would mean falling back into a
mechanistic conflict between opposing interests: "According to his 'organic' conception, the division of powers has another meaning: that of the differentiation and
development of the universal will"—that is, of a single will that can be expressed in
a single individual. "Only an individual will ultimately guarantees that these [groups
or organizations] are not blocked or make themselves self-sufficient, but continue
to be subordinate to the existence of the state" (p. 321).

78. "The development [*Ausbildung*] of the state to constitutional monarchy
is the achievement of the modern world" (§ 273 R).

79. Marcuse 1941 (1960), p. 217. Others, however, have found motifs that go
far beyond contingent historico-political considerations. Michael Theunissen (1970),
for example, saw a significant theological background in this solution. Not only
does the king "assume the features of the God that revealed Himself in Christ" (p.
444), but the merely natural character of the person of the king is itself an expres-

sion of the theological figure of Christ's incarnation, of God's "making Himself human nature and flesh." As we have seen, Theunissen's entire interpretation is designed to show the Christological background of Hegel's doctrine of the state, as evidenced by the "numerous theological predicates Hegel attributes to the state" and his "discourse on the sovereignty of the state as the 'veritable absolute final end.'" Indeed, the concept of absolute final end [*Endzweck*] is "used by Hegel to characterize the *eschaton*, which God anticipated with the life, death and resurrection of His son" (p. 443). Ludwig Siep (1992) follows this line of interpretation when he writes that "the unification of the divine Idea with nature and human spirit in the person of Christ," which "for Hegel is the most speculative dogma," constitutes "the theological pendant of his theory of monarchy" (p. 323). But, at the same time, this "necessary 'contraction' of the supreme legitimation of the sovereignty of the state in a natural individual" is one of the most "problematic" aspects of his political philosophy, since it rests "on ontological premises" that "perhaps have to be completely abandoned" (p. 327).

80. See also the corresponding paragraphs in the *Philosophy of Right*, in particular sections 321–322, where Hegel emphasizes this *excluding* character of the state's individuality, characterized by the old conception of individual freedom and identity as grounded exclusively in a negative relation toward the other.

81. This nemesis of the state is curious indeed, with the state now reduced to a mere "ideality" in the face of world history, when it had itself represented the true "actuality" (§ 257) with respect to the spheres of the family and civil society, reduced in their turn to the rank of mere "ideal spheres" (§ 262).

82. Miguel Giusti (1987) showed how the world spirit's transcending of ethical life means, *first*, that *Sittlichkeit* is downgraded to a "moment of world history" and to the "phenomenal form of a *Weltgeist* at a higher level" (p. 323) and, *second*, renders the process of the subject's recognizing himself in historical substantiality incomplete, since "this substance is a contingent moment within world history" (p. 324).

83. The *unwillingness* of the historical occurrence with respect to the will of the subject is a central element in Hegel's conception of history: it is impossible to act in history and claim at the same time to reduce historical events to determinations of one's own will and consciousness. This is the real basis of Hegel's critique of the French Revolution: in an excess of rationalism, the revolutionaries claim to reduce history to a theater in which their will and consciousness is realized, holding objectivity hostage to their subjectivity. But *the subjects do not have history at their disposal* and, whatever their "scenario" may be, in the end historical objectivity will not play it out according to their subjective intentions. In this sense the revolution proves, willy-nilly, to be *more Hegelian than Hegel*, because it thinks—hyperidealistically—it can realize in history the complete identity of subject and object. On the relation between theory and praxis in Hegel against the background of the more complex relation between practical subjectivity and historical objectivity, see Habermas 1963/71.

84. For Bubner locating ethical life within the nation state does not compromise its universalist character, since the experience of the citizen of a state is itself an experience of liberation from the egotism and particularism of a class or race (Bubner 2002, p. 188). In any event, for Bubner no other form of universalist experience is imaginable in the political domain. At the same time, however, Bubner's substantially legitimate justification of the Hegelian viewpoint risks legitimating a de facto historical experience (the existence of individual nation states) as the only possible actualization of the universalism of ethical life, failing to recognize in *Hegel's own theory of ethical life* the elements that lead it beyond the borders of the nation state.

85. Ottmann 1982, p. 383.

86. Ibid., p. 390. While he did take account of Theunissen's reading in which the three parts of the *Philosophy of Right* (abstract right, morality, ethical life) are correlated with the three parts of the *Science of Logic* (being, essence, concept), Ottmann saw the conclusion of the work as a manifestation of the ground of its entire course—and this, clearly, calls Theunissen's reading into question. In any event, as we shall see, the *Philosophy of Right* does *not* conclude with the war between states.

87. "Spirit as a second nature is the negation of the spirit, and this negation is all the more profound the more the self-consciousness of spirit is blind to its own naturalness. This is what happens to Hegel. His world spirit is the ideology of natural history" (Adorno 1966–67, trans. p. 356, translation modified). Adorno's thesis is that the "higher" rationality of Hegelian history masks a perfectly mechanical natural logic, which now takes its revenge by violently forcing itself on subjects.

88. Ottmann 1982, p. 391.

89. Ibid., p. 391.

90. Hösle 1987b, p. 221. For the same reason, following the logic of the concept, Hösle maintained that the Hegelian notion of war as something necessary and even affirmative must be rejected.

91. Ibid., pp. 219–220.

92. Hegel described this third subject as "the absolute substance that is the unity of the different independent self-consciousnesses which, in their opposition, enjoy perfect freedom and independence: 'I' that is 'We' and 'We' that is 'I'"; he specifies that "with this, we already have before us the concept of *spirit*" (PhG 108/PS 110).

93. Marx 1927, trans. p. 16.

94. Ibid., p. 16.

95. Marcuse 1941 (1960), p. ix.

96. Ibid., p. ix.

97. In modern society "man remained subject to the laws of an unmastered economy, and had to be tamed by a strong state, capable of coping with the social contradictions. The final truth had therefore to be sought in another sphere of reality" (ibid., p. 164). And: "Although Hegel says that the stage of historical development attained at his time reveals that the idea has become real, it 'exists' as the comprehended world, *present in thought*, as the 'system of science'" (ibid., p. 164).

Chapter 4

1. The "left-wing" critics of Hegel (such as Marcuse) who reproach him for separating theory and praxis and failing to apply freedom to sociohistorical relations remain prisoners of this emphatic conception.

2. Ilting 1983, p. 246.

3. Ibid., p. 246.

4. Ilting 1982, p. 226 (but, on the subject, see the entire essay, pp. 225–253).

5. Becchi and Hoppe, editors' *Nachwort* [Afterword] to Ilting 1993 (in particular, pp. 359–360).

6. Vittorio Hösle was sharply critical of Ilting's position. For Hösle, Hegel's identity of the rational and the actual refutes Ilting's thesis that the *Philosophy of Right* presents a merely descriptive theory. Indeed, Hegel's formulation entails the selective individuation of the *rational* within the numerous manifestations represented by historical *reality*. For Hösle, Hegel's own assertion that the *Philosophy of Right* is "an attempt *to comprehend and portray the state as an inherently rational entity*" (PR 15/21) confirms this approach. Hence Hegel's work has the explicit "intention of developing what within the factually existent can be comprehended as rational. Hegel's *Philosophy of Right* must therefore be understood as a *normative theory* on a determinate subject area" (Hösle 1987a, pp. 29–30, my italics).

7. Schnädelbach 2000, p. 351.

8. For Joachim Ritter this hermeneutic role is, for Hegel, the true task of philosophy: to be "its own time comprehended in thoughts" (Ritter 1957, trans. p. 40; cf. PR 15/21). Günther Rohrmoser (1961) concurred: "In contrast to the positing of abstract postulates and to continual planning incessantly renewing itself, Hegelian philosophy is distinguished by a hermeneutics of existing historical reality, a hermeneutics of the world as it is, and not as it ought to be" (p. 85). Rüdiger Bubner (1970) agreed, as did Schnädelbach who, however, harshly criticized the consequences: "The price of Hegel's speculative and, at the same time, normative historicism is high: the place where the question of the normative rightness of action is decided is no longer the self-conscious individual, reflectively certain of his moral identity, but world history. There is no room here for a Kantian moral principle. Hegel's practical philosophy knows only legal norms and institutional duties and, beyond them, the boundless normative power of world-historical facts" (Schnädelbach 2000, p. 352). This criticism is quite different from Ilting's: while Ilting maintained that in Hegel it is *historical objectivity* that determines the rationality and ethicality of a sociopolitical order (relativistic historicism), Schnädelbach insisted that the criterion is at a higher level, in the *philosophy of history*—that is, in an absolutist philosophical gaze capable of establishing the rationality of world development (speculative historicism) independently of the opinions of the individuals who live in that world and that society.

9. It is in virtue of concretely existing individuals that spirit has a "sense of itself" [*Selbstgefühl*] that is actualized only in this type of historical subject. As we

have seen, "the subject bears *spiritual witness* to them [the ethical powers] as to *its own essence*, in which it has its *sense of itself*" (PR § 147).

10. The reference here is to Theunissen 1982.

11. Vittorio Hösle (1987a) insisted that the transition from ethical life to absolute spirit entails a loss of the intersubjective perspective attained by objective spirit and a return to the perspective of isolated subjectivity. But this position is hardly tenable. Monological subjectivism characterizes the *Philosophy of Right* from beginning to end, despite Hegel's many openings to intersubjectivity and recognition. In short, the premise of this "last word of the Hegelian system" constituted by the "absolute spirit that withdraws ever more into its own subjectivity" until it reaches the "solitude of the thinking philosopher who cannot associate with the world" (p. 53) resides precisely in objective spirit, of which it cannot be said—as Hösle did—that it "constitutes intersubjectivity" (p. 48).

12. Hösle agreed that the transition from ethical life to the viewpoint of absolute spirit is perfectly consistent with the general structure of the Hegelian system and in particular with the coordinates of the *Science of Logic*. The *logic of the concept* is the necessary reference for the philosophy of spirit, and if "right and the state only correspond to the first two sections of the logic of the concept," we have to conclude that "only absolute spirit corresponds to the third section, to the Idea as such" (Hösle 1987a, p. 45). Accordingly, even though the Hegel of the *Philosophy of Right* employs an "objectivistic" notion of the Idea, in the end he asserts the meaning of the Idea elaborated in the third section of the *Science of Logic*, in which it is clear that the category of "objectivity" investigated in the second section has been overcome. "The Idea, which is the object of the third section, is not exactly this objectification of the concept but, rather, its withdrawal into ever purer ideality" (ibid., p. 45).

13. It is clear that the *Science of Logic* intends to tackle the problem of otherness in earnest. Its great challenge consists in finding a way to speak of a true otherness without calling the primacy of the logical into question, and—even more radically—in the fact that otherness itself cannot be spoken of outside the logical (on this complex question see Bellan 2002). But this complex engagement with otherness risks being nullified precisely by Hegel's conclusive claim to resolve the process of mediating in an ultimate immediacy capable of preserving the *whole* truth of the process within itself. In any event, without this final claim the Hegelian system as we know it today would not have been possible.

14. The references are to Theunissen 1978 and Theunissen 1982.

15. On this premise Robert Pippin affirmed the structural intersubjectivity of Hegelian *Sittlichkeit* in its different spheres. His thesis is that not even in the *Philosophy of Right* did Hegel abandon the intersubjective logic of recognition—he only transformed it: "I want to treat Hegel's mature theory of ethical life or the ethical community [. . .] as an extension of the original, or Jena-period theory of recognition, not as its abandonment" (Pippin 2008, pp. 183–184). If individual freedom has social bases, it must presuppose reciprocal recognition between individuals: "The standpoint of objective spirit, or the standpoint of the *Philosophy of Right*,

presupposes that some mutuality of recognition has been achieved, and that this achievement establishes 'objectively' a level of freedom necessary for true sociality. (That is, he makes clear that he is very far from having abandoned an intersubjective theory of freedom for a monological one)" (p. 199). In fact, as my examination of Hegel's texts has shown, the *intersubjective* logic of recognition remains merely *implicit* in the *Philosophy of Right*—particularly in the sphere of the state—where it is replaced by a logic of the citizens' *bottom-up recognition* of the state and by a logic of the *self-recognition* of spiritual substance.

16. On a number of occasions I have traced the general lines of a theory of recognition that I have described as "normative" in order to distinguish it from other competing theories. The fullest exposition is the one expressed schematically in 163 "provisional theses" (Cortella 2005a). The other essays on the subject are in Cortella 2002, pp. 373–396, and in Cortella 2003, 2004, 2005b, 2008a, 2008b, 2010.

17. Adorno 1966–67, trans. p. 191. (Note: In the translation *Negative Dialectics* the first sentence of this passage is omitted. I quote the German in full: "Über die Romantik hinaus, die sich als Weltschmerz, Leiden an der Entfremdung fühlte, erhebt sich Eichendorffs Wort 'Schöne Fremde.'")

18. It is clear that my use of the notion of "ethics" is substantially different from the contextual, pluralistic, and particular notion utilized in the contemporary debate. Jürgen Habermas (1983 and 1991), for example, pits a notion of contextual "ethics" connected with subjective conceptions of the "good life" against his proposal for a universalist "morality." By contrast, in my approach ethics indicates a normative structure that is completely universal, insofar as it is connected with the formation of our subjectivity. In this sense I uphold the tradition of Hegel himself, whose challenge to modernity consisted precisely in his proposal of a universal ethical life.

19. See Honneth 1991 and 1992.

20. On this point see Cortella 2008b.

21. Forst 1994, trans. pp. 283–292. In characterizing political recognition as a separate sphere, Forst criticized Honneth's attempt to locate social esteem in the domain of the political community: for Forst, this would be possible only at the price of considering the political community to be an "ethical" community (in the Habermasian sense)—that is, a community founded on a sharing of the same value orientations (ibid., pp. 281–283). I think Forst is quite right about this, but I do not understand why he then went on to correct Honneth's differentiation between the sphere of social esteem and that of family love, unifying both in the context of "ethical" recognition. As I see it, the relational medium of affection has nothing to do with an "ethical" sharing of values and life plans and must therefore be kept distinct from it.

22. Ibid., pp. 280–281.

23. Honneth 2001, trans. p. 8.

24. Calogero 1962, p. 370.

25. Bubner 1996, pp. 188–189.

26. Schnädelbach 1986, p. 57.

27. Ibid., pp. 56–57.

28. Wellmer 1993, trans. p. 50.

29. Ibid., p. 52. The expression "democratic ethical life" [*demokratische Sitt-lichkeit*] arose in the context of the German participation in the debate between liberals and communitarians as an attempt to employ Hegelian conceptuality to reconcile communitarian positions with a universalist paradigm. Albrecht Wellmer used it for the first time in his 1989 essay, written in English, *Models of Freedom in the Modern World* (in German in Wellmer 1993; see trans. pp. 3–37, in particular pp. 14–15). Axel Honneth (1992) then took up the expression, emphasizing its root in the Hegelian theory of ethical life: "The idea of post-traditional, democratic ethical life [. . .] was first proposed by the young Hegel and further developed, on postmetaphysical premises, by Mead" (trans. p. 175). Wellmer re-presented it at a congress dedicated to the liberal-communitarian controversy titled *Gemeinschaft und Gerichtigkeit* [Community and Justice] in Frankfurt in May of 1992 (see Brumlik and Brunkhorst 1993), with his lecture "Bedingungen einer demokratischen Kultur. Zur Debatte zwischen Liberalen und Kommunitaristen" (later published in Wellmer 1993, trans. pp. 3–37, "Conditions of a Democratic Culture: Remarks on the Liberal-Communitarian Debate"). Forst (1994), too, used the expression, which, in the end, was also adopted by Jürgen Habermas (1996, trans. p. 385), renowned for his procedural and formalistic approach to practical questions.

30. Habermas 1992, trans. p. 302.

31. "One can easily understand this accommodating lifeworld context in the sense of a 'postconventional *Sittlichkeit*' or a democratic ethos" (Habermas 1996, trans. p. 385). However, it must be said that Habermas's endorsement of the idea of an ethical democracy is not without reservations. He specified, in fact, that it is to be assumed in a "weak reading," in which one must not "ultimately place the burden of democratically legitimating law *entirely* on the political virtues of united citizens" (ibid., p. 385). In other words, ethical life is to be understood as a psychological-functional precondition for the necessities of the democratic state but not as a fully legitimating condition. Legitimation rests exclusively on argumentative formality: "Processes of deliberation and decision making must be set up in such a way that discourses and bargaining function like a filter: only those topics and contributions that are supposed 'to count' in reaching a decision are permitted to pass through" (ibid., p. 385). For Leonardo Ceppa "in Habermas the expression 'postconventional ethical life' has the same semantic ambivalence as 'constitutional patriotism': in both cases it is a question of combining [. . .] the universalism of validity with the particularism of factuality" (Ceppa 2009, pp. 19–20). But this combination is not perfectly balanced: the good, that is, the ethical background, only has a "genetic priority" (ibid., p. 21) over the right but not a "methodological priority" (ibid., p. 20); which is to say, liberal-democratic habits precede argumenta-tive procedures but cannot replace them. From this point of view Habermas remains a Kantian who, even when he "exalts Hegelian ethical life against Kantian morality" (ibid., p. 21), will not permit—in the context of justification—the universality of norms to depend on the ethics that stands behind our backs. In my opinion, this formalist claim that places the entire burden of justification on discursive procedure

is destined to remain unsatisfied, for at least two reasons. The first is that the ethical background cannot be neutralized by any type of formal procedure: it enters into the argumentations and conditions the rational agreements that are reached on the basis of these argumentations. The second is that without this shared ethical background no argumentative engagement would be possible: no dialogue and no agreement is imaginable between individuals who have not recognized one another and accepted one another as "worthy" to participate together in a discussion. In short, contemporary ethical life is *constitutive* of democratic legitimacy both in the sense of genesis and in that of validity.

32. Habermas 1990, trans. p. 446.

33. Ceppa 2009, p. 121.

34. Walzer 1990, p. 21.

35. Ibid., p. 14.

36. This accounts for the *difficult coexistence* between the individual who has become autonomous and the ethical institutions that have generated him. Although Hegel thought differently, a complete reconciliation between this individual and the social totality is not possible. It is precisely the failure to attain this reconciliation that makes the relation between individuality and the world of right and legality *structurally unstable*, despite the many elements they share.

37. Walzer 1991, p. 301.

38. Ibid., p. 302.

39. Wellmer 1993, trans. p. 34.

40. Ibid., p. 14 (my italics).

41. Schaber 1989, p. 133.

42. Ibid., p. 133.

43. "Hegel's philosophy of right is an attempt to construct the concept of ethical life beyond the 'standpoint of ethical life'" (Wellmer 1993, trans. pp. 14–15).

44. Wellmer 1993, trans. p. 50.

45. Ibid., p. 51.

46. Habermas 1993, trans. pp. 138–139.

47. Wellmer 1993, trans. p 51.

48. Ibid., p. 60.

49. Ferrara 1992, p. LIII.

50. As Ceppa wrote, "the complexity of modernity is neither *systemically* coordinable nor *democratically* administrable by the imperialistic and centralized perspective of a universal particularistic *ethical life.*" Hence when the "Pax Americana" rejects "multilateralism and democratic decentralization" it becomes inadequate not only on the plane of functionality but above all "on the plane of legitimacy" (Ceppa 2009, p. 97). The ethical life I propose is based on a *political*, not a *cultural* universalism; an ethical life of *rules*, not of *values.*

51. Adorno 1966–67, trans. p. 310.

52. Menke 1996, p. 12.

53. Menke 1993, pp. 230–231.

54. Wellmer 1993, trans. p. 61.

55. Ibid., p. 36.

56. Habermas 1981.

57. Wellmer 1993, p. 36.

58. Honneth 1992, trans. p. 177.

59. "After the tragic loss of ethical life, the integration produced by the good can be constituted only by the specific (and therefore *plural*) 'decision' of the subjects involved. The reflection of the good does not lead to an objective order that serves as a criterion for the selective reflection of those involved: the integration produced by the good comes about subjectively" (Menke 1996, p. 305).

60. Honneth 1992, trans. p. 173.

61. Honneth 1993, p. 263.

62. Ibid., p. 269.

Bibliography

Hegel's Works Cited

with the abbreviations of their titles used in the text

1. German Editions

[GW] *Gesammelte Werke*, in Verbindung mit der deutschen Forschungsgemeinschaft, hrg. von der Rheinisch-Westfälischen Akademie der Wissenschaften. Hamburg: Felix Meiner Verlag, 1968, ff.

- Band 1: *Frühe Schriften. Teil 1*, hrg. von F. Nicolin u. G. Schüler, 1989.
- Band 3: *Frühe Exzerpte (1785–1800)*, hrg. von F. Nicolin u. G. Schüler, 1991.
- Band 4: *Jenaer Kritische Schriften*, hrg. von H. Buchner u. O. Pöggeler, 1968. Works from this volume cited in the text: **[DFS]** *Differenz des Fichteschen und Schellingschen Systems der Philosophie*; **[GuW]** *Glauben und Wissen*; **[NR]** *Über die wissenschaftlichen Behandlungsarten des Naturrechts*.
- Band 5: *Schriften und Entwürfe (1799–1808)*, hrg. von M. Baum u. K. R. Meist, 1998.
- Band 6: *Jenaer Systementwürfe I*, hrg. von K. Düsing u. H. Kimmerle, 1975.
- Band 7: *Jenaer Systementwürfe II*, hrg. von R. P. Horstmann u. J. H. Trede, 1971.
- Band 8: *Jenaer Systementwürfe III*, hrg. von R. P. Horstmann, 1976.
- Band 9: **[PhG]** *Phänomenologie des Geistes*, hrg. von W. Bonsiepen u. R. Heede, 1980.
- Band 10: *Nürnberger Gymnasialkurse und Gymnasialreden (1808–1816)*, hrg. von K. Grotsch, 2005.
- Band 11: **[WL11]** *Wissenschaft der Logik. Erster Band. Die objektive Logik (1812/13)*, hrg. von F. Hogemann u. W. Jaeschke, 1978.

- Band 12: **[WL12]** *Wissenschaft der Logik. Zweiter Band. Die subjektive Logik oder die Lehre vom Begriff (1816)*, hrg. von F. Hogemann u. W. Jaeschke, 1981.
- Band 13: *Enzyklopädie der philosophischen Wissenschaften im Grundrisse (1817)*, hrg. von W. Bonsiepen u. K. Grotsch, 2001.
- Band 14.1: **[PR]** *Grundlinien der Philosophie des Rechts. Naturrecht und Staatswissenschaft im Grundrisse*, hrg. von K. Grotsch u. E. Weisser-Lohmann, 2009.
- Band 15: *Schriften und Entwürfe I (1817–1825)*, hrg. von F. Hogemann u. Chr. Jamme, 1990. Work from this volume cited in the text: **[JW]** *Über Friedrich Heinrich Jacobis Werke.*
- Band 16: *Schriften und Entwürfe II (1826–1831)*, hrg. von F. Hogemann u. Chr. Jamme, 1999.
- Band 17: *Vorlesungsmanuskripte I (1816–1831)*, hrg. von W. Jaeschke, 1987.
- Band 18: *Vorlesungsmanuskripte II (1816–1831)*, hrg. von W. Jaeschke, 1995.
- Band 19: *Enzyklopädie der philosophischen Wissenschaften im Grundrisse (1827)*, hrg. von W. Bonsiepen u. H.-Chr. Lucas, 1989.
- Band 20: **[ENC]** **[ENC-L]** *Enzyklopädie der philosophischen Wissenschaften im Grundrisse (1830)*, hrg. von W. Bonsiepen u. H.-Chr. Lucas, 1992.
- Band 21: **[WL21]** *Wissenschaft der Logik. Erster Band. Die Lehre vom Sein (1832)*, hrg. von F. Hogemann u. W. Jaeschke, 1984.

[V]　　*Vorlesungen. Ausgewählte Nachschriften und Manuskripte.* Hamburg: Felix Meiner Verlag, 1983, ff.
- Band 1: *Vorlesungen über Naturrecht und Staatswissenschaft (1817/18)*, hrg. von C. Becker, W. Bonsiepen, A. Gethmann-Siefert, F. Hogemann, W. Jaeschke, Chr. Jamme, H.-Chr. Lucas, K. R. Meist, H. Schneider, 1983.
- Band 2: *Vorlesungen über die Philosophie der Kunst (1823)*, hrg. von A. Gethmann-Siefert, 1998.
- Band 3: *Vorlesungen über die Philosophie der Religion. Teil 1: Der Begriff der Religion*, hrg. von W. Jaeschke, 1983.
- Band 4 a/b: *Vorlesungen über die Philosophie der Religion. Teil 2: Die bestimmte Religion*, in zwei Bänden, hrg. von W. Jaeschke, 1985.
- Band 5: *Vorlesungen über die Philosophie der Religion. Teil 3: Die vollendete Religion*, hrg. von W. Jaeschke, 1984.
- Band 6: *Vorlesungen über die Geschichte der Philosophie. Teil 1: Einleitung. Orientalische Philosophie*, hrg. von P. Garniron u. W. Jaeschke, 1994.
- Band 7: *Vorlesungen über die Geschichte der Philosophie. Teil 2: Griechische Philosophie I: Thales bis Kyniker*, hrg. von P. Garniron u. W. Jaeschke, 1989.

- Band 8: *Vorlesungen über die Geschichte der Philosophie. Teil 3: Griechische Philosophie II: Plato bis Proklos,* hrg. von P. Garniron u. W. Jaeschke, 1996.
- Band 9: *Vorlesungen über die Geschichte der Philosophie. Teil 4: Philosophie des Mittelalters und der neueren Zeit,* hrg. von P. Garniron u. W. Jaeschke, 1986.
- Band 10: *Vorlesungen über die Logik (1831),* hrg. U. Rameil, 2001.
- Band 11: *Vorlesungen über Logik und Metaphysik (1817),* hrg. von K. Gloy, 1992.
- Band 12: *Vorlesungen über die Philosophie der Weltgeschichte (1822/23),* hrg. von K. Brehmer, K. H. Ilting u. H. N. Seelman, 1996.
- Band 13: *Vorlesungen über die Philosophie des Geistes (1827/1828),* hrg. von F. Hespe u. B. Tuschling, 1994.
- Band 14: *Vorlesungen über die Philosophie des Rechts (1819/20),* hrg. von Emil Angehrn, Martin Bondeli u. Hoo Nam Seelman, 2000.
- Band 15: *Vorlesungen über philosophische Enzyklopädie (1812–1813),* hrg. von U. Rameil, 2003.
- Band 16: *Vorlesungen über die Philosophie der Natur (1819/20),* hrg. von Martin Bondeli u. Hoo Nam Seelman, 2002.
- Band 17: *Vorlesungen über die Philosophie der Natur (1825/26),* hrg. von K. Bal, G. Marmasse, Th. Posch, K. Vieweg, 2007.

[EZ]   *Enzyklopädie der philosophischen Wissenschaften im Grundrisse.* Mit Erläuterungen und Zusätzen versehen von L. von Henning, K. L. Michelet und L. Boumann, in G. W. F. Hegel, *Werke in zwanzig Bände,* auf der Grundlage der Werke von 1832–1845 neu edierte Ausgabe, Redaktion E. Moldenhauer und K. M. Michel, Bände 8–10. Frankfurt am Main: Suhrkamp, 1970.

[RZ]   *Grundlinien der Philosophie des Rechts.* Mit Hegels eigenhändigen Notizen und den mündlichen Zusätzen, in G. W. F. Hegel, *Werke in zwanzig Bände,* auf der Grundlage der Werke von 1832–1845 neu edierte Ausgabe, Redaktion E. Moldenhauer und K. M. Michel, Band 7. Frankfurt am Main: Suhrkamp, 1970.

[PhWg]   *Vorlesungen über die Philosophie der Weltgeschichte,* hrg. von G. Lasson, Bände I–IV. Leipzig: Meiner, 1917–1930 (vol. I rev. by J. Hoffmeister 1955; reprinted by Hamburg: Meiner,1968).

[GPh1]   *Vorlesungen über die Geschichte der Philosophie,* hrg. von K. L. Michelet, in G. W. F. Hegel, *Werke. Vollständige Ausgabe durch ein Verein von Freunden des Verewigten,* Bände XIII–XV. Berlin: Duncker und Humblot, 1833–1836, now in G. W. F. Hegel, *Werke in zwanzig Bände,* hrg. von E. Moldenhauer und K. M. Michel, Bände 18–20. Frankfurt am Main: Suhrkamp, 1971.

[GPh2]   *Vorlesungen über die Geschichte der Philosophie*, hrg. von K. L. Michelet, in G. W. F. Hegel, *Werke. Vollständige Ausgabe durch ein Verein von Freunden des Verewigten*, Bände XIII–XV. Berlin: Duncker und Humblot, 1840–1844.

2. English Translations

[DIF]   *The Difference Between Fichte's and Schelling's System of Philosophy*, translated by W. Cerf and H. S. Harris. Albany: SUNY, 1977. Also: *The Difference Between the Fichtean and Schellingian Systems of Philosophy*, translated by J. P. Surber. Reseda, CA: Ridgeview Press, 1978.

[ENC]   *Philosophy of Mind* (Part Three of the *Encyclopaedia*) (referred to in the text as *Philosophy of Spirit*), translated by W. Wallace; Zusätze translated by A. V. Miller. Oxford: Oxford University Press, (1894) 1971. Cited by section (§) number. "R" indicates "Remarks," although the distinction between section proper and Remarks is not evidenced in the English translation.

[ENC-L]   *Logic* (Part One of the *Encyclopaedia*), translated by W. Wallace. Oxford: Oxford University Press, (1873) 1975.

[FK]   *Faith and Knowledge*, translated by W. Cerf and H. S. Harris. Albany: SUNY, 1977.

[HP]   *Lectures on the History of Philosophy*, three volumes, translated by E. S. Haldane and F. H. Simson. Atlantic Highlands, NJ: Humanities Press, (1896) 1983.

[JAC]   "Review, Freidrich Heinrich Jacobi's Works, Volume III," (1816), in Hegel, *Heidelberg Writings: Journal Publications*, translated by B. Bowman and A. Speight. Cambridge, UK: Cambridge University Press, 2009, pp. 3–31.

[NL]   "On the Scientific Ways of Treating Natural Law," in Hegel, *Political Writings*. Cambridge, UK: Cambridge University Press, 1999, pp. 102–180.

[PH1]   *Lectures on the Philosophy of World History, Introduction: Reason in History*, translated by H. B. Nisbet. Cambridge, UK: Cambridge University Press, 1975.

[PH2]   *The Philosophy of History*, translated by J. Sibree. New York: Dover, 1956. In a number of cases (indicated by "Cf.") this abridged translation does not include the passages cited in the text.

[PR]   *Elements of the Philosophy of Right*, translated by H. B. Nisbet. Cambridge, UK: Cambridge University Press, 1991. Cited by section (§) number. "R" indicates "Remarks"; "A" indicates "Addition" [*Zusatz*].

[PS]   *Phenomenology of Spirit*, translated by A. V. Miller. Oxford: Oxford University Press, 1977. But see also *The Phenomenology of Mind*, translated by J. B. Baillie. New York: Harper Torchbooks, 1967 (1st ed., London: Macmillan, 1910).

[SL]   *Science of Logic*, translated by A. V. Miller. London: George Allen & Unwin, 1969.

At some points the English translations have been modified, to make them more faithful to the original text or to standardize terminology. Throughout this book, *Geist* has been translated as *spirit*, *Begriff* as *concept*, *aufheben* as *supersede*, and *Aufhebung* as *supersession*.

General Bibliography

When a text first published in one work is indicated as republished in another, page numbers in the book refer to the later edition.

Adorno, Theodor Wiesengrund. *Negative Dialektik*. Frankfurt am Main: Suhrkamp, 1966–67. Trans. *Negative Dialectics*. New York: Continuum, 1990.

Angehrn, Emil. *Freiheit und System bei Hegel*. Berlin and New York: De Gruyter, 1997.

———. "Il principio della soggettività e l'ambivalenza del moderno," in V. Vitiello (ed.). *Hegel e la comprensione della modernità*. Milan: Guerini & Associati, 1991, pp. 15–33.

Apel, Karl-Otto, Claus von Bormann, Rüdiger Bubner, Hans-Georg Gadamer, Hans-Joachim Giegel, and Jürgen Habermas. *Hermeneutik und Ideologiekritik*. Frankfurt am Main: Suhrkamp, 1971.

Aristotle. *The Nicomachean Ethics*. The Loeb Classical Library. Cambridge, MA: Harvard University Press, 1926.

———. *Politics*. The Loeb Classical Library. Cambridge, MA: Harvard University Press, 1932.

———. *History of Animals:* Books VII–X. The Loeb Classical Library, Cambridge, MA: Harvard University Press, 1991.

Bellan, Alessandro. *La logica e il 'suo' altro*. Padua: Il Poligrafo, 2002.

Biral, Alessandro. "Per una storia della sovranità." *Filosofia politica* 1, (1991): 5–50. Also in A. Biral, 1999, pp. 275–318.

———. *Storia e critica della filosofia politica moderna*. G. Duso (ed.). Milan: Angeli, 1999.

Bonito Oliva, Rosella. *L'individuo moderno e la nuova comunità. Ricerche sul significato della libertà soggettiva in Hegel.* Naples: Guida, 2000.

Brumlik, Micha and Hauke Brunkhorst (eds.). *Gemeinschaft und Gerechtigkeit.* Frankfurt am Main: Fischer, 1993.

Bubner, Rüdiger. "Philosophie ist ihre Zeit, in Gedanken erfaßt," in R. Bubner, K. Cramer, and R. Wiehl (eds.). *Hermeneutik und Dialektik. Festschrift für Hans-Georg Gadamer,* vols. 1–2. Tübingen: Mohr, 1970, pp. 317–342. Also in K. O. Apel, C. von Bormann, R. Bubner, H. G. Gadamer, H. J. Giegel, and J. Habermas, 1971, pp. 210–243.

———. "Rousseau, Hegel und die Dialektik der Aufklärung," in J. Schmidt (ed.). *Aufklärung und Gegenaufklärung in der europäischen Literatur, Philosophie und Politik von der Antike bis zur Gegenwart.* Darmstadt: Wissenschaftliche Buchgesellschaft, 1989. Also in R. Bubner, 1995, pp. 97–109.

———. "Hegels politische Anthropologie," in R. Bubner, *Innovationen des Idealismus.* Göttingen: Vandenhoeck & Ruprecht, 1995, pp. 72–85. Trans. *The Innovations of Idealism.* Cambridge, UK: Cambridge University Press, 2003.

———. *Welche Rationalität bekommt der Gesellschaft?* Frankfurt am Main: Suhrkamp, 1996.

———. *Polis und Staat. Grundlinien der Politischen Philosophie.* Frankfurt am Main: Suhrkamp, 2006.

Bubner, Rüdiger, Konrad Cramer, and Rainer Wiehl (eds.). *Hermeneutik und Dialektik. Festschrift für Hans-Georg Gadamer,* vols. 1–2. Tübingen: Mohr, 1970.

Calogero, Guido. *Filosofia del dialogo.* Milan: Edizioni di Comunità, 1962.

Cesa, Claudio. "Tra Moralität e Sittlichkeit. Sul confronto di Hegel con la filosofia pratica di Kant," in V. Verra (ed.). *Hegel interprete di Kant.* Naples: Prismi, 1981, pp. 147–178.

Cesarale, Giorgio. *La mediazione che sparisce. La società civile in Hegel.* Rome: Carocci, 2009.

Ceppa, Leonardo. *Il diritto della modernità. Saggi habermasiani.* Turin: Trauben, 2009.

Chiereghin, Franco. *Dialettica dell'assoluto e ontologia della soggettività in Hegel. Dall'ideale giovanile alla Fenomenologia dello spirito.* Trento: Verifiche, 1980.

Cortella, Lucio. *Dopo il sapere assoluto. L'eredità hegeliana nell'epoca post-metafisica.* Milan: Guerini & Associati, 1995.

———. *Autocritica del moderno. Saggi su Hegel.* Padua: Il Poligrafo, 2002.

———. "Etica del discorso ed etica del riconoscimento," in C. Vigna (ed.). *Libertà, giustizia e bene in una società plurale.* Milan: Vita e Pensiero, 2003, pp. 225–248.

———. "Il fondamento della normatività. Discutendo con Axel Honneth," in E. Bonan and C. Vigna (eds.). *Etica del plurale. Giustizia, riconoscimento, responsabilità.* Milan: Vita e Pensiero, 2004, pp. 75–94.

———. "Tesi provvisorie per una teoria del riconoscimento." *Fenomenologia e società* XXVIII, no. 2 (2005a): 3–19.

————. "Originarietà del riconoscere. La relazione di riconoscimento come condizione di conoscenza." *Giornale di metafisica* XXVII, (2005b): 145–156.

————. "Riconoscimento normativo. Da Honneth a Hegel e oltre." *Quaderni di Teoria sociale*, no. 8 (2008a): 15–32.

————. "Per una teoria politica del riconoscimento," in Seminario di Teoria critica, 2008b, pp. 79–98.

Ferrara, Alessandro. Introduction to *Comunitarismo e liberalismo*. A. Ferrara (ed.). Rome: Editori Riuniti, 1992, pp. IX–LVII.

————. *Reflective Authenticity. Rethinking the Project of Modernity.* London: Routledge, 1998.

————. *The Force of the Example.* New York: Columbia University Press, 2008.

Finelli, Roberto. "Note sulla filosofia della natura e della storia in Schelling e Hegel." *La ragione possibile* I, no. 2 (1990): 65–81.

Forst, Rainer. *Kontexte der Gerechtigkeit. Politische Philosophie jenseits von Liberalismus und Kommunitarismus.* Frankfurt am Main: Suhrkamp, 1994. Trans. *Contexts of Justice. Political Philosophy Beyond Liberalism and Communitarianism.* Los Angeles: University of California Press, 2002.

Fulda, Hans-Friedrich, Rolf-Peter Horstmann, and Michael Theunissen. *Kritische Darstellung der Metaphysik. Eine Diskussion über Hegels "Logik."* Frankfurt am Main: Suhrkamp, 1980.

Giusti, Miguel. *Hegels Kritik der modernen Welt. Über die Auseinandersetzung mit den geschichtlichen und systematischen Grundlagen der praktischen Philosophie.* Würzburg: Königshausen und Neumann, 1987.

Habermas, Jürgen. "Hegels Kritik der französischen Revolution," in *Theorie und Praxis. Sozialphilosophischen Studien.* Frankfurt am Main: Suhrkamp, 1963/71, pp. 128–147. Trans. *Theory and Practice.* Cambridge, UK: Polity Press, 1988.

————. "Die Moderne—ein unvollendetes Projekt," in *Kleine politische Schriften I–IV.* Frankfurt am Main: Suhrkamp, 1981, pp. 444–464.

————. *Moralbewußtsein und kommunikatives Handeln.* Frankfurt am Main: Suhrkamp, 1983. Trans. *Moral Consciousness and Communicative Action.* Cambridge, UK: Polity Press, 1990.

————. "Moralität und Sittlichkeit. Treffen Hegels Einwände gegen Kant auch auf die Diskursethik zu?" in W. Kuhlmann (ed.). *Moralität und Sittlichkeit. Das Problem Hegels und die Diskursethik.* Frankfurt am Main: Suhrkamp, 1986, pp. 16–37. Also in J. Habermas. *Erläuterungen zur Diskursethik.* Frankfurt am Main: Suhrkamp, 1991, pp. 9–30.

————. *Eine Art Schadensabwicklung. Kleine politische Schriften VI.* Frankfurt am Main: Suhrkamp, 1987.

————. Preface to *Strukturwandel der Öffentlichkeit. Untersuchung zu einer Kategorie der bürgerlichen Gesellschaft.* Frankfurt am Main: Suhrkamp, 1990, pp. 11–50. Trans. "Further Reflections on the Public Sphere," in C. Calhoun, *Habermas and the Public Sphere.* Cambridge, MA: MIT Press, 1992, pp. 421–461.

————. *Erläuterungen zur Diskursethik.* Frankfurt am Main: Suhrkamp, 1991.

————. *Faktizität und Geltung. Beiträge zur Diskurstheorie des Rechts und des demokratischen Rechtsstaates*. Frankfurt am Main: Suhrkamp, 1992. Trans. *Between Facts and Norms*. Cambridge, MA: MIT Press, 1996.

————. "Kampf um Anerkennung im demokratischen Rechtsstaat," in C. Taylor, *Multikulturalismus und die Politik der Anerkennung*. Frankfurt am Main: Fischer, 1993, pp. 147–196. Trans. "Struggles for Recognition in the Democratic Constitutional State," in C. Taylor, K. A. Appiah, J. Habermas, S. C. Rockefeller, M. Walzer, and S. Wolf, 1994, pp. 107–148.

————. "Replik auf Beiträge zu einem Symposion der Cardozo Law School," in *Die Einbeziehung des Anderen. Studien zur politischen Theorie*. Frankfurt am Main: Suhrkamp, 1996, pp. 309–398. Trans. "Reply to Symposium Participants, Benjamin N. Cardozo School of Law," in M. Rosenfeld and A. Arato (eds.). *Habermas on Law and Democracy: Critical Exchanges*. Los Angeles: University of California Press, 1998, pp. 381–452.

————. *Wahrheit und Rechtfertigung. Philosophische Aufsätze*. Frankfurt am Main: Suhrkamp, 1999. Trans. *Truth and Justification*. Cambridge, UK: Polity Press, 2003.

Henrich, Dieter and Rolf-Peter Horstmann (eds.). *Hegels Philosophie des Rechts. Die Theorie der Rechtsformen und ihre Logik*. Hegel-Tage Fontenay-aux-Roses 1979. Stuttgart: Klett-Cotta, 1982.

Hofmeister, Heimo E. M. "Moral Autonomy in Kant and Hegel," in J. J. O'Malley, K. W. Algozin, and F. G. Weiss (eds.). *Hegel and the History of Philosophy*. The Hague: Martinus Nijhoff, 1974, pp. 141–158.

Honneth, Axel. *Kampf um Anerkennung. Zur moralischen Grammatik sozialer Konflikte*. Frankfurt am Main: Suhrkamp, 1992. Trans. *The Struggle for Recognition*. Cambridge, UK: Polity Press, 1995.

————. *Posttraditionale Gemeinschaften. Ein konzeptueller Vorschlag*, in M. Brumlik and H. Brunkhorst (eds.). Frankfurt am Main: Fischer, 1993, pp. 260–270.

————. *Leiden an Unbestimmtheit. Eine Reaktualisierung der Hegelschen Rechtsphilosophie*. Stuttgart: Reclam, 2001. Trans. *The Pathologies of Individual Freedom*. Princeton: Princeton University Press, 2010.

Hösle, Vittorio. "Die Stellung von Hegels Philosophie des objektiven Geistes in seinem System und ihre Aporie," in C. Jermann (ed.). *Anspruch und Leistung von Hegels Rechtsphilosophie*. Stuttgart: Frommann-Holzboog, 1987a, pp. 11–53.

————. "Der Staat," in C. Jermann (ed.). *Anspruch und Leistung von Hegels Rechtsphilosophie*. Stuttgart: Frommann-Holzboog, 1987b, pp. 183–226.

Ilting, Karl-Heinz. "Rechtsphilosophie als Phänomenologie des Bewusstseins der Freiheit," in D. Henrich and R. P. Horstmann (eds.). *Hegels Philosophie des Rechts. Die Theorie der Rechtsformen und ihre Logik*. Hegel-Tage Fontenay-aux-Roses. Stuttgart: Klett-Cotta, 1982, pp. 225–254.

————. *Naturrecht und Sittlichkeit. Begriffsgeschichtliche Studien*. Stuttgart: Klett-Cotta, 1983.

————. *Grundfragen der praktischen Philosophie*, P. Becchi and H. Hoppe (eds.). Frankfurt am Main: Suhrkamp, 1993.

Kant, Immanuel. *Grundlegung zur Metaphysik der Sitten*. Riga, Latvia: Hartknoch, 1785. Trans. *Groundwork of the Metaphysics of Morals*. New York: Harper and Row, 1964.

————. *Kritik der praktischen Vernunft*. Riga, Latvia: Hartknoch, 1788. Trans. *Critique of Practical Reason*. New York: Macmillan, 1993.

————. "Über den Gemeinspruch: Das mag in der Theorie richtig sein, taugt aber nicht für die Praxis." *Berlinische Monatsschrift* XXII (1793): 201–284. Trans. "On the Common Saying: That May Be Correct in Theory, but Is of No Use in Practice," in *Practical Philosophy*. Cambridge, UK: Cambridge University Press, 1996, pp. 273–310.

————. *Metaphysik der Sitten*, Königsberg: Nicolovius, 1796–97. Trans. *The Metaphysical Elements of Justice. Part I of The Metaphysics of Morals*. New York: Bobbs-Merrill, 1965.

Kuhlmann, Wolfgang (ed.). *Moralität und Sittlichkeit. Das Problem Hegels und die Diskursethik*. Frankfurt am Main: Suhrkamp, 1986.

Larmore, Charles. *Patterns of Moral Complexity*. Cambridge, UK: Cambridge University Press, 1987.

Laska, Peter. "Kant and Hegel on Practical Reason," in J. J. O'Malley, K. W. Algozin, and F. G. Weiss (eds.). *Hegel and the History of Philosophy*. The Hague: Martinus Nijhoff, 1974, pp. 129–140.

Lübbe, Hermann. *Politische Philosophie in Deutschland. Studien zu ihrer Geschichte*. Basel and Stuttgart: Benno Schwabe & Co., 1963.

Marcuse, Herbert. *Reason and Revolution. Hegel and the Rise of Social Theory*. Boston: Beacon Press, 1941 (1960).

Marini, Giuliano. *Libertà soggettiva e libertà oggettiva nella 'Filosofia del diritto' hegeliana*. Naples: Morano, 1978–90.

Marquard, Odo. "Hegel und das Sollen." *Philosophisches Jahrbuch* LXXII (1964–65): 103–119. Also in O. Marquard, 1973, pp. 37–51 and 153–167.

————. *Schwierigkeiten mit der Geschichtsphilosphie*. Frankfurt am Main: Suhrkamp, 1973.

Marx, Karl. *Aus der Kritik der hegelschen Rechtsphilosophie. Kritik des hegelschen Staatsrechts* (1843), in *Marx-Engels Gesamtausgabe*, Abt. I, Bd. 1, Hb. 1, pp. 401–553. Moscow: Marx-Engels-Lenin Institut, 1927. Trans. *Critique of Hegel's Philosophy of Right*. Chicago: Aristeus Books, 2012.

Massolo, Arturo. *La storia della filosofia come problema e altri saggi*, L. Sichirollo (ed.). Florence: Vallecchi, 1973.

Menke, Christoph. "Liberalismus in Konflikt. Zwischen Gerechtigkeit und Freiheit," in M. Brumlik and H. Brunkhorst (eds.). *Gemeinschaft und Gerechtigkeit*. Frankfurt am Main: Fischer, 1993, pp. 218–243.

————. *Tragödie im Sittlichen. Gerechtigkeit und Freiheit nach Hegel*. Frankfurt am Main: Suhrkamp, 1996.

O'Malley, Joseph J., Keith W. Algozin, and Frederick G. Weiss (eds.). *Hegel and the History of Philosophy.* The Hague: Martinus Nijhoff, 1974.

Ottmann, Henning. "Hegelsche Logik und Rechtsphilosophie. Unzulängliche Bemerkungen zu einem ungelösten Problem," in D. Henrich and R. P. Horstmann (eds.). *Hegels Philosophie des Rechts. Die Theorie der Rechtsformen und ihre Logik.* Hegel-Tage Fontenay-aux-Roses 1979. Stuttgart: Klett-Cotta, 1982, pp. 382–392.

Pelczynski, Zbigniew Andrzej (ed.). *Hegel's Political Philosophy. Problems and Perspectives. A Collection of Essays.* Cambridge, UK: Cambridge University Press, 1971.

Pippin, Robert. *Hegel's Practical Philosophy. Rational Agency and Ethical Life.* Cambridge, UK: Cambridge University Press, 2008.

Rawls, John. *A Theory of Justice.* Cambridge, MA: The Belknap Press of Harvard University Press, 1971.

Riedel, Manfred. *Studien zu Hegels Rechtsphilosophie.* Frankfurt am Main: Suhrkamp, 1969. Trans. *Between Tradition and Revolution.* Cambridge, UK: Cambridge University Press, 2011.

———. *Bürgerliche Gesellschaft und Staat bei Hegel. Grundproblem und Struktur der Hegelschen Rechtsphilosophie.* Neuwied and Berlin: Luchterhand, 1970.

———. "Natur und Freiheit in Hegels Rechtsphilosophie," in Z. A. Pelczynski (ed.). *Hegel's Political Philosophy. Problems and Perspectives. A Collection of Essays.* Cambridge, UK: Cambridge University Press, 1971, pp. 136–150. Also in M. Riedel (ed.), 1974, vol. II, pp. 109–127.

———. (ed.). *Materialien zu Hegels Rechtsphilosophie.* Frankfurt am Main: Suhrkamp, 1974.

Ritter, Joachim. *Hegel und die französische Revolution.* Köln and Opladen: Westdeutscher Verlag, 1957. Trans. *Hegel and the French Revolution.* Cambridge, MA: MIT Press, 1984.

———. "Zur Grundlegung der praktischen Philosophie bei Aristoteles." *Archiv für Rechts- und Sozialphilosophie* 46 (1960): 179–199. Also in M. Riedel (ed.). *Rehabilitierung der praktischen Philosophie.* Freiburg: Rombach, 1974, vol. II, pp. 479–500.

———. *Metaphysik und Politik. Studien zu Aristoteles und Hegel.* Frankfurt am Main: Suhrkamp, 1969. Three of the essays are translated in Ritter, *Hegel and the French Revolution*, 1984, pp. 124–191.

———. *Subjektivität. Sechs Aufsätze.* Frankfurt am Main: Suhrkamp, 1974.

Rohrmoser, Günther. *Subjektivität und Verdinglichung. Theologie und Gesellschaft im Denken des jungen Hegels.* Gütersloh: Mohn, 1961.

Ruggiu, Luigi. *Logica Metafisica Politica. Hegel a Jena.* Milan and Udine: Mimesis, 2009.

Schaber, Peter. *Recht als Sittlichkeit. Eine Untersuchung zu den Grundbegriffen der Hegelschen Rechtsphilosophie.* Würzburg: Königshausen & Neumann, 1989.

Schnädelbach, Herbert. "Was ist Neoaristotelismus?" in W. Kuhlmann (ed.). *Moralität und Sittlichkeit. Das Problem Hegels und die Diskursethik.* Frankfurt am Main: Suhrkamp, 1986, pp. 38–63.

―――. *Hegels praktische Philosophie. Ein Kommentar der Texte in der Reihenfolge ihrer Entstehung*. Frankfurt am Main: Suhrkamp, 2000.

Seminario di Teoria critica. *Che cos'è la politica?* Rome: Meltemi, 2008.

Siep, Ludwig. *Anerkennung als Prinzip der praktischen Philosophie. Untersuchungen zu Hegels Jenaer Philosophie des Geistes*. Freiburg and München: Alber, 1979.

―――. "Hegels politische Philosophie," in L. Siep, *Praktische Philosophie im Deutschen Idealismus*. Frankfurt am Main: Suhrkamp, 1992, pp. 307–328.

Smith, Adam. *An Inquiry into the Nature and Causes of the Wealth of Nations*. Aalen: Otto Zeller, 1776 (1963).

Taylor, Charles. *Hegel and Modern Society*. Cambridge, UK: Cambridge University Press, 1979a.

―――. "What's Wrong with Negative Liberty," in *The Idea of Freedom: Essays in Honour of Isaiah Berlin*, A. Ryan and I. Berlin (eds.). Oxford: Oxford University Press, 1979b. Also in C. Taylor, *Philosophy and the Human Sciences. Philosophical Papers II*. Cambridge, UK: Cambridge University Press, 1985, pp. 211–229.

Taylor, Charles, K. Anthony Appiah, Jürgen Habermas, Stephen C. Rockefeller, Michael Walzer, and Susan Wolf. *Multiculturalism: Examining the Politics of Recognition*. A. Gutmann (ed.). Princeton: Princeton University Press, 1994.

Theunissen, Michael. *Hegels Lehre vom absoluten Geist als theologisch-politischer Traktat*. Berlin: De Gruyter, 1970.

―――. *Sein und Schein. Die kritische Funktion der Hegelschen Logik*. Frankfurt am Main: Suhrkamp, 1978.

―――. "Die verdrängte Intersubjektivität in Hegels Philosophie des Rechts," in D. Henrich and R. P. Horstmann (eds.). *Hegels Philosophie des Rechts. Die Theorie der Rechtsformen und ihre Logik*. Hegel-Tage Fontenay-aux-Roses 1979. Stuttgart: Klett-Cotta, 1982, pp. 317–381.

Tugendhat, Ernst. *Selbstbewußtsein und Selbstbestimmung. Sprachanalytische Interpretationen*. Frankfurt am Main: Suhrkamp, 1979. Trans. *Self-Consciousness and Self-Determination*. Cambridge, MA: MIT Press, 1986.

Verra, Valerio (ed.). *Hegel interprete di Kant*. Naples: Prismi, 1981.

Vitiello, Vincenzo (ed.). *Hegel e la comprensione della modernità*. Milan: Guerini & Associati, 1991.

Walzer, Michael. "The Communitarian Critique of Liberalism." *Political Theory* XVIII no. 1 (1990): 6–23.

―――. "The Idea of Civil Society." *Dissent* (Spring 1991): 293–304.

Wellmer, Albrecht. *Endspiele. Die unversöhnliche Moderne*. Frankfurt am Main: Suhrkamp, 1993. Trans. *Endgames*. Cambridge, MA: MIT Press, 1998.

Wildt, Andreas. *Autonomie und Anerkennung. Hegels Moralitätskritik in Lichte seiner Fichte-Rezeption*. Stuttgart: Klett-Cotta, 1982.

Index

209

136, 156–161; morality and, 1–2,
54–55, 97–100, 119–120, 184,
185; nature and, 6–7, 85–88, 180;
otherness and, 151–152, 157; posttraditional, 161–162, 194, 195;
pluralism of, 163–165; as primacy
of the object, 114–120; as process of
formation (*Bildungsprozess*), xix, 66,
76–77, 162; religion and, 106–107;
as reconciliation (*Versöhnung*),
105–113, 131, 151–152, 195;
as second nature, 95–100, 183,
190; as solution of the conflicts of
modernity, 100–105, 195; as (self-
knowing) substance, xvii, 91, 96,
144, 150, 161; as tradition, 6–8, 83,
93–95, 157–158, 164, 169, 170;
as unity of freedom and history,
88–93; as unity of freedom and
nature, 85–88; as unity of individual
and universal, 114–116; as unity of
subjectivity and objectivity, 57–58,
105–113; as unity of universality
and ethos, 93–95; universality of,
94–95, 130–131, 158, 165, 195
ethical state, xx, xxiii, 99
ethics, 193; fundamental norm of,
153–154; institutions and, xxiii,
97–98; politics and, 98–100; as
product of ethical life, 99–100,
153–154; as product of recognition,
150, 152–153
Europe, xxv, 165
exposition and critique, 73, 178–
179

Faith and Knowledge, 16–17
family, 68, 72, 76–77, 169
Ferrara, Alessandro, 164, 176, 195
Fichte, Johann Gottlieb, 15, 56–57,
85, 111, 116, 187
Finelli, Roberto, 68, 178
Forst, Rainer, 155, 193, 194

freedom: abstract, 19–20; arbitrariness
and, 26–28; Aristotle and, 18,
30; as autonomy, 18–19, 48–58;
Christianity and, 31; concrete, xiii,
21, 22, 107; defeat of, 127, 131;
emphatic conception, xvi–xvii, 11–12,
135; finitude and, 20–21; formal,
65, 69; God and, 15; good and,
87–88, 184; as ground of ethical life,
84, 85–88, 143, 147; Idea and, 88,
143–144, 145–146; Kant and, 18,
20–21, 25, 27, 51–58, 88; logic and,
15, 29, 143–144; modern philosophy
and, 11, 50–51, 57–58; modernity
and, 18–19, 29–30, 48–51; nature
and, 62–65, 84, 85–88, 181–182;
necessity and, 14, 69, 183–184;
negative and positive, 20–21, 49,
55, 92, 118–119; negativity and,
16, 19–20; objectivity and, xvi–xvii,
2–3, 24–28, 55, 57–58; ontology
and, 11–17, 57; particularity, 20–22;
Plato and, 30; as reality, 88, 94,
95–96; relation and, xvii, 21–24, 55,
67, 77, 109, 119, 146, 150–151,
161; Rousseau and, 25–26; self-
consciousness and, 28–30, 48;
self-transparency and, 14–15, 17–19;
subjective, 19, 28–30, 48–58; as
thought, 25–26; as totality, 11–12,
15; two competing conceptions of,
xvii, 145–147, 150–151; work and,
63–66
French revolution, 20, 98, 176–177,
189
friendship, 22, 154, 167
Fulda, Hans-Friedrich, 180

Giusti, Miguel, 189
God, 15, 25, 29, 31, 50; death of,
16–17; ethical world and, 56;
incarnation of, 31, 182–183, 188,
188–189; state and, 90, 182–183